Happy 50th A

1955-2005

Home of Defence Industries Limited

Victory is our business

Congratulations and Best Wishes, Ajax, on your Outstanding Achievements!

Alan Paul Longfield

Lynn Philip Hodgson

Blake Books Distribution

Lynn Philip Hodgson, Alan Paul Longfield

Library and Archives Canada Cataloguing in Publication Data
Ajax Arsenal of Democracy
The Inside Camp-X Blake Grey Series. 2nd . Includes index.
ISBN 0-9735523-1-X

Distributed by:
Blake Books Distribution
467 Fralick's Beach Road
Port Perry, Ontario
Canada L9L 1B6
(905) 985-6434
lynniso@idirect.com
Website: http://www.camp-x.com/

Cover Design and Page Layout:
© APL Consulting
Whitby, ON L1N 6B6
Adobe Creative Suite®
Alan Paul Longfield
(905) 668-1173
alongfi@sympatico.ca

Editor: Barbara Kerr

1. Great Britain. Special Operations Executive. Special Training School 103 (Whitby, ON)--Fiction.
2. World War, 1939-1945—Secret Service--Great Britain--Fiction.
3. World War, 1939-1945--Secret Service--Canada--Fiction.
4. World War, 1939-1945--Military intelligence--Canada--Fiction.
II Title. III. Series: Inside Camp-X series ; 2.
PS8565.O324A74 2005 C813'.6
C2005-900522-X

Printed and Bound in Canada by:
WEBCOM LIMITED books and beyond
3480 Pharmacy Avenue, Toronto, Ontario M1W 2S7 1-800-665-9322

I am ready to meet my Maker...But whether my Maker is prepared for the great ordeal of meeting me, is another matter.

Sir Winston S. Churchill (1874-1965)

Dedication

Ajax Arsenal of Democracy is respectfully dedicated to the men and women of DIL-Defence Industries Limited, Ajax, Ontario

Will a desperate enemy make it happen here?

Can it happen here? Yes, experts say, it can. Faced with the grim certainty of his ultimate defeat as long as the Arsenal of Democracy – Canada and the United States—continue to pour the munitions of war, food, and fighting men to the aid of his enemies, Hitler, in desperation may well command his Luftwaffe to level our cities, wreck our industries, demoralize our citizens. Then it would be our churches and our worshippers, our homes and their families, or school and our children, our industries and their workers that would know the hate that is the Hun's.

Yes, it could happen here. And it will if we pursue the path of complacency engendered by the news of victories won. We've just won a few battles so far; we haven't won the war yet. It will take a lot to do that... in men, munitions and money. We've got the men and we can and will make the munitions. The money? We've got that too. And it's badly needed; it too, is an essential 'materiel' of war. It is needed to fight for our churches, our homes, our schools and our livelihood. Let's lend it to our country for the sake of these things. Buy War Savings Stamps and Certificates regularly.

Commando. Defence Industries Limited, Ajax, Ontario. February 1 1943.

Foreword

Ajax Arsenal of Democracy

Prior to the Second World War, the Town of Ajax did not exist. There were simply miles of rolling hills and open farmland with the occasional farmhouse sprinkled here and there in South Pickering Township. With the outbreak of hostilities in 1939 and Canada's entry into the war, the Allies had a rapidly mounting need for munitions manufacturing plants. What we now know as the Town of Ajax on the eastern outskirts of Toronto was an ideal location for establishing one of these factories.

The Canadian Government and military called upon Canadian Industries Limited (CIL) for their co-operation and the name became DIL, for Defence Industries Limited. Thus Defence Industries Limited, DIL, was the official name of Ajax during the Second World War.

The City of Oshawa, logically because of the General Motors plant situated there, was seen as a primary source of skilled personnel. Subsequently a number of workers were engaged to work at DIL. However, General Motors' own wartime production quotas of military vehicles and a myriad of other strategic products limited the number of workers available to go elsewhere. In response to DIL's critical needs, the wives, daughters and sisters of GM's workforce were well-represented among the many women recruited by DIL.

As the munitions manufacturing plants began to push up across the farmland, there grew a necessity for short-term housing. What are now called 'war homes' were erected in a controlled fashion. A visitor to Ajax today would see hundreds of these war homes, all strategically placed just outside what was the entrance gate to DIL on the north side of 401 Highway starting at Harwood Ave. Today, a large percentage have been creatively upgraded and imaginatively renovated so as to be almost unrecognizable as original 'DIL homes'. Although the houses were small and inexpensively built, typically without garages, they were, in fact, well constructed. The (almost) instantly constructed town consisted of the war munitions complex, homes, stores, schools, churches, community halls, and a post office: everything a small town would need.

The entire town was heated by one source, a steam plant powerhouse. The entire (approximately) three thousand acres of DIL were heated by an underground system of ductwork originating at the powerhouse, connecting all of the buildings over the entire area, and then returning back to the source of the steam plant. It is amazing that, to this day, many buildings are still heated from that original steam plant.

It soon became apparent that the local population was not large enough to support both General Motors and Defence Industries Ltd. An appeal was sent out across Canada. Advertisements offering a lucrative opportunity for people to live and work at DIL were placed in local papers in the towns in Northern Ontario, as well as in other provinces. The town quickly established a bus system for the workers. Buses would pick them up at their residences to transport them to DIL where they were required to produce nametags as proof of identification. The rate of pay was approximately fifty cents an hour, an excellent wage during World War II.

Security was extremely tight at DIL. There was even an elaborate system to illuminate the entire area at night giving it a daylight effect and there were eight-foot barbed wire fences surrounding the entire area of the plant. Safety was one of the highest concerns. When a worker first came to DIL he or she was required to take a safety course, which had to be completed successfully before the worker could be assigned to a workstation on the assembly line. So safety conscious was management, that smoking was banned outright. There was a penalty of imprisonment if an employee was caught with matches or a lighter, and cigarettes were not allowed anywhere inside the munitions factory area.

The normal weekly shift consisted of six days, eight hours per day. There were three shifts each day and a worker was on a two-week swing. The plant was closed on Sunday. At the height of the war, DIL employed over ten thousand people who filled over fifty million shells of every size and calibre.

Not surprisingly, DIL was obviously a very convenient source of munitions used in training at Camp X. There were special training techniques, which placed the agents on a mock mission to infiltrate DIL. These exercises would be pre-arranged similar to the General Motors exercises. The supervisor of a particular building would be made aware that he could expect a 'visitor' sometime during his shift. It then became the foreman's responsibility to be on the watch constantly and be prepared to inform the DIL guards immediately of any irregularity. This particular exercise was beneficial not only of benefit to Camp-X, but DIL also. Depending upon the success of the infiltration attempt, the information obtained from each exercise or 'scheme', would be used to alert Camp X instructors and DIL defence managers as to what steps needed to be taken in order to correct the breach.

One might imagine that this training was taken very seriously, as the outcome could be catastrophic-locally and for Allied forces that depended upon the steady flow of DIL munitions to the front lines.

Which leads us into our story…

But first, an introduction to the two symbols used throughout the book:

•Crest of Special Operations Executive (SOE)

Created in 1940 by British Prime Minister Winston Churchill to 'Set Europe ablaze', **SOE's** operational mandate was, '...to confuse and confound the enemy...' through guerilla warfare tactics, principally subversion and sabotage behind enemy lines. Canada's Camp-X, STS 103, a.k.a. 'The Farm', a unique Canadian/British **SOE** training school, was to be the model adopted by the American OSS, Office of Strategic Services, later to become the CIA (1947).

•The '25 pounder' (pdr) Artillery Shell

The quick firing '**25 pdr**', called by many 'one of the best guns in the world', undeniably among the most versatile and effective artillery pieces of WWII, fired three types of shells: Smoke, Armour Piercing, High Explosive. All were produced at **DIL**. Its rapid fire capabilities could put up to 5 shells in the air at a time. At El Alamein in 1942, 824 25 pdr German tank 'killers' fired over one million rounds during the 12 day battle. **DIL**'s huge output of 25 pdr shells was vital to the Allied ultimate victory in Europe,1945.

Living History

The remarkable Ajax/DIL steam plant, still operational, (2005), provided heating to DIL and the entire town.

In Appreciation

Alan Paul Longfield and Lynn Philip Hodgson wish to thank our **Editor**, Barbara Kerr and acknowledge the contributions of the ***Inside Camp X Series*** Advisory Team without which ***Ajax Arsenal of Democracy*** would not have been possible: Marlene, Judi, Michael and Anne-Marie.

We are indebted to the following people for their generous support and assistance:

Cris Anderson, for his expert advice and demonstrations as portrayed in our books by the character Major Robert Samson, a fictional adaptation of the legendary William E. Fairbairn.

George Blackmore and William H. 'Bill' Davies, for their photographs and authoritative information on '25 pounder' artillery shells and field pieces.; Major Bruce Clayton, PMC, Officers' Mess, Ontario Regiment, Oshawa, ON, for historical references to the 'Ontario's'; Robbie Cressman, President of Underwood Systems and Bill Underwood's official historian, for background information on Bill Underwood and his fighting systems: Combato and Defendo. www.UnderwoodSystems.com

Bonnie Gerrow (née Stephen) for her fascinating background stories of life at DIL, which we have taken care to honour through preserving their historical authenticity and integrity.

Mr. Sydney T. Hopkins FCGA C.A.

John and Dale Montgomery for permission to use John's grandparents' names, Jim and Lillian Montgomery, and their wonderful stories of DIL.

Pickering-Ajax Digital Archive (PADA) http://www.pada.ca/ the **Pickering** and **Ajax Public Libraries**, for so generously providing access to their superb online archive, including permission to use the cover and back page photograph.

The Friends of The Ajax Library for hosting our Book Launch; Mayor Steve Parish, Town of Ajax and Cherry Sevigny the Mayor's Secretary, for her kindness and patience in responding to our many 'calls for help'; Leona Barrington and Brenda Kriz, Town of Ajax; Mayor Marilyn Pearce of Scugog Township for all of her support in the past.

Mrs. Harry Smith, whose late husband, Harry, was the first Mayor of Ajax; Deirdre Stuart for kindly making the Camp-X Museum available for our launches; Russel Gregg, for his research with former DIL employees, Ajax Legion; Marion Carter and Helen Redman, two of our most loyal and intrepid fans.

Our families and close friends- thank you as always for your advice, patience, continuing support and understanding.

And you, our faithful readers, and those for whom this may be their first encounter with the ***Inside Camp-X Series***, and now the ***Blake Grey Series***, our gratitude and heartfelt thanks for helping keep the eternal flame of remembrance burning bright. We are sincerely grateful.

Thank you.

LPH APL May 2005

Table of Contents

Arsenal of Democracy

Chapter 1 *Baker 3525*

Richmond-upon-Thames, England

September 1943

He's nearly unconscious, Adara!"

"What? Who's unconscious?" her voice drifted downstairs.

"It's Clifford! He's lying at the doorway. There's blood everywhere; it's coming from his mouth! Hurry!"

Throwing on a housecoat, Adara rushed down the stairs to see Blake knelt on the vestibule floor, cradling Clifford Jackson's head. "Oh, my God! What happened?"

"Quiet! Quiet! He's trying to say something." Blake leaned closer. "Clifford, it's Blake. Blake Grey. Adara's right here. What happened?"

Faintly, Jackson replied, "Motorbike…motorbike policeman...pulled me... over..." He paused.

"A policeman on a motorcycle pulled you over," Blake repeated. "Then what?"

There was no reply. "We're losing him, Adara. We need an ambulance. Call the operator, quickly. And throw me that blanket on the sofa! Go upstairs for the ice and a towel. The champagne bucket. In the bathroom!

"An ambulance will be here, very soon, Clifford! Do you know who attacked you?" Blake prompted.

"It was a…set-up," Jackson muttered. "Not…not a copper," he continued, his voice rising barely above a whisper.

"No, not a copper," Blake confirmed softly.

"The ambulance is on the way!" Adara called. "Here's the blanket. I'll go upstairs for the ice!"

"Moroccan Embassy...fascist..." Jackson gasped. His eyelids fluttered, and then closed.

"Adara! Come!" Blake called out. "He's unconscious! Adara! Are you coming? Hurry! Now!" Blake insisted. "Clifford muttered something about a fascist at the Moroccan Embassy before he passed out."

Cupping his hands, Blake shouted, "Adara? Where are you? Adara! We can't wait for the ambulance! We'll have to drive him!"

"Coming! I'm getting dressed as quickly as I can!" Seconds later, Adara appeared, clutching a bundled white bath towel to her chest. Her lustrous black hair had been pulled back and fastened at the nape of her neck with a black ribbon; her cameo-like features showed no trace of makeup.

"Oh, there you are. For a moment I thought you'd been kidnapped," he snapped.

"That's not funny."

"What about the bloody ice?"

"It's wrapped inside the towel. Here. We'll put Clifford into the back seat of the car. I'll drive," Adara calmly directed. "Bring him out. I'll go get the car started."

"Open both back doors, Adara." Blake wrapped Cliff's head in the towel to staunch the flow of blood, and carried him outside to the sedan. He and Adara managed to pull Cliff through until he lay sprawled across the rear seat. "I never realized how tall he is!" she remarked, now out of breath.

"Well, he's in. I'll look after the doors. Done. Ready, Adara?"

"Ready."

Leaning forward, Blake ordered, "Gun it! Good. Hold that speed." He studied Cliff's face for a moment, recalling his training as a boxer. "Do you think it's alright if I put a small piece of ice on his mouth? His lips look all dry and cracked."

"Only enough to keep them moist, mon chéri. Otherwise he could choke."

"Okay. How far to the hospital?"

"Less than a half hour. Actually, it's a clinic where I worked a few years ago. Doctor Grant and his staff are very capable. They don't have much in the way of sophisticated equipment, but they should be able to stabilize him. Try to keep him warm and comfy and hope to heavens the bleeding stops."

"It seems pretty well stopped now, but he's unconscious. Thank God he's not a bleeder," he commented, recalling the story told by Sal, his adoptive father and trainer, about a promising young light-weight whose career was ended abruptly with a slight cut above his eye. "Are we almost there?"

"Just ahead," she nodded reassuringly.

After what seemed like an eternity to Blake, Adara abruptly turned right into a small parking lot. As the front bumper was about to strike the brick wall, she jammed on the brakes. Quickly shutting off the engine and ratcheting up the hand brake, she stepped from the car calling back to Blake, "You stay here with Cliff; I'll get help."

"Trust me, Adara. Cliff and I aren't going anywhere. Go quickly. His breathing is very shallow."

The driver's door slammed shut. Blake looked around, thrumming the tips of his fingernails on the window as he waited for Adara to return. She re-appeared, running, accompanied by three figures in white jackets, two of whom carried a folding stretcher.

One took charge and introduced himself as Blake opened his door. "I'm Dr. Grant. We will take over now. Please be good enough to step out of the automobile, Sir. Thank you."

Once Clifford was secured in the stretcher, Dr. Grant motioned Blake and Adara to follow him. As they entered the door at the rear of the clinic, a female attendant met them and led them to a small waiting room. "Doctor Grant will be out as soon as he knows something." Then, with sudden flash of recognition, she added, "Adara! How have you been? I haven't seen you in dog's years. You look smashing, dear, as always!"

"I'm fine, thanks, Liz," Adara smiled. "This is my colleague, Mr. Blake. I have been living for the past while in Casablanca."

"Liz Thomason. How do you do, Mr. Blake?" she remarked with an approving smile.

"Casablanca! My, that sounds romantic, Adara! You must tell me all about it, but first, I'll go check on your friend. Dr. Grant should know something by now. In the meantime, be a pet and complete this Patient Admittance Form. I'm sure that you can do it with your eyes closed. Pen? Here. And do help yourselves to some tea."

"Blake, what names shall I use?" Adara whispered, as she began filling out the register.

"Cliff's and yours. That should be good enough," he commented while looking over her shoulder.

"Shall I use my maiden name, or, you, know, Peter's?"

"Go with what they know. By the way, Adara, what is your last name?"

"Zekara. It's Moroccan. Berber," she added for clarification.

"Adara Zekara. A to Z. All inclusive. Very appropriate." He smiled meaningfully.

"Oh, do be serious for once, Blake, and help me, please? Would you happen to know Clifford's date of birth?"

"It's likely on his driver's license somewhere in his billfold. They'll find it."

She concentrated on the task for a minute and then without looking up, asked quietly, "What did Cliff say again?"

Blake stared at her uncomprehendingly. "Oh, at the house, you mean! Let me think. 'Motorbike, policeman, pulled me over.' Then he said, 'Not a copper. Moroccan Embassy. Fascist.' That was it. Why?"

"What do you make of all that?" Adara wondered. "There were some very strange characters at the Embassy the night that I met Cliff, including some of the officials. One in particular; the host, made it clear that he was an admirer of Adolf Hitler, and a shameless Nazi sympathizer."

"So you've said. I can only speculate that the attacker was a hired thug."

"Hired by whom, Blake?"

"The Abwehr or Sicherheitsdienst, Foreign Branch. Or, maybe the Bulgarians or the Italians. Who knows? I'm willing to bet that Clifford was a prime target of opportunity for every Axis assassin and freelance thug. I do know one thing for sure, Adara; I will find out who it was."

"Ssh. I'm sure you will, darling. Changing the subject: how shall we pay for this?"

"Not a problem. I have cash. More than enough to cover it. Or rather, I'll slip you the money and that way, I'll stay off the scoreboard." He arose and stood looking out the window. Then, turning to Adara he blurted, "Dammit! I am mightily burned about this, Adara! Murderous bastards! Sorry." His outburst was interrupted by the appearance of Doctor Grant.

"Miss Zekara. In the rush, I forgot to say how good it is to see you again. And you are…?"

"Blake, Dr. Grant. A pleasure."

"Indeed," he smiled. "I'm happy to say that your friend Mr. Jackson is going to pull through. He has sustained a deep scalp wound, contusions, and a moderate to severe concussion. Thanks to you, the bleeding had all but stopped when he arrived. His pulse and blood pressure are stable, but he's not out of the woods quite yet.

"Our facilities for dealing with post accident trauma here are rather limited, as you might imagine. I'm requesting your approval to have him transferred to a hospital in London. He will require an X-ray to determine if there's a fracture of the skull. If not, I expect that they would keep him in for two to five days for observation and recovery. The concussion does worry me. We're keeping him awake, but he's resting quietly now. The sooner we transfer him to a properly equipped facility, the better. May I have your permission to telephone London, Miss Zekara?"

"Yes, absolutely, Doctor Grant!"

"Very good. Mrs. Thomason, ring the Maudsley Hospital, please."

Turning again to Adara and Blake, he inquired, "What happened to him? I shall have to put in a report to inform the Maudsley."

"That's what we would like to know Doctor," replied Blake. "He showed up at our door like that and just collapsed."

"Have you contacted the police?"

"No," Blake replied.

"In my opinion, it…" The telephone rang shrilly.

Liz answered it, listened briefly, and then interrupted. "Excuse me, Doctor Grant. It's for you."

"Please ask them to call back, Mrs. Thomason. Or, take a message." Turning again to Adara and Blake, he continued, "Sorry. It's my responsibility to inform you…"

"Doctor?"

"Yes, Mrs. Thomason?"

Covering the mouthpiece with her hand, she continued "I think you'd best take it, Doctor. The caller insists on speaking with you directly. He's calling from The Home Office, London."

"Very well. Transfer it to my office. One moment, please, Miss Zekara, Mister..."

"Blake, Doctor," he repeated.

Minutes later, Dr. Grant opened his door and motioned to Adara and Blake. They rose and entered. As he closed the door, Grant cleared his throat nervously and ventured, "Do either of you know anything about the nature of Mr. Jackson's, er, employment?"

"Yes, Doctor," admitted Adara. "Clifford is with the Home Office."

"Indeed. That was a call from his supervisor in London. It seems that Mr. Jackson, er, Clifford, failed to report in and was about to be listed as missing due to 'unexplained circumstances'. Somehow, they tracked him down here. I've no idea how, nor did the gentleman elaborate.

"When I told him that Mr. Jackson is waiting to be transferred to the Maudsley, he gave the go ahead, on the condition that both of you accompany him. I gather that you are rather well known to Mr. Jackson's department," he smiled thinly. "A representative of the Home Office will be waiting at the hospital upon your arrival. Oh, yes, the caller also stipulated that the local constabulary are not to be involved and added that all expenses are to be billed to him directly. Mrs. Thomason will look after those arrangements, of course. Well, Miss Zekara, Mr. Blake, I expect that the ambulance will be around shortly. Is there anything else?"

"No, thank you, Doctor Grant. Both you and Mrs. Thomason have been extremely kind and helpful," Blake replied.

"Our pleasure! Now, if you don't mind, I have a minor surgery to prepare for. You're more than welcome to wait in here for the ambulance. The caller indicated that someone will be around to pick up Mr. Jackson's auto to take it to London for 'examination'. Miss Thomason will give you Mr. Jackson's personal belongings. Best wishes!"

An overbearing Home Office representative refused to allow them to accompany Clifford into ADMITTING and insisted on taking possession of Jackson's personal effects, without an explanation. Officiously, he directed that they find a suitable place to wait until they were paged. In an unexpected gesture of attempted goodwill, he reached into a slim, black patent briefcase and produced a folded newspaper. He handed it to Blake stating, "It might be a longish wait; something to read, Mr. Blake." Turning to Adara, he selected a crisp, one-pound note from his billfold, offering in an undertone, "Take this please, and purchase some refreshments for yourselves, Miss Zekara."

"Thank you, but…"

He had vanished. "Odd sort of duck," Adara remarked casually as they searched the large YOU ARE HERE floor plan for directions.

"Old Quaker saying: 'All the world is strange except thee and me and sometimes I wonder about thee.'"

"Old Moroccan saying: 'Among walnuts, only the empty one speaks'," she countered.

"Touché, my dear," replied Blake, smiling gallantly.

Relegated to a gloomy, institutional green basement cafeteria, they decided to make the best of things. "Something to drink, my dear?"

"You can cut out the 'my dear' chivalry. A person would think we're stuffy characters in a Jane Austen novel," she chided. "Don't sulk. It doesn't suit you. Here." She kissed him gently.

"How about then, 'Something to drink, cara mia?'"

"Cara Mia. That is sweet. Yes, please. Coffee, avec beaucoup de lait, milk, Blake, and a half-spoon of sugar."

"Surely you jest. We'll be lucky to find ersatz coffee that's not made out of pencil shavings and dandelions."

"Use the old Blake magic," she smiled, encouragingly. "Here's The Odd Duck's money."

Adara picked up the newspaper that Blake had left lying on the table, unfolded it, and scanned the front page, occasionally glancing over the top at the serving counter. Even at a distance, it was apparent that Blake and the pretty young girl were engaged in an animated discussion. Adara smiled watching the attendant primp and pose.

He returned with two ceramic cups and a metal pot on a nondescript Bakelite tray. "'Sorry, ducks, no coffee, only tea. Even then it's weaker than sin as I have to use the tea bags twice over,'" he quoted. "'That's quite alright,' I told her, 'hold the tea bag for the servicemen. I'll have two hot waters instead.'"

"How very thoughtful and patriotic of you. Did you pay her for it?"

"Of course, and a tip," he answered. "Here's your change." Shifting gears quickly he continued, "Where did you get The New York Times?"

"Odd Duck. Remember him, 'ducks'?"

"Oh, I thought it was The Times, as in London. Mind if I look at a section?"

"You can have it all. Ghastly war photos. Reports of fresh disasters. And some child has been scribbling on the inside front page. Blake, in spite of, or perhaps because of, Odd Duck's thinly veiled threats, I think that it's time to go and find out for myself if there's any news about Clifford. We can't leave here until I'm absolutely certain that he is going to be all right." Adara stood up. "Back soon, chéri. Be good."

"Always. Don't get lost, Adara. Ciao!" Glancing at the front-page article headings and accompanying photographs of war-torn Europe, he turned over to Page Two. His attention was immediately drawn to the bottom right margin. There, printed in small but clearly legible characters was 6/3/2/3. 'That's no child's scribble. It's a message.' Rapidly he deciphered, 'Section 6, page 3, column 2, item 3.' Quickly turning to Section Six, Classified Ads, and then page three, he found Column two, and scanned down to the third entry:

World-famous Rockettes! Limited number of select seats available for the Thanksgiving Gala Special Preview Show, at New York's Radio City Music Hall. Why line up? Simply call Baker 3525. Phones open November 13 at 10:00 a.m., until this special offer is sold out!

He didn't have to read it again to know that he, Special Agent 3525, had been recalled to New York without delay after checking in at Clifford's, and presumably, Odd Duck's office on London's Baker Street. 'But why?'

His musing was interrupted when Adara returned. "Clifford's going to be fine. I just spoke with him. There are two plain-clothes coppers outside his room. His private room, that is. Odd Duck must be flexing his Home Office muscle. I got in though. Said I was his stepdaughter. Clifford caught on straightaway and went along with it, thank goodness. He said that there are no fewer than a half-dozen SIS/MI5 agents assigned to the assault investigation. Oh yes, Odd Duck, he truly loved that, is a man called Jenkins; foursquare, a top echelon 'handler' and 'fixer' and can be trusted with your life. Clifford's exact words. Sorry, darling, I'm rambling." Seeing Blake's expression, she paused. "What's wrong?"

"The New York Times, Adara. The scribbling? It's a message for me. I've been called to New York."

"Oh, I see," she replied coolly. "When do you have to leave?"

"Right away, darling. When this happens, it means 'drop everything and get back soonest! I'll have to take the first available flight out of London. I am so sorry, Adara. I'm concerned about you and Clifford. We don't know what's going on here yet and we have to find out."

"Look, don't worry about me, Blake. I lived in London for a year and I know scads of people. I'll be fine. If nothing works out, I'll just ring up Granny Zekara. She has a lovely little walk-up flat not far from the hospital. I want to spend as much time here with Clifford as I possibly can."

"I agree. Here's what we'll do. Jenkins and company may be exactly as Cliff said, but I'm from Missouri when it comes to 'secret operatives'. There are just too many unanswered questions. I'll speak to the Director of the hospital and say that the situation warrants his keeping an eye on things, and on you, for my peace of mind, and ask his permission for both of us to stay overnight. Then I'll take a cab to Baker Street and demand to speak with Sir Willson Cunnington. I'll come back as soon as I have his word that Jenkins is a boy scout. If it's a ploy, you can expect to see Sir Willson, his bullyboys, me, and a lot of very serious bother for Jenkins' lads. Do not leave here under any circumstances. I will be back, alright, love?"

"Yes, you have my word, Blake," replied Adara. "Be careful and come back soon. Love you!"

"Good. Love you, too."

64 Baker Street, London, W1

Recalling his first visit, Blake smiled when the same seemingly ageless gentleman in a bespoke navy blue Savile Row suit and Tartan tie complete with a bushy regimental moustache answered the doorbell, intoning with a courteous Scots burr, "Good afternoon. How may I help you, Sir?"

"Good afternoon. I'm Major Blake Grey. I wish to see Admiral Cunnington."

"Is the Admiral expecting you, Major Grey?"

"Well, not exactly, however it is essential…"

"Major Grey! Come in! Thank you, Angus; I'll take full responsibility for verifying the Major's bona fides," boomed Cunnington. "I saw you alight from the cab. Please come down the hall to my lair." Sir Willson Cunnington, Chief of the British Secret Service, closed the door behind him. "Here, have a seat. Thank you for stopping in on your way to the airport. It was imperative that I speak with you before you leave."

"Thank you, Sir Willson."

"Call me, 'Will', please, Blake. Care for a dram?"

"Thank you, no, Sir Will. Actually, I'm not flying out until 0700 tomorrow. I'm here to verify a few details concerning Clifford Jackson."

"Go ahead, Blake."

"Forgive me if I'm direct, Sir Will, but who is the man, Jenkins?"

"Tony Jenkins. MI5."

"And is he balding, rather plump, and somewhat condescending in manner?" Blake inquired.

"Yes, that's Jenkins to a 'T'," Cunnington chuckled. "Despite all that, he's as reliable as rain."

"Well, Sir, I'm relieved to know that. Of course, he did hand me The New York Times. And can I assume that he, or rather you, are on the Jackson case, Sir Will?"

"Oh, Lord, yes, Blake. Full throttle. This incident involving Clifford is most likely linked to your mission in Morocco. Jerry has enough of the blue asbestos fibre for the present, but they'll use up what they have quick time. In typical fashion, they want to be assured that we don't interfere in future negotiations; so, they reasoned that by eliminating Jackson, you'd be sufficiently intimidated to give it up. The Abwehr also have it in for you for Mueller's abrupt termination in Morocco. Actually, Blake, Jenkins' crowd have been keeping an eye on you, and on Miss Zekara, as well."

"Sir?"

"Care to guess?"

Blake grinned. "I think I have it, Sir! The attractive counter girl?"

"Mm, full marks, Blake. Lana's one of our youngest and brightest. One could hardly know it from her Bow Street accent that she's not English-born. She's a Latvian stage actress. She and her company were touring the provinces in '39 doing *Pygmalion*. They sought asylum here just before the Russkie's invaded in '40. I happened to see her playing Eliza Doolittle in Manchester and knew she was just what we were looking for: brains, beauty, and that je ne sais pas quality."

"Lana. The same as the glamorous Hollywood actress, Lana Turner?"

"The same. Sure that you won't join me?" Cunnington stood, indicating his sideboard. "I have brandy, scotch, vodka, and the devil's own gin in the cupboard."

"If you insist, Sir Will. Scotch, neat, two fingers, please." Blake paused while Cunnington poured the drinks. "Thank you. Cheers!" Blake offered, acknowledging Admiral Cunnington's toast. "Well, your Lana certainly had me fooled, Sir Will." Blake shook his head and chuckled in admiration. "Excellent scotch, Sir!"

"Yes, it is rather unusual to be able to find twelve year single malt in these troubled times. Thank you. I shan't tell you how I keep supplied for fear that your Chief, Erik Williamson would attempt to winkle it out of you," Cunnington confided dryly.

"Now, to get to my point, Blake. Something rather big has come up. Something just as important as the Moroccan blue fibre business and even more urgent, if that's possible. Erik Williamson and I are agreed that it can't be divulged until you are safely in America, in his Manhattan office, to be precise. If the other side had any inkling that we know what they're about, thousands, perhaps hundreds of thousands, of lives would be in jeopardy. How and why, I can't say."

"Of course, Sir Will." 'There'd be all hell to pay, literally, if the Germans knew we can eavesdrop on their communications,' Blake correctly inferred. "Very well, Sir. And what of Miss Zekara? As you must know, I've grown very fond of her. I'm quite concerned about her safety and well being," replied Blake, "particularly in that she was mixed up with that scoundrel, Graziano, in Casablanca…the Abwehr …"

"Naturally. She is one of us, Blake, and a damn fine agent, at that. Her protection will continue without interruption. On that, you have my solemn word. Additionally, while you're otherwise occupied, given her involvement from the 'get go', as the Cousins say, she can perhaps assist my chaps in their search for fresh leads to the blue fibre contraband trade. Does that meet your expectations?"

"Yes, extremely so, Sir Will. Thank you. I do appreciate it, Sir. Now, I should be getting back to the hospital. I understand that I'm off to Radio City Music Hall in New York. Pity that I won't get to see the Rockettes, knowing Erik," he smiled, placing the empty glass on a silver serving tray.

"Yes, unfortunately it's simply a rendezvous point. Be waiting outside the Music Hall on the thirteenth and a car will be along to pick you up at 1000h. Williamson will brief you in his usual meticulous manner."

"Very good, Sir Will. I'll be off then. Thanks again." Blake rose from his chair.

"Hold on, old man. There have been slight changes to your plans. You're flying courtesy of RCAF Ferry Command."

"I am, Sir? But why, if I may ask?"

"Erik's idea. Now, they normally fly out of Prestwick, Scotland, but Erik has arranged with his Canadian pal, Air-Vice Marshall Shearer, to have a Lockheed Hudson diverted in order to pick you up here at Croydon Airport.

"Isn't...isn't that flying in the wrong direction, for Ferry Command, Sir? I mean, isn't their job to bring aircraft here, from North America?"

"Yes, you're right," Cunnington chuckled. "But they do have to get the pilots back to Canada. They hardly have the luxury of time to sail home."

"Of course." Blake smiled slightly, silently giving thanks that he would not have to endure another transatlantic crossing as a galley assistant, third class.

Pushing back his chair, Cunnington opened his desk drawer and produced a small manila envelope. "Take this, Blake. You'll find an itinerary, hotel reservations, and sufficient funds to cover your out-of-pockets. Open it, please."

"Very well." He extracted a typewritten sheet and a sheaf of bank notes: British, Canadian, and American. "Whew, that's more than I'll likely need, Sir."

"Consider it danger compensation for past and future exploits. A few more details and then we're done. You will take off from Croydon tonight at 1930h."

Blake glanced at his wristwatch. 'Six hours.'

"Please read your agenda, memorize and return it." Cunnington waited while Blake complied. "Questions or concerns?"

Shaking his head, Blake handed back the paper. "No, it all seems well-planned."

"Now, one or two items that weren't included. An agent, Anderson, has been assigned to look after transporting you and Miss Zekara, Adara. He will drive you back to the Maudsley to pick her up and from there convey you both to her grandmother's flat. We have conducted the usual thorough background security checks, including the neighbours, of course. He will have you at Croydon airfield at 1900h. Oh, and one last thing. This came in the post for you. I've been holding it for your return."

"Thanks, Sir Will. As usual, your thoroughness is impressive and sincerely appreciated. From Canada?"

"Read it in private, Blake."

Blake looked up at Cunnington questioningly.

"No, no. I have absolutely no idea. Word of honour!" Cunnington affirmed. "I just thought it might be the sort of thing you might want to digest in peace. You'll find it's delightfully quiet around this hour at The Fox and Thistle. Only minutes away. Out the door, left, and turn left onto Marylebone Road. It's two doors past the Waxworks. I highly recommend the fish and chips or the proprietor's specialty, steak and kidney pie, if you're famished. And when you're ready to return to the Maudsley, 1430h say, your host will have your ride waiting curb side. Every good wish,

Blake, and please give my best to Erik Williamson. I know that you're still concerned about Adara and Clifford, but I am doing everything within my power to see to their safety."

"I know, Sir Will. I just hope that you can chase down the culprits."

"Oh, be assured, Blake, we will. You have my word on it!"

As the proprietor cleared away the plate and cutlery, Blake nodded thanks and took a sip of his half and half. Reaching into his jacket's inner pocket he retrieved the mysterious letter from Canada, opened it, and smoothed it out carefully on the table. It was undated.

Dear Blake,

I hope this letter finds you well.

I regret to have to tell you this, but I feel that I must. I recently met a man who is working at Father's office. His name is James Catherwood. James is a lawyer. Father has known James' family at the Country Club for many years. James and I didn't mean for this to happen, but it did. As we are to announce our engagement within the month, I thought it only fair and honourable to let you know now.

I have thought about this for many sleepless nights. How would my life be with you? I could only envision more years of secrecy and long unexplained absences. I only know that whatever it is you do, it must be of invaluable benefit to Canada.

Please do not think ill of me, Blake. I will always hold you in the highest regard and hope that you will do the same for me.

Kindest regards,

Trudy Bristol

'Trudy *Bristol*. Just on the off-chance there are two or three Trudy's on my dance card, I suppose. Should have seen this coming, Blake,' he sighed, refolding the letter and placing it in the envelope. And I should have let you know about Adara. Can't say that I blame you, Trudy, old girl. The going was getting rocky. I suppose it began to fall apart in the spring, when Erik and Robert Brooks recruited me. Trudy must have suspected that there was someone else. The irony is, there wasn't. Not then. I know I damn well would have been suspicious. All of my mysterious coming and goings without any explanation except the occasional feeble, 'duty calls'. Part of the price you agreed to pay, Blake. But should I complain? I have Adara. Do I deserve her? Probably not. Am I lucky? Yes. Look at Robert Brooks. Wife killed in an accident. Sophisticated, handsome, brilliant. Putting in sixteen-hour days as Erik's top man in Canada. What chance for a relationship is there in that?'

'You were right, Trudy,' he reflected, 'I deserved the *Dear Blake* treatment. I could have made more of an effort to set things right at the train station, when I think about it now.'

"Blake, darling, do you have to leave tomorrow? Ken and Charlotte Davis have invited us to their dinner party at Auberge des Deux Monts after the races! It will be so much fun! Daddy and scads of his horsey chums will be there, perhaps a cabinet minister or the American Ambassador. I so want you to meet Father."

"I'm afraid I'll have to pass on this one, darling. King and country," Blake shouted from the bathroom over the sound of running water. 'Oh, God, Ken and Charlotte's. The last one was a disaster.' "But that's no reason to mess up your plans. You go and dazzle Daddy's horsey set. Why, hello!"

"I need a kiss, now, foam face!"

"In the midst of my manly ritual?" he asked in mock seriousness.

"Ritual be damned. You heard me. Ah, I feel much better. You wouldn't abandon me, now, would you?" Trudy asked coyly. Tenderly, Blake wiped a speck of shaving cream from her chin as she walked past to the bedroom.

The drive down to Montréal in Trudy's magnificent right hand drive British racing green Jaguar roadster should have been magic. Its top down, the magnificent SS100 roadster's six-cylinder overhead valve engine produced a throaty snarl as only that finely engineered power plant was capable. The trip had begun positively enough. He had even commented several times, admiring her impressive double-clutching and perfectly-timed down shifts.

Trudy, however, was not to be seduced or swayed from her agenda. Her probing into the whys and wherefores of this latest unexplained departure was spurned with non-committal shrugs. He was not being intentionally evasive; he simply had no idea himself as to his assignment. The discussion quickly deteriorated into bickering and finally, into silence. Later, Blake smiled inwardly at how charitably she had dismissed their quarrelling as she kissed him goodbye at Central Station:

"Silly back and forthing. Sorry, Blake, darling. My doing. I'll miss you terribly, that's all. I don't do at all well when you're on the 'missing in action' list." He brushed her cheek lightly with his fingertips; her iridescent tears were genuine. He felt terrible.

"Damn this bloody war!" Blake muttered, taken back momentarily to their bittersweet parting. Startled by his own outburst, he made a vain attempt to cover up by clearing his throat.

"Couldn't have said it better myself, Sir," remarked the owner, collecting Blake's dish and cutlery.

"Oh, sorry. Must have dozed off for a minute," Blake remarked sheepishly.

"Not a problem, Sir. I won't be bothering you until it's time."

"Thanks, everything was delicious!"

'I must remember to send a telegram to wish her and her lawyer Catherwood kindest regards,' Blake reflected. 'Wonder why he's not in the service? Maybe he... Hold on! James Catherwood. Yes, Catherwood. Ha, now I remember! He's that slick, silver-haired attorney whose Bay Street firm turfed him for certain undisclosed 'irregularities'. Escrow money mysteriously vanished, widow's mortgages in default, orphans out on the street: that sort of dismal business, as I recall. Lost his Rosedale mansion, his Cadillac, his Packard, his trophy wife, and two children. Or so he claimed. Front page news for days. Seamy, steamy reading. Who was his co-conspirator? Ah, yes. How could I forget? His secretary. Quite a babe, she was. A stunner. Likely skiing and playing kneesies with some sleazy Count Drago of Ruritania at Davos, Switzerland. She ditched the shifty old scoundrel PDQ when his house of cards came down. Case hasn't gone to court yet, as far as I can remember. Technicalities! Uh, huh. Some dark hints and rumours swirling about war profiteering, too. In the millions. Munitions. Maybe that's why it's been hushed up. Quite a piece of work, Catherwood, if any of it's true.

'Why would Mr. Bristol take him on in the first place and why on God's green earth would he allow his only daughter to be mixed up with such an unsavoury old scoundrel? The old school tie network, no doubt. Or? Or what? Should I send an engagement present? Um, perhaps a matched set of hacksaw blades? Oh, Trudy, Trudy, my dear friend. Watch your assets.'

"Another, Sir?"

"Oh, no thanks. Here, will this cover it?"

"It's been taken care of, Sir. The driver will be around in two shakes."

The two-hour meeting with BSO Chief Erik Williamson and Deputy Chief of Operations, Robert Brooks, was to be a routine debriefing, or so had Blake expected. That is until Erik had dropped a bombshell, literally. The taxi ride from Rockefeller Centre to Grand Central Station was punctuated by blaring horns and squealing tires, accompanied by a frenzied and often hilarious running commentary by the cabbie consigning all others who drove the streets of his New York City, including its traffic officers, to unusual acts, unspeakable agonies, and eternal flames.

Exhausted from the long, cold, uncomfortable flight, and still slightly hung-over, thanks to a 'deadheading' pilot bound for Gander who had packed a large canteen of coffee well-laced with Newfoundland 'screech', Blake nevertheless managed to concentrate on his assigned task, despite the man's highly entertaining, scatological tirade.

It seemed too bizarre to be believed, and he would not have done so had it come from anyone other than Erik Williamson. German Intelligence, likely the Abwehr, was actually planning to obliterate the massive Canadian munitions plant, Defence Industries Limited, located at Ajax, twenty-five miles east of Toronto, only eight miles from STS 103, Camp-X.

Blake recalled Robert Brooks' words: "Even if they were to only partially succeed by disrupting operations, the results would be catastrophic for the Allies. DIL is the single largest munitions production complex in the British Commonwealth. Erik and I have selected you as BSO's principal operative, Blake. Naturally, others will be assigned as the case unfolds and circumstances warrant." Brooks then added, "Your first stop: The Farm."

'At least I'll see my old pal Hamish Findlay at Camp-X, unless he's been shipped out by now to Swaziland or Timbuktu.'

"Did ya see that moron?" The cabby's nasal New York twang brought Blake back into the moment.

"That's a police car!" he corrected.

"Ya, well maybe the dumb bastard shoulda learned to read before putting on that badge. The sign says, NO U TURN."

"Funny. I could have sworn you did the same in front of Rockefeller Centre."

"That was different, Mac. Us cabbies do it there all the time. Time's money, if ya know what I mean, buddy. Gotta hustle to make a buck these days. So, tell me, what's your line of work?"

"Encyclopaedias. Have any children?"

"Uh, nope." As he shifted uncomfortably, Blake noted the family snapshot proudly displayed on the dashboard. "Uh, two actually. Boy and a girl. But both are too young to read."

"That's nice." After an appropriate period of silence, Blake offered, "These days, I specialize in custom bound Bibles actually."

"Bibles! No kiddin'! You a reverend of some kind? Gees, Sir, sorry about the language."

To Blake, he sounded contrite. "Think nothing of it, my son. Now if you wouldn't mind, I must cogitate."

"Sure whatever, Reverend. You just go ahead and do that. To your heart's content. Maybe say one for me, would ya? And I'll shut my gob."

Which to Blake's great relief, he did.

Arsenal of Democracy

Chapter 2

The Twenty Percent Solution

Ajax – DIL, South Pickering Township, east of Toronto, Ontario, Canada
Fall 1943

Rinsing his coffee cup, Jim Montgomery looked out the kitchen window; a light rain had just begun. He and Lillian lived in a second-hand twenty-five foot trailer located on an otherwise bare patch of land at the northwest corner of what is now Harwood Avenue and the King's Highway Number Two. It was, they declared, only temporary, adding that at least it was conveniently near their workplace.

"It's starting to come down. It'll likely be a downpour by the time we get out of church."

"Jim, don't put that back in the cupboard. Let it dry in the rack."

"Ooops, sorry, Lil. By the way, I was talking with James Gillard last night at the Foreman's Club."

"Who?"

"James Gillard. You know his wife, Christine. The one you play Bridge with Thursday evenings."

"Yes, Christine, of course. She hasn't been there the last couple of weeks," replied Lillian.

"I'm not surprised. James was pretty down...telling me that their boy, Freddie, he's only eighteen-years old, has just joined his two brothers, Jimmie and Bob, overseas. Can you imagine what those parents are going through?"

"No, Jim, I can't. I don't even like to think about it. Did you know that besides James and Christine working at Ajax, their youngest son, Sandy, and daughter, Ellin, both work at DIL too?"

"Really? Where do they work?"

"On Line One," replied Lillian.

"Well, I'll be…I've seen their names but didn't put it together with James and Christine."

"That family has been through so much. James's mother was killed in an air raid in England and Christine's grandmother also died in an air raid. On top of everything else, Christine has two brothers fighting in Europe."

"My god Lillian, that family deserves a special medal when this war is over," Jim declared. "What shift are you on next week, Lil? I know you told me…".

"Days," Lillian replied. "It's marked on the calendar. Why?"

"So it is. Just trying to keep track of whose turn it is to make dinner tonight. You're on days; I'm graveyard, so that means that it's my turn."

"That's right, Jim, which also means that we'll likely be eating your famous Sunday roast leftovers' stew all week, and roast beef sandwiches in the lunch boxes."

"Yes, dear."

"No bother," Lillian sighed, washing the remaining breakfast dishes. "I'm so bushed when I get home that I can hardly taste food anyway. Go put on your suit coat. I'll finish up. Oh, dear, look at the time: ten-twenty. If I don't shake a leg we'll be late for church."

"I'll be out front, Lil, warming up the Buick. I have to check the tire pressure before it runs flat. Noticed yesterday that it was down a bit. Don't forget the collection envelope!"

"It's in my purse, on the bureau. My, you do look spiffy, Jim! I'm very proud of you, Mr. Shop Foreman!"

"You say that to all the boys!" he answered, gently kissing her cheek. "Hurry, Lil! You know how Rev Peebles glares at latecomers."

"'Reverend' Peebles, Jim! I'll be out in two shakes!"

British Commonwealth Air Training Plan (BCATP) Centre

Elementary Flight Training School No. 20, (EFTS) Oshawa

"Do you hear that, John?" Albert shouted above the idling 145 hp deHavilland four-cylinder engine.

"Hear what? I don't hear anything," John called back. "She sounds real swcct to mc!"

"The pinging, man! It's as clear as day. The timing's off. Goose it. There it is again. Hear it now?"

"Go on. I can't hear anything, Al. You're imagining things."

"I think it's the valves; I'm going to make an adjustment. Hold on." Albert turned a nut a fraction of an inch securing the valve assembly. "There, that's better."

Albert Cowan and John Billington had been best friends since grade one at South Simcoe Public School in South Oshawa. A recess-time scrap over a game of Red Rover had resulted in a tussle and a subsequent visit to the principal's office where the two boys settled the dispute and, from that moment forward, became inseparable. As they grew up, they designed and built model airplanes and began tinkering with cars. In Grade 12 (Form 4), they jumped at the chance to apply for the apprenticeship program at 'The Motors', General Motors of Canada. Upon completion, they were recommended for training as aircraft mechanics at deHavilland Aircraft in Toronto. Qualifying in less than two years, they were posted to EFTS No. 20, Oshawa's Elementary Flight Training School.

"That'll do it, John. You can wheel her out. Lieutenant Colonel Findlay will be over to take her up this afternoon."

"Right." John climbed into the cockpit of the Tiger Moth biplane, the basic trainer of the British Commonwealth Air Training Plan. "He'd better treat this baby with care. Last time the cockpit was half-filled with flour, remember, Al?" he shouted, shaking his head.

"Yeah, sure. Findlay's an officer, and we're not, so you might as well go cry in your beer at the Genosh! Now roll this crate out of here, John! The next job up's a complete five-hundred hour mechanical!"

Badge of Elementary Flight Training School No.20, Oshawa,ON

Ajax – DIL, Defence Industries Limited

South Pickering, Ontario, Canada

"Good morning, Dorothy. Mr. Caldwell wants to see me?"

"Hi, Jim. Yes, he does. He's on the telephone but you're to go right in."

"Thanks, Dorothy. Any idea what's cookin'?"

"Not a clue, Jim," she smiled. "How's Lillian?"

"Great, thanks. Are you and Trevor coming to the wiener roast Saturday night?"

"Wouldn't miss it! You and Lil?"

"We'll be there. Hope the weather holds up," Jim replied.

"It should be fine unless Trevor washes the car!" she laughed. "You know his luck!"

"Do I? Two golf tournaments back-to-back rained out. Hide his bucket and chamois," he smiled. "I'd better go in."

Dave Caldwell looked up. "Morning, Jim! Just give me a minute to finish this business and I'll be right with you; have a chair," offered Caldwell affably, his hand over the receiver.

"I'm fine, thanks." Jim looked out the General Manager's window onto the shop floor below, where row upon row of young women filled metal artillery shells with deadly high explosives. The majority of the women wore coloured bandanas to cover their heads, keeping stray hairs from contaminating the chemicals. Jim Montgomery was constantly amazed at the women's resourcefulness in creating a Canadian fashion fad with a triangle of coloured material. Replacing the receiver, Dave Caldwell pushed back his chair. Crossing his legs, he reached back with both arms to cradle his head in his hands. "So, how's it going, Jim?" "Good. Real good, Dave. Everything's back to normal since that conveyer belt was replaced last weekend. Why, do you see a problem, Dave?"

Sitting forward, Caldwell confided, "No. But they do. The Brass. Two problems, actually. Ottawa and Head Office want a twenty percent increase in production. Any ideas, Jim?" asked Dave.

"Twenty percent?" Jim sank into the wooden chair. "Good Lord, Dave. The women are working twenty-four hours a day, three eight-hour shifts, six days a week as it is. How in blazes can I ask any more of them?"

"I know, I know, Jim. But it's not a matter of whether or not we can.

We have to do it. DIL's under the gun, and so are our lads overseas. It's a twenty percent increase here or they'll be firing blanks there. It's that simple. End of story."

Jim sat in silence. "So, that's it, Dave? Do it or bust?"

"Pretty much, Jim."

"Okay, Dave, I'll give it some serious thought. But offhand I don't see how we can swing it. Unless…"

"Unless what?"

"Unless we can expand the place and hire more help. Fat chance of either one, eh?"

Shell assembly line DIL

"About the same as that proverbial snowball," grunted Caldwell. "'Do more with what you've got.'"

"So, what's the other piece of cheer, Dave?"

"If we don't come up with a workable plan within forty-eight hours, I was told a team of Defence officials from Ottawa and supervisors from Montreal will be landing on our doorstep. I'll be lucky to be counting rolls of toilet paper in the warehouse. So far, Jim, it looks like you're okay."

"Come on, you can't be serious, Dave? This shop's production figures are the best in the whole Empire and Commonwealth!"

"That was yesterday, Jim. I am, or rather they are, deadly serious. Canadian sons, brothers, and dads are being outgunned and it has to be stopped. Now. Is it political as well? Of course. But these days, what isn't?"

"I remember a sign in the manager's office where I worked before the war: 'We don't expect miracles, we depend on them.' Seems to apply to this situation, eh?"

"True, too true," Caldwell sighed as he pushed back his chair, stood up and walked over to his window. Jim Montgomery walked toward the door, opened it, and then paused.

"Wait a minute...!" Jim ventured.

Turning around, Dave Caldwell asked, "You forget something, Jim?"

"It's just a thought. It might just be wishing for the sky; might not fly at all. Probably won't," replied Jim.

"For heavens sake man! What is it? I can't decide whether it has a chance or not," retorted Caldwell, "unless you tell me!"

Walking back to the chair in front of Dave's desk, Jim sat down. Leaning forward, his head in his hands, he muttered, "No, that won't work, but maybe if we…"

"Jim! Tell me! Now!" Dave shouted. "Sorry!"

"That's okay. See what you think. What if we hold a contest?" asked Jim.

"A contest," Dave repeated unenthusiastically. "What kind of contest? Hoop tossing? Guess my weight and win a cigar?" he asked sullenly.

"No, Dave. An efficiency improvement contest!" exclaimed Jim.

"Go on."

"The person putting forward the best idea for improving the quality and quantity on the production lines will win either a first, second or third prize, depending on the increase in productivity."

"How would it work?" asked Dave.

"Okay. First, we set up suggestion boxes in all of the buildings. Then, we'll announce the contest in the ***Commando Newsletter***, you know, rules and all that. Put up posters everywhere and have Payroll include flyers in all personnel pay cheque envelopes," replied Jim.

"Go on Jim, this is sounding interesting."

"Okay, up to a ten percent increase in production or quality would win you third prize, twenty percent, second prize and thirty percent, first prize. Anything above that, the prize would be decided by the Management Committee. How does that sound?" asked Jim tentatively.

"Jim, my boy, I think you're onto something. Sound management strategy. Very up-to-date, too. You want production increased, get the producers involved. Yes, indeed. Something like that worked for Western Electric at their Hawthorne plant in Illinois, if I remember correctly. Basically, don't tell, ask and pay attention! The Hawthorne Effect. The study found that just by paying attention to the workers on the line, by varying the lighting, their productivity zoomed. Why?"

"Maybe because they felt management was noticing them."

"Yes, and taking it one step further, they had a sense of being part of 'the team', of being valued. I say it's worth trying. You know, James, you should be taking modern management courses at night school. I think you'd take to it like a duck to water. And Lord knows, we need more managers who know the theory and the realities of the line." Walking over to his desk, Caldwell pressed the intercom button to page Dorothy.

Opening the door, Dorothy inquired, "Yes, Mr. Caldwell?"

"Dot, I want you to have a seat and take down what Jim is about to tell you."

"Yes, Mr. Caldwell."

"Get hopping on it right away. Jim, I want it all laid out today so that I can call the Brass with the good news. One big caution, Jim, and this has to be a major factor in whatever plan we come up with. We don't have the luxury of time as the Hawthorne team did. We can't mess around, spending forever analyzing it to death. It's twenty percent, no BS excuses, or delays, or it's bye bye!"

"I understand, Dave. Oh, one other thing. I've been thinking about prizes."

"What did you come up with, Jim?"

"Well, how about Victory Bonds? Say, top prize one thousand, second, five hundred and third, two hundred."

"Not a bad idea and very fitting for the kind of competition we're looking at. I'll pass it on to the Brass when I call."

"Good. Thanks, Dave." Seating himself beside Dorothy, Jim began, "Well, here's what we're going to do…"

Bus depot at DIL main gate 1943 (Harwood Ave. south of Highway 401)

Highland Creek, Ontario, Canada

Christoph Hartt, Master Mechanic, closed the top of his eight-drawer tool chest and snapped shut the combination lock. "See you tomorrow, Rolf."

"Wait a minute. I'll walk with you to the bus stop," replied Rolf Enders.

The two men had just finished their shift at the Highland Creek Machine Shop.

"Fine. But hurry, Rolf! The bus is coming in seven minutes!"

"*Kein Problem,* Christoph. One minute! We need to talk."

"Ya? What about? Hang on, I've got to go to the washroom. Keep talking," Christoph shouted.

"About things."

"Hey, where the hell did you hide the toilet paper, Rolf?"

"Check your lunch box. You think I didn't see you sneaking…?" Rolf said accusingly.

"There's a war going on! I have a wife and two kids!" Christoph snapped.

"Ya, ya, tell me about it," Rolf replied glumly.

"That's all Herta talks about these days: 'How can you expect the four of us to live on your wages? Can't you get a better-paying job?' Whining. It makes me crazy! Your minute's up, Rolf!"

"Okay, I'll talk with you on the way to the bus," replied Rolf.

"So you see, Christoph, there is an opportunity to make some quick money, and no one will find out."

"But Rolf, what makes you think that they'll go for it?"

"Look, remember Günther? He used to work here."

"Yes, I do. And, I remember what happened to his Italian friend, Marco: garrotted at the Genosha Hotel as I recall," replied Christoph. "Damn the English to hell!"

"And the Canadians! Well, I know where Günther went into hiding after Marco was murdered."

"Get to the point, Rolf," demanded Christoph.

"Okay, okay. Here is the idea. Günther was sending coded messages back to Germany through the U-boats in the St. Lawrence. Don't you know anything? The St. Lawrence River, Christoph! These messages he was receiving from Marco who had managed to get himself established at the spy-training place, Camp-X down by the lake. Are you with me so far?"

Christoph shrugged. "I suppose so. Go on, Rolf."

"So, it's obvious that Günther would pay dearly for any information about Camp-X. In fact, it could be that his life is in danger after Marco was done in. He would likely do anything to redeem himself in the eyes of Berlin."

"I'm beginning to see where you're going with this Rolf. So what exactly is your plan?"

"Okay, don't think that I'm crazy, Christoph. Give me a chance to tell you my whole plan before cutting me off, like you usually do. Promise?"

"I promise."

"Good. I have a friend who works at the EFTS in Oshawa. He's a mechanic."

"What's an EFTS?" asked Christoph.

"Elementary Flight Training School, where they train Allied pilots before going overseas," replied Rolf.

"What's your friend's name?"

"Albert Cowan. He has mentioned to me many times that anytime I want, he would take me up. Apparently Sundays are the student pilots' day off."

"How do you know this Albert Coward?"

"Cowan. We belong to the same model airplane club."

"Fine. And how is this going to make us some extra money?" asked Christoph.

"I'll ask Albert to teach me to fly an airplane. He says I already have very good 'air sense' from flying models, which shouldn't surprise you. Apparently the planes, they're called Tiger Moths, are very easy to learn on. And 'moths' is very hard to say," he remarked. "Anybody can learn to fly a Tiger Mo... trainer in a short time."

"And just what do we do after learning how to fly this plane?" asked Christoph.

"Here's my plan. We will fly over both Camp-X…"

"Yes, Camp-X! Now I remember! Günther was always going on about it when he wasn't supposed to. Big braggart that he was," replied Christoph.

"Very good. Anyway, we'll fly over Camp-X taking photographs as we go and then travel west toward Ajax where they have the largest munitions works in North America."

"Now I'm sure you're crazy. What makes you think that they are just going to let us fly over these secret military installations, Rolf? They'll shoot us down!"

"There are no anti-aircraft guns at either place. I'll bet my life on that. You gave me your word you wouldn't interrupt. So please, be quiet. Here's where my plan becomes brilliant. John told me one time that the head officer of Camp-X often comes up to pick up a Tiger Moth to fly down to the Camp. Apparently they use them for some type of training. He always flies in the same plane: number 9666. I've actually seen him flying around this area. Always in 9666," said Rolf.

"And so?"

"I have an uncle who has a farm in Orono. Once we can fly the plane, which shouldn't take more than a few weeks to learn. I'll ask my friend John if I can take it up for a solo. I know he'll let me, as he likes to play the big shot. I'll build up his ego first. You'll drive out to my Uncle's farm with the camera equipment. There's an old barn in the backfield, which isn't used anymore. I'll land there. You bring with you stencils, and black water-based paint, which we will use to replace the numbers on the plane with 9666. We'll then fly out over the lake and come back on land just before we get to the Camp. What do you think?"

"You realize that if we're caught, we'll be in prison for life or hanged as spies. Next point: if we do this thing, how would we get the photographs to Berlin? Air mail?" Christoph sniggered.

"Günther!" stated Rolph.

"And how in hell will he accomplish this?"

"That's up to him. Are you in or out, Christoph?"

"What about the money?"

"What about the money!"

"How much are you going to ask for?"

"Five thousand."

"Five thousand…dollars? Whew!"

"Yes. We'll split it in half."

"Well, what if he says he doesn't have it?"

"What if… what if. What if we drop dead tomorrow? What if Germany loses the war? What if I just do this myself?" he added with finality.

"Okay, okay, I'm sorry."

"Günther will have to come up with it if he wants to get back in favour with Berlin. He can deliver them personally for all I care. I'm going to ask you this just once more, Christoph: Are you in or out?"

"I'm in."

"Shake on it and solemnly swear: word of honour."

"*Ehrenwort*. I swear."

"Good, so we're in business, are we, Christoph?"

"Let's get started!"

Ajax – DIL, Defence Industries Limited
South Pickering, Ontario, Canada

Popping his head inside Dave Caldwell's office, Jim Montgomery called, "Are you ready, Dave? We've stopped the line for five minutes during lunch, as you requested."

"Excellent Jim. And I have more good news from the Brass."

"You do?"

"Yep, they've sweetened the pot. Considerably. Wait till you hear!" Stepping out onto the metal catwalk, Dave looked down at the shop floor. All of the employees were now standing, waiting quietly beside their machines.

"Thank you, ladies and gentlemen for taking five minutes out of your lunchtime to allow me to address you about a very important subject. As you know, thanks to Foreman Jim Montgomery here, we have a great contest underway at DIL. I have to tell you that it has paid off handsomely already. So, without further ado, it is my pleasure to announce our first finalist: Fred Prasse. Fred, come up here!"

"Who, me? Holy Toledo!" His face beaming, Fred bounded up the steep flight of stairs to be greeted warmly by General Manager Dave Caldwell and Supervisor Jim Montgomery. "Congratulations, Fred!" Dave declared. "Now, Jim, since this is your baby, read the citation, please."

"Thanks, Dave. Fred, your suggestion to eliminate the daily dismantling of the presses and replace it with a bi-weekly cleaning has saved the company at least thirty percent in downtime and, a substantial increase in production. Great job, Fred!"

"What does he get?" shouted Val Linton from below.

"Good question, Val," Dave responded. "Fred, I'm delighted to tell you that your name, along with two other finalists' chosen by Jim and me, goes to Management Committee next Monday, for a final decision. The contest ends this Friday, five p.m., don't forget, folks. Keep filling those contest boxes with your ballots. Oh, yes, the most important thing of all: Defence Industries Limited is pleased to announce that each 1st place winner will receive a one week, all-expenses paid holiday at the beautiful Muskoka Pines Inn."

A roar of approval and applause rose from the floor.

"That's in addition to the Victory Bonds!" Dave shouted. "For the rest of you, get your thinking caps on. You have two more days to drop your brilliant idea into the box. Winners will be announced next Tuesday: same time, same place. Now, enjoy your lunch. And remember, folks, this is a quarterly contest. So, if you don't win this time, keep filling that box and you could be up here, like Fred, next time."

Workers on Line 3 removing shipping caps and cleaning shell casings

The Montgomery's Trailer
Plant Road (Harwood and Highway No. 2)

Jim Montgomery burst in through the door of the trailer shouting, "Lillian! Lillian!"

"What is it, Jim?"

"Where are you, Lil?"

"It's a small trailer, Jim. I'm in the bedroom getting changed."

"Hey, Lil, I've got some great news! Guess where we're going to be vacationing next summer?"

"I can't guess, Jim. Wasaga Beach, again. Don't tease me about things like that," Lillian replied.

"I'm not teasing you. You know my idea of holding the contest in order to improve production?"

"Well, sure. I work there too, remember."

"Well, it's been so successful that Dave awarded *me* a prize!"

"Oh, my gosh! A prize! What kind of prize?" asked Lillian.

"A one-week paid vacation at a terrific resort in Muskoka!" exclaimed Jim. "I-I forget the name. Oh, here it is," he exclaimed excitedly, taking an envelope out of his pocket. "The Muskoka Pines Inn! Look at that picture! Can you believe it?"

"Jim, I'm so proud of you! Coming up with that idea! And now this. I'd love to go out and buy some end-of-season clothes this weekend while they're still on sale. Oh, well, I can make do with what I have."

"You should go shopping. Hey, Lil, we'll go fishing and canoeing."

"You'll go fishing, I'll be reading on the dock with my feet up," replied Lillian.

"Whatever you want. What's for dinner? I'm starved!"

"Beef stew and leftovers from your Sunday dinner. Remember, Chef Montgomery?"

"Yes, yes, I remember. Overdone and too salty for you," he commented glumly. Brightening, he remarked, "Lil, I picked up the ***Commando***."

"Oh, it was fine, dear. Shucks, Jim, you can't be perfect at everything.

Would you read me the editorial while I get dressed?"

"Sure, dear. Just let me find my glasses. There, now I can make it out. Okay, it says:

Capping shells

"All Out" Effort Means "All In" Every Shift

Anyone who would deliberately absent himself or herself from a defence job today is as guilty of desertion as any soldier, seaman, or airman who would shirk his duty in the face of the enemy. This is a critical time-acutely so. The summer offensives of our enemies, the war-mad dictatorships, are under way. Their blood-drunk armies are pressing on every front. Sevastopol has fallen, Tobruk and Barbia are lost, Egypt is threatened; yes, even at our north western ramparts the Aleutian Islands, they are hamming with everything they've got. On the seas and under the seas they menace our convoys of sorely needed help and supplies, and from the air they hurl their hate and mass murder on our kinfolk and allies. They must- will be- stopped.

The gallant men and women of the United Nations who are facing the brunt of this war are sacrificing everything, including their very lives, in their efforts to do so. But, their sacrifices - ironically - are not enough. They have to be more than a match for the enemy; they must have the

```
means of resistance and aggression, as well as the
spirit of sacrifice.
```

```
And that is a challenge to every defence worker.
It is not only a challenge, but also a test of
our patriotism. It is up to us, every one of us,
to measure up to the test. We can do it; it is a
simple job. It is to keep the munitions of war
constantly, continuously, and amply supplied to
our fighting men. That is a production job and
we have the plant, the brains, and the brawn to
do it. Don't let us jeopardize that job- and
absenteeism is doing just that. Production cannot
be maintained without a vast army of workers on
the job, on time, everyday. Let Hitler's munitions
workers take the odd day off, let his labour
slaves take it easy; but, let us answer the
whistle as the soldier responds to the bugle. Let
us remember that an ALL OUT EFFORT MEANS ALL IN
EVERY SHIFT.
```

"Look at it as a celebration for my award. Besides, next summer we don't have to pay for a vacation. How much are we going to save there?" asked Jim.

"I guess you're right. We will save a lot on our holiday. I suppose we should. Yes, let's go. Heaven knows we haven't had a night out *together* in dog's years," replied Lillian meaningfully. Seeing his reaction, she held out her arms. "Oh, come here." They hugged and kissed warmly.

"And I want you to get those summer clothes. No arguments. Okay?" Jim whispered.

"If you say so. And you need new shorts, Mr. Montgomery. Those ugly plaid ones you bought without me are covered with paint. We can't have you traipsing around a fancy resort looking like no one takes care of you, now can we? Say, Mr. Prize Winning Foreman, dinner's not ready for um… twenty-three minutes…"

VICTORY IS
R BUSINESS!
Commando
OF DEFENCE INDUSTRIES LIMITED • AJAX • ONTARIO
AJAX, ONTARIO, AUGUST 5, 1942
NUMBER
"Each to our part, each to our station."

Arsenal of Democracy

Chapter 3 Puzzling *Times*

Ajax DIL Ajax DIL Ajax DIL Ajax DIL

Special Training School 103 Camp-X

Whitby/Oshawa, Ontario

Fall 1943

Camp-X, aerial view

Blake! Blake! Behind you! On your left!" shouted Hugh Mason. "The bloody fool's going to blind-side you!"

"I see him!" Gathering momentum, Blake Grey suddenly feinted to his right in an attempt to shake off his rapidly approaching adversary.

"Blake! Over here! I'm in the clear!" Mason called. Oblivious to Mason's plea, Blake bobbed and weaved, executing a brilliant sequence of broken-field running manoeuvres. But relentlessly his pursuer gained ground, nimbly countering each evasive tactic.

Intending to throw a shoulder block at the onrushing attacker's knees, Mason slipped on the soggy field and fell, face down. The momentum rolling him onto his back, he looked on helplessly as Blake flew forward with the violent collision.

Staggering as though pole axed, Blake buckled, collapsing sideways. The sickening snap of shattering leg bones rang like rapid-fire pistol shots across the field. Lieutenant Colonel Hamish Findlay dashed from the sidelines to Blake's assistance.

As Blake hit the ground, the ball squirted out of his arms. Arcing end-over-end, it drifted lazily into the outstretched hands of his stunned opponent.

Enraged, Mason scrambled to his feet and launched an attack aimed below the perpetrator's knees. Having deftly sidestepped Mason, the ball carrier lumbered onward for ten yards, picking up momentum until he was clipped from behind by two Yugoslav 'client-trainees'. Winded and tottering, he struggled to maintain his footing until Mason threw a perfectly executed flying mare, finally taking him down. "You crazy Yank bastard! You've broken his leg!"

Taking Captain Mason's lead, his teammates turned on their American rivals. A wild melee ensued as punches and furious insults flew.

"Gentlemen! That will do! I said that will do!" Lieutenant Colonel Findlay thundered above the pandemonium as he reached Blake's side. The scuffling players froze, staring at the Commandant in shocked silence. "Captain Mason, you will get off that man, immediately! Help him up, Captain!"

"Yes, Colonel." Reluctantly, Hugh Mason released his grip on the American's neck, and slowly stood up.

"Captain DuBose, on your feet, Sir," Findlay continued matter-of-factly, removing his jacket and covering Blake who was now exhibiting signs of shock.

Scowling, Mason reluctantly held out his hand to the gasping, red-faced American officer.

"Very well. You will all shake hands, gentlemen." The teams formed two ragged lines in compliance with his order. Unimpressed with the lacklustre display of fellowship, Hamish snapped, "Gentlemen! I mean it! Much better. Good show!

"Captain Mason, I need a blanket, a stretcher, and leg splints. That's on the double, Captain!"

Panting and perspiring heavily, Mason fumbled on the ground for his left shoe.

"And bring two stout lads with you! Not in a fortnight, Captain, immediately!"

"Yes, Colonel, right away, Sir!" Breaching camp protocol, Mason saluted his commanding officer before hobbling toward the Camp office building.

American OSS 'client'-trainees on manoeuvres north of Camp-X

"Oh, good Lord! Lord, I'm deeply, deeply sorry, Sir!" The disembodied Southern drawl drifted downward to Blake Grey.

Blinking, Blake searched the sea of blurred faces. "Was, was that you, Captain?" he whispered.

The distraught six-foot two-inch Captain leaned over Major Blake Grey.

"Captain DuBose. Rufus Dagget DuBose II, Sir. I, I apologise deeply, M, Major Grey," he stammered. "I accept full responsibility, Major. I just got carried away with the c, consarned excitement, Sir," admitted DuBose, shaking his head in despair.

A smile flickered faintly across Blake's ashen features. "Well, let me tell you something, Captain Rufus Dagget DuBose II." Blake slowly wet his lips, and then continued in a hoarse whisper, "I don't know what it's called at West Point… but in the Canadian football rule book, it's Rough Play… likely to get you tossed… out for the… remainder." Blake blanched, wincing with pain. "Damn! Is my leg broken, Colonel?"

Findlay declined to answer, looking instead at his wristwatch. "Help is on the way, any moment, old man," he reassured, patting Blake's arm.

"Adara won't believe this. Maybe she will: "Mon Dieu, que tu es idiote, Blake!"

Despite himself, Hamish chuckled. "I'd dearly love to meet this lady!"

"I am some kind of idiot!" Blake reiterated with a grimace. "She's over there doing something useful and I'm here playing football and now I'm no… damned use to anyone," Blake's muttering trailed off. "Could you let her know, gently, Hamish?"

"Sssh, lad, I'll take care of it. Promise."

"Thanks," replied Blake with a slight smile. Looking up at DuBose, he continued weakly, "You were an all-star line-backer at the Academy. 'Freight Train Dubose' or some such, wasn't it?"

"Yes, Sir," DuBose replied solemnly. "I have no excuse. I should have known better, Sir." Obviously distraught, his lips trembled as he spoke. Despite the pain, Blake experienced a fleeting moment of alarm at the prospect of this gigantic youth falling prostrate on the field, blubbering childlike for forgiveness. He was relieved when Dubose stood up to make way for Captain Mason, accompanied by the two sturdy Yugoslav trainee-client tacklers carrying a folding field stretcher.

"Yes, you should have, but I understand…the game. There's one other thing, Captain…" Blake's face contorted with pain as the two men attempted to raise him.

"Stop!" Findlay shouted at the Yugoslavs. "It might be a compound fracture! Bloody hell! Have you two yobs never heard of first aid? Give me the blanket! Stand aside. Please." As Hamish's fingers gently probed Major Grey's grotesquely twisted right leg, he watched the injured officer's face for signs of distress.

"Double fracture…the fibula and tibia. Fortunately, not compound," Findlay concluded gravely. "Blake, can you squeeze my finger? Good lad! Now let's try it again, with your left hand. Very good. Rest, man, rest.

"There appears to be no spinal trauma, apart from severe bruising of the upper torso region," Hamish muttered. "Lord only knows, but I wouldn't rule out a shredded knee ligament. Once I've secured the leg splints, we'll transfer him onto the stretcher. There, that should do it. Mason, immobilise his head. Excellent. You two lads, cross his arms. Then, by the shoulders…ready, on a three count. Easy!"

When Blake finally rested on the stretcher, DuBose addressed the Commanding Officer. "Permission to speak with Major Grey, Colonel Findlay? Briefly?"

"Briefly, very briefly, Captain DuBose. He's losing consciousness."

Captain DuBose knelt by the stretcher. "Begging your pardon, Major, you were going to say…?"

"Major Beck, high-tail it up to the office! Have Betty call Doc Miller. Tell him to meet us at The Oshawa General in fifteen minutes!" Findlay instructed. "He's to insist that their top orthopaedic surgeon be scrubbed and standing by! If he's not available, I want Doc to have Major Grey on an operating table in Toronto within the hour!"

"Oh, yes. There is one other thing, Captain DuBose," Blake responded faintly. "I am…definitely…taking you with me for…backup the next time I'm ordered to haul our boys' butts out of The Genosha. In the meantime, Captain, keep your head down and your powder…d, dry." Fluttering briefly, Blake's eyelids closed.

"Sir! Thank you, I will. God keep you, Sir!" DuBose called out as Blake's stretcher was borne away. Head bowed, DuBose offered a silent prayer for Blake's recovery.

"Captain DuBose?" a friendly voice queried. "Are you alright? Captain DuBose?"

"Sorry," Dubose answered. "More or less, thank you, Sir. I was curious about the Major's mention of, was it, The Genosha?"

"Major Michael Heaviside, Explosives, and Small Arms. Yes, The Genosha. It's a respectable hotel in Oshawa: one of the more popular watering holes on a Saturday night. Oh, Lord knows there are others: the Queens for example, on Simcoe Street, cheek by jowl with the Ontario Regiment McLaughlin Armouries, but we stick to 'the Genosh' or the Blue Swallow up the road. Some of the Yanks before you lot renamed the Genosha's bar *Dodge City*. A bit over the top, actually. Quite civilised, mostly. That's not to say that some of the local lads can't get quite belligerent with our chaps from time to time, for God knows what reason. Silly buggers don't have a clue with whom they're dealing. Anyway, you'll find out, Captain. That is, if you can refrain from beating the stuffing out of the senior brass here. Care to walk with me, Captain DuBose?"

"Why, thank you, Major. But I'm not very good company. I'm so disgusted with myself…" DuBose' voice trailed off.

Consolingly, Heaviside placed his hand on the despondent U. S. Ranger Captain's shoulder. "Don't worry about Major Grey, son. He's a survivor. He's a piece of work, believe me. I know first hand, lad. Only three months ago, a gang of hooligans set upon Blake, a bloke we called 'The Prof', and me in an alleyway. There were six of them. Major Blake disposed of two of the villains in the time it takes to tell. The Prof and I were dealing with one apiece and when Blake turned his attention to the other two they didn't know whether to wind their watches or haemorrhage," he chortled, "So off they scarpered like startled rabbits.

"Yes, the Major is a deceptive blighter all right. By his appearance and manner, you'd think he'd be more at home in a tuxedo, romancing a sighing flock of debutantes at some fancy-dress soirée, than he would be here. But in truth, Captain, Major Grey was a street-smart urchin schooled in the hardscrabble ways of Toronto's Cabbagetown. He's quick-witted, a dodgy rascal, altogether too clever by half. His charm and unusually dark good looks combined with his rapid-fire mouth got him girls by the boatload and more than a spot of bother from the boys, naturally. Fortunately, his fists and feet were faster than theirs. As for the girls," grinned Heaviside, "that's an ongoing saga. But he's the soul of discretion and never tells tales. Good thing, too.

"Getting back to the story: quite by chance, a boxing coach from the Cabbagetown YMCA spotted him mixing it up with a gang of toughs, thrashing them single-handedly in a street punch-up. After the man, Salvatore, or Sal, sorted out the combatants who were still standing, he took Blake to a local greasy spoon for a nosh, and invited him to the Y for a try-out the next day."

"Was Salvatore a professional boxer?" inquired DuBose.

"No, amateur. Welterweight. Unfortunately, when he was in his early twenties he contracted polio and that put paid to his future aspirations, inside the ring, at any rate. Up until then, he was considered a gold medal contender, primed to go to Amsterdam as Canada's welterweight pride in the '28 Olympics. A real tiger, Sal, but with a heart of gold. And as fate turned out, a gifted coach and mentor, luckily, for a score of budding juvenile delinquents, including one young Blake Grey.

"Of course, he was pleased to have caught the coach's interest and agreed straightaway. Sal soon realized that he had discovered a thoroughbred, you might say. He saw in the Major all the qualities of a champion: a superbly talented, albeit raw and undisciplined athlete blessed with truly extraordinary intellectual gifts. Sal and his wife, Heike, sought Blake's mom's permission to take over as stand-in parents before Blake could get himself into any serious pickles with the gendarmes, the direction in which he was headed. Blake's mother, perennially in and out of the sanatorium with tuberculosis, was very happy to accept their offer. His father had gone missing when the Major was a tad of three.

"Blake continued to thrive under Sal's tutelage and, as well, took to the books, graduating from high school with top honours. The couple, Sal and Heike, without kids of their own, scraped and saved enough to put him through university. Thanks to them, and gobs of god-given talent, he's as fluent in Italian and German as they. Anyway, after completing a Master's degree at Toronto in lord-knows-what, he sailed off to Cambridge on a scholarship.

"So, that's the story of Major Blake Grey, PhD. Despite Major Grey's well-earned reputation as a formidable adversary, Captain DuBose, he is not a vindictive sort of fellow, generally," Heaviside grinned.

"It's Dag, Major, if you feel so inclined," smiled DuBose. "May I ask, how do you know so much about Major Grey?"

"Sal Musso was my coach too, Dag. I was a scrawny, lonely street brat, a Brit émigré from Manchester who had taken to hanging around the gym after school doing whatever I could to be noticed. Anxious to impress Sal, I volunteered to be Blake's punching bag, read 'sparring partner'. Lord, he was good and was he fast! Like the proverbial greased lightning! He pummelled the tar out of me regularly. Naturally we became best chums."

"Did Major Grey know his real father?"

"Not open for discussion," Heaviside stated emphatically. "Now, Captain, care for a beer in the Mess? You look as though you could use one, or perhaps something even more potent. On me, lad. What say you?"

Camp-X

A few weeks later

"Miss Robertson!"

"Coming, Colonel Findlay." Elspeth 'Betty' Robertson, Executive Secretary of Camp-X since its opening on December 6, 1941, materialised in front of Hamish's desk.

"Exactly where is Major Grey?" demanded Hamish irritably.

"Well, Colonel, the Major is convalescing. On Doctor Miller's orders, Sir," she added pointedly.

"I know that, lass. But exactly where is he convalescing? Tahiti? The Outer Hebrides?"

"Not quite, Sir. Major Grey is staying at a resort lodge in the Laurentians…"

"All by himself?" Hamish queried dryly and then continued, "Tell me, has the Major called here in the last fortnight?"

"Indeed he has, Colonel; Monday past and yesterday, 0900h, as you agreed. He's been out of commission only a few weeks, Sir. It was the concussion, mild, thank goodness, on top of the double fracture that kept him from getting up and about sooner, Doc Miller said. Thank goodness there were no other complications."

"Yes, of course," Hamish commented, his tone softening. "I do miss the fellow. Major Heaviside's doing a sterling job as his replacement, mind. Tell me; is Major Grey fully mobile yet? You know, capable of more than sitting up and taking nourishment?"

"Oh, yes. He says he's becoming quite active, now that the cast has been removed. He's getting about with crutches. I'd say that must present an elegant sight," she reflected, smiling.

"Oh, aye, to be sure.

"Listen, Betty, ring him at the lodge and tell him he is expected in Manhattan at the British American Overseas Importing offices, Thursday morning, 0900h. A telegram with instructions, hotel reservations, and all will be awaiting 'Mr. Blake' at the CNR telegraph office, Montréal Central Train Station, tomorrow evening, 1730h. He rolls out from Montréal at 1830h hours. Thank you, Betty. That is all."

Hamish Findlay resumed signing the endless stream of situation reports, payroll vouchers, and requisitions. 'Damned pens. When is someone going to invent something so that a left-handed person can write without smearing ink all over the page?'

Auberge des Deux Monts
Lac Riopelle, Province of Quebec

Blake surprised even himself by choosing to return to the place that had marked the beginning of the end of the affair with Trudy Bristol. Ken and Charlotte Tessier's first dinner party there had been memorable in one sense: it had been a colossal bore. Most of the guests had been drunk, crude and rude, and the few who were sober seemed obnoxiously self-absorbed. Blake's suggestion that they leave just after dessert at ten had led to a heated exchange on the patio. He had actually been ready to depart by eight, but had indulged Trudy out of consideration for another two hours.

Nevertheless, he reflected as he packed, he had enjoyed his two-week stay this time. The meals were superb, as was the service, and he received an hour of physio every other morning with Guy, a pleasant fellow and competent practitioner. His leg was on the mend, according to Guy, 'Tanks be to God, but dere'll be no limp, hardly, Mr. Blake.'

'Now I know what I can look forward to when I retire,' chuckled Blake. The afternoon hands of bridge with the blue-rinse crowd and even the shuffleboard weren't so bad. 'But Bingo! Once was enough, thank you very much.' "Under the B…four!" "Before what?" the jokesters in the room insisted upon shouting in unison. 'And the cigar smoke! Ah, but the deck shuffleboard… Now, that's my style. On crutches, shooting doubles with the Recreation Director, the divine Mlle. Valérie, from Senneville. What was a single, nineteen-year-old, brainy, brunette dish like her doing at a resort populated with a clientele of over-fifty snots and fourflushers on the prowl for an easy mark while the missus was shopping in town or taking the waters? Husband hunting? Nah! Fortune seeking?' He had thought so at first. Although she was prohibited from after-hours socialization with the guests, she was expected to be the soul of hospitality while on duty. They had chatted almost daily while he lay on a chaise lounge well back from the pool as she supervised exuberant water polo games. His conclusion: 'None of the foregoing and none of your damn business, Blake! She speaks English, French, German, Italian, and Spanish, all of them fluently. I should pass her name along to Robert Brooks. Mm, on second thought, no.'

The bellhop toted his suitcase to the front desk where the concierge discreetly informed him that his bill had been paid in full, and then added that a limousine was waiting to whisk him to Central Station in Montréal.

"That's great. Thank you very much. One question: What about my bar chits?"

"Looked after, Monsieur."

"And gratuities?"

"Oui, Monsieur, that as well. Do you need assistance?"

"Just the suitcase. Merci."

"Please do visit us again, Monsieur Blake."

'Amazing! Thank you Erik!' Blake sighed as he sank into the Packard's luxurious leather upholstery.

After depositing his single piece of luggage in his compartment, Blake started out for the club car, as Colonel Findlay's telegram had instructed. Lowering himself gingerly into a window seat, he stowed his crutches, casually surveyed the crowded coach, then at ease finally, sat back to gaze out the window.

Watching the upper New York State countryside slip by in the twilight, Blake wondered what prompted Erik to recall him to Manhattan. The only conclusion that made sense was that he was being taken off the operation.

"Everything to your liking, Mr. Blake?"

Blake didn't look up. "Yes. Fine. Thanks."

Unfazed by Blake's non-committal response the attendant explained, "We just passed Albany, state capitol of New York, or the outskirts, I should rightly say." The reflection in the coach window continued, "Quite majestic, the Governor's mansion, and the Assembly buildings. I'm Augie." The face beamed. "Care for a copy of *The Times*? May I bring you some refreshment, Sir?"

"I suppose a small one wouldn't hurt," Blake laughed. "Yes, to both, thanks. Two fingers of scotch, single malt if you have it, with one ice would be just fine. Thanks, Augie." Blake looked up at his cheerful host.

"Just what the doctor ordered for that leg," Augie winked, "and coming right up. Here, let me put this cushion under your foot."

"Thanks, but that's really not..."

"All part of the service, Sir. Back in two shakes!"

Steam locomotive of the era

Augie returned with a silver serving tray bearing a matching bucket of ice, tongs, a shot glass of generous size containing an amber liquid, a glass, *The New York Times,* and a cocktail straw encased in a thin paper sheath. Setting it all down on a folding serving table that had been tucked under his left arm, Augie prepared the drink, reciting, "Twelve year old single malt, special reserve, one cube of ice and *The Times."*

Blake watched as Augie dispensed the beverage and then carefully arranged the straw on the paper serviette. "Okay, thanks, Augie. That's perfect. You can hold onto the straw."

"I believe you'll find it quite helpful, Sir, along with the crossword. Seven down, eighty-six across!" Augie remarked quietly and returned to the bar.

'A straw for a glass of whiskey, and a crossword? Helpful? God bless

America.' Blake shrugged, savouring his first sip. Setting down the glass, he reached for the newspaper. Out of curiosity, Blake consulted **The Table of Contents** to locate the crossword page, a feature that, up to now, he had diligently avoided as a time-filler comparable to crokinole or dominoes, suitable only for pensioned army officers, wealthy widows, and tenured professors of English. 'Seven down, seven down. There it is. *Tail*. Now, what was it? Right, eighty-six. *Straw man*.'

Folding the page, he looked down at the paper napkin. Lying on it, the straw was pointing directly at a male, seated mid-car, his back to Blake. Blake glanced over at the bar and nodded slightly in the stranger's direction. Augie, engaged in a lively conversation with the Conductor, acknowledged his gesture with a barely perceptible tilt of his head.

'What the hell is this? Beaulieu's finest at work? If that guy's trying to be a "no see' um", he flunked basic training,' reflected Blake. Amused, he was reminded of a hilarious weekend training 'scheme' misspent with an English chum, a.k.a. "Tony," in Southampton. The exercise, intended to gauge an agent-in-training's ability to 'shake a tail', was crucial to his or her satisfactory completion of the Special Operations Executive program at Beaulieu, the SOE 'finishing school'. Blake and Tony not only managed to outwit their instructor, but 'fell among the Philistines' in a seedy waterfront pub, as Tony had laughingly observed, where they holed up overnight, enjoying the food and drink and endless generosity of their hostess and her doughty band of irregulars.

Upon their return to Beaulieu, he and Tony were summoned to a debriefing with their case officer, Captain Angus Mutton, a dour, fuddy-duddy of a Presbyterian lay preacher, who by their misfortune, was a life-long teetotaller *and* a dyed-in-the-wool bachelor. Motioning that they be seated, Mutton proceeded to recite the complete catalogue of their sins, errors of commission and omission, and procedural gaffes, all in excruciatingly accurate detail, pausing with a sigh as he turned each page. Tony, quoting Dickens' Mr. Bumble, in a moment of insanity when Mutton had excused himself briefly, had whispered, chortling, "The law is a ass-a idiot. Thc law is a bachelor."

Reaching now for his whiskey glass, Blake smiled at the memory of them both, *in extremis*, squirming, 'sweating buckets', listening with acute embarrassment and drop-jawed astonishment as Mutton recounted the exact times, locations, and persons with whom they had 'had social intercourse.' "...And on the third instance, the female subject in question, the, shall I say, *proprietress*, known to the civil authorities as Sally Mae Ford, a.k.a. Jewel, Sally Tingle, and a person of interest to the local constabulary, etcetera..." At that moment they realised it was hopeless.

"Old Mutton-face had us pegged, chapter, verse *and* page. Dead to rights. Guilty as charged, Your Honour...the innocent victims of a criminal conspiracy. Abducted and held against our will," they had guffawed afterwards.

Cringing mentally at the memory, Blake glanced in the direction of the 'straw man', while recalling how much pleasure Captain Mutton seemed to get in recounting every sordid detail of their misadventures.

But the straw man had vanished. As had Augie.

Arsenal of Democracy

Chapter 4

But I’m due in Manhattan at 0900h!

South Finger Lakes Region, New York State
Fall 1943

Will you be having another, Sir?”

“Uh, no. No thanks, Augie. I’m fine.”

“Perhaps you’d care for something to eat? A menu, Sir? May I suggest the rack of spring lamb? It’s our chef’s speciality. With tangy mint sauce, oven-baked new potatoes sprinkled with fresh parsley. Well, I declare! I’m making myself hungry.”

“That sounds delicious, Augie, but perhaps a little overwhelming. May I have a minute?” In truth, Blake admitted to himself, he was finding Augie’s non-stop, one-man show quite irritating.

“Of course, Mr. Blake. No rush at all, Sir. You take your time. May I suggest, Sir, if a complete meal sounds too much, our superb lighter fare selections are listed on a separate page. And our desserts are well worth a look. Yes, well worth it.”

Opening the menu, Blake examined the light offerings, and decided on the turkey club sandwich, on freshly baked whole wheat, lightly toasted. Casually skimming *Our Delectable Desserts*, his eye was caught by ‘Bundt Cake’. It appeared to have been faintly circled in pencil. ‘Bundt Cake. Hmm, that sounds all right. So why is Bundt circled? Maybe someone’s recommendation?’

“Ready, Sir?” Augie stood by, pencil poised.

Blake gave Augie his order. “Excellent choice the Bund cake, Mr. Blake,” Augie observed with an approving smile.

All at once, it dawned on Blake. ‘He said Bund. Not Bundt. *Bund.* Another of Augie’s clues! The mysterious stranger is a member of the pro-Nazi *German American Bund.*’

"Yes, I agree," concurred Blake, handing Augie his empty glass. "Good work!" he confided.

"And you, Sir! We're keeping an eye on things. Clear sailing at present. Your meal will be ready in short order. If you wish to freshen up, the washroom facilities are located just ten feet behind and on your left. Your crutches, Mr. Blake. Let us know if we can be of any further assistance."

"Thanks. I think I should be able to navigate that far on my own," Blake grinned. "If I don't show up within a half-hour, consider your offer taken." Shifting his weight to stand, Blake mused, '*We*; who's *we*?'

"That was truly delicious, Augie. My compliments to the chef."

"Why, thank you, Mr. Blake; we do try not to disappoint. Will there be anything else this evening? A nightcap perhaps?"

"No, thank you. I think I'll turn in soon. Perhaps a little reading before I call it a day," replied Blake.

"Sounds like a good plan, Sir. Your meal has been taken care of. Breakfast will be served at 6:45 a.m. With the two-hour lay by, and the good Lord willing, we'll arrive at Grand Central Station, New York City, at 7:44."

"Very good, Augie. See you then. Bright and early."

"Sleep well, Sir!"

Blake made his way along the narrow corridor to his private berth without encountering any of his fellow passengers. Quietly closing the cabin door and securing the lock, he then reached for the light switch and limped to the sink. Bending over, he examined his leather shaving kit. "Son of a gun! Someone has been messing around in here. How did Hamish know I'd be tailed?" Blake exclaimed softly. Reading Hamish's cryptic telegram at Montréal Central, Blake had almost laughed aloud. It was the oldest chestnut in the book, *The SOE Training Syllabus*. Colonel Findlay had insisted that Blake follow procedure by placing an inconspicuous hair across the zippered opening of the pouch.

"Well, Herr Strawman-Bund, whoever in blazes you are, I've got your number," Blake whispered. "Or maybe it's *we*: me, good old Augie, and… whoever."

Gradually, Blake Grey became accustomed to the sounds and rhythms of the train. Folding *The Times* in half, he tossed it to the foot of the bed and lay back, cradling his head in his clasped hands. "*L'esperienza di questa dolce vita*. The sweet life!" He smiled, recalling his 'father', Salvatore, bedridden with arthritis, moved to tears when Blake recited the entire canto of Dante's *Divine Comedy,* after only one night of study.

"Time to turn in." He yawned and undressed. Supported by one crutch, he brushed his teeth, then rinsed and dried his face. Rifling through his bag he found his current book, *A Concise History of the English Civil War*. Switching on the feeble bedside lamp, he then turned back the bedclothes, and lay down.

Ten minutes later, the tome slipped from his hands, landing with a loud thud on the cabin floor. Blake sat up with a start. Realising that the disturbance was self-inflicted and thoroughly annoyed as a result, he lay down again, watching the flickering shadow and light show playing hide and seek on the sleeping compartment wall, while wondering who had entered his cabin earlier, and why. 'Probably the Porter. Maybe if I pull down the shade, I can get back to sleep.' Stiffly, he swung his legs over the edge of the bed and attempted to reach the blind, but it was beyond his reach. 'Damn. I'll have to stand up.' Then, hopping over to the washbasin, he fumbled in the pitch dark for the cup dispenser.

A narrow slit of light glinted in the mirror. As Blake watched, the slit became a narrow rectangle as his cabin door continued opening slowly, and silently. The image from the book of an Irish Roman Catholic clergyman being bodily dragged from the darkness of his secret 'Priest Hole' by Oliver Cromwell's marauding Roundheads flashed in through his mind.

Turning, Blake caught sight of the dull glint of a snub-nose pistol barrel with a silencer protruding into the compartment just as two suppressed flashes and muffled gunshots filled the air with the reek of cordite and fluttering puffs of feather. Lunging at the opening in an attempt to trap the intruder's hand, he was only able to slam the door's metal edge against the end of the silencer. Then it withdrew. As the door slammed shut, Blake pitched forward, striking his forehead. He cursed involuntarily as he raised both hands to his head. Just then the train braked abruptly, hurling him onto the floor.

Dazed, he struggled to stand up. Mixed with the not-disagreeable smell of cordite was the heady aroma of dime-store cologne, or hair tonic. A half-forgotten memory flashed before his eyes: the only boxing match he had lost, KO'd as flat and cold as mackerel, as his Dad, Sal, had remarked, during the sixth round at Hart House, Toronto, by a fancy-dancing, flying-fisted freshman the size of Captain Rufus 'Freight train' DuBose. The shriek of steel grating on steel confirmed that the train was reducing speed. As he wrenched the door open to peer into the passageway, the metallic din suddenly intensified as a nearby interconnecting coach door swung open. 'Ready, bum leg or not!' he half whispered, determined to take down his assailant.

"Hey, is that you, Mr. Blake?" called a familiar voice.

"Augie?"

"The very same! Good Lord, what are you doing out here at two o'clock in the morning, Sir?

"I might ask you the same thing," Blake replied warily.

"Fair question: I was up front playing double deck pinochle with the conductor and railway security fellows. Won a ten spot!" he exclaimed holding out a crumpled ten-dollar bill.

"Bully for you, mate. Come on in; I need a drink," Blake commented, his tone softening. "Did you see anyone between the time you left your friends and now?"

"Excepting you, Sir? Nary a soul. Why?"

Reaching into his suitcase, Blake produced a Moroccan leather case containing a twelve-ounce bottle of Adams Private Stock whiskey, and two oversize shot glasses. While filling both, he recounted the incident, summarizing with a display of the bullet-riddled pillow. "Exhibit A. Whoever did that was a respectable shot: twelve o'clock and six o'clock. The top one would have finished me off and the other one, well... Cheers!

"So, tell me, just for interest's sake, Augie, what in blazes were you really doing skulking around at this hour?" Blake asked casually. "Insomnia? A secret rendezvous? Pinochle with the boys, you say. Come on! I'm listening, Augie, if that is your name, and it had better be good," added Blake. Taking his .32 Webley and Scott automatic pistol from the suitcase, and placing it on the night table, Blake sighed. "I have the feeling this is going to be a very long night, old man. Sit down, please, over there, slowly." Blake pointed to the only chair in the suite. "And relax. Now, as you were about to tell me..."

In fact I was playing pinochle in the next car instead of sleeping, you see, because I've been assigned to be your *minder*."

"My *minder*?" Blake asked, taken aback. "Another drink?"

"No, thanks. I have to be at work in another two hours. Your *minder*-shepherd, keeper, watchdog, whatever you wish to call it, Mr. Blake," Augie replied.

"Who sent you to *mind* me, Augie?"

"HQ NYC, I would imagine. However, I never receive orders directly. They always come through...channels."

"HQ NYC? What's that?"

"Please, Mr. Blake, that is fairly lame. BSO HQ, Rockefeller Centre, of course."

"And the cover name?"

"British American Overseas Importing."

"And the Vice President is?"

"Mr. Robert Brooks."

"And have you ever met this Mr. Brooks?

"Oh, yes, many times when I'm assigned to the Toronto Union - New York Central run. About five feet ten, light blonde hair, blue eyes. Canadian I'd venture. Slight accent; perhaps the by-product of a private school upbringing. A real lady-killer type but quite reserved. A real gentleman."

"Is he a drinker?"

"Mmm, yes. Moderate, though. I always serve him two fingers of Glen Laird Scotch whisky, with a straw. It's a long-standing joke between us," Augie added, chuckling.

"Okay, it's good to know that you do know. I did wonder what was going on with your straw, crossword clues, and the menu folderol. A bit too cloak and daggerish for my taste. Why didn't you just tell me, you know, whisper it quietly? On the q. t.? The suspect was quite far away and …"

"I couldn't."

"Oh? Why not?"

"HQ has reason to believe there are two, but the other was not identified. So he or she could have been within earshot."

"Makes sense. By the way, have you noticed that we're not moving, Augie?"

"Yes, it's normal for this run. We pulled off to a siding. It's known as a *lay by* to railroaders. We'll be changing engineers and…"

Suddenly, loud shouts and running footsteps filled the corridor. "What's the bloody racket out there?" As Blake was about to get up from the bedside, Augie stepped over to the door.

"I'll have a look. You'd best stay here," Augie advised. "Back in a flash."

Blake was reaching for his revolver as Augie re-entered. "The yard crew found a man's body, mangled beyond recognition. It was caught in the undercarriage; likely dragged a mile or thereabouts," Augie reported.

"The shooter?" Blake queried softly. "He must have jumped out just before you came through the passageway door."

"Possibly. New York State troopers and more railway police are on the way, according to Willy the Conductor. A full investigation will be necessary and all passengers will be detained and interviewed. Naturally, foul play is suspected."

"But I'm due in Manhattan at 0900h!"

"Trust me in this, Mr. Blake. I will send a telegraph to my contact immediately for orders. One thing is clear; you cannot afford to be mixed up with a police investigation. My suspicion is that something very, very big and nasty is behind this set of events. Sit tight, please, and lock the door after I leave."

As Blake dressed, he reflected that Augie's corn-fed rural Alabama 'y'all' drawl had assumed the hard edge of a person well accustomed to issuing orders. 'Just who in blazes are you, Mr. Augie? Friend, foe, or both?'

Ajax-DIL Defence Industries Limited

South Pickering, Ontario, Canada

Dave Caldwell ducked his head into Foreman Jim Montgomery's office. "Jim! They're due in five minutes! Is everything ready?"

"Relax, Dave, you could eat off the floor. Everything's tickety-boo." Looking at his reflection in his office window, Jim straightened his tie for the tenth time. "There. All set!"

"Fine, Jim. Put your jacket on. My office."

"Yes, Sir." As Montgomery followed Dave Caldwell along the corridor, Dave maintained a steady stream of commentary. "This means a lot to us, Jim. A hell of a lot! You know that. Everything has to be top notch. I don't want anything to go wrong when we've put so much work and preparation into this. You're sure, eh?

"Any word, Carol?" Caldwell nervously inquired of his secretary.

"Not..." Her telephone rang. "Mr. Caldwell's office. May I help you? Hi, Charley. One moment, please." Using an elegantly long, Cleopatra Red, lacquered index finger nail, she gracefully pressed the hold button.

"It's Charley at the front gate. They're here, Sir."

"Okay! Thanks, Carol. Have Charley send them through. And Carol, make sure he remembers to have them park as close to the entrance as possible. Last time he had the corporate Secretary –Treasurer walking all the way from darn near Kingston Road!"

"Will do, Sir!" she smiled, switching back to the telephone connection. "Hi, Charley. It's Carol again. Charley, Mr. Caldwell said…"

"Right, Jim, this is it. Let's go meet them." The two men hurried down the flight of stairs to the front foyer where two of the visitors were examining the small gallery of photographs adorning one wall while the other two inspected a display of munitions.

Bayly and Harwood (circa 1940)

His every fibre exuding charm, Dave extended his right hand in greeting. "Welcome To DIL, gentlemen. Dave, Dave Caldwell. General Manager. This is one of my top Foremen, Jim Montgomery. I've asked Jim to join us, as he is one of our longest-serving employees. That is, as long as 'long-serving' can be around here," he joked.

"Pleased to meet you, Mr. Caldwell, Mr. Montgomery. Joseph Jelecanin,

Executive Assistant to Mr. Allan MacDonald, Vice-President of CIL."

"Dave, please. A pleasure to meet you. And you, Mr. MacDonald."

Jelecanin continued, "And I would also like to introduce you to Dr. Lorne Willis, Director of Chemical Engineering from CIL Head Office, Montréal, and from Ottawa, The Honourable Mr. Charles Taylor, Parliamentary Secretary to the Minister of Defence. Mr. Taylor has kindly agreed to rearrange his busy schedule in order to be with us today."

"Excellent. Well, gentlemen, I want to thank you so much for joining us today. And a very special thanks to Dr. Willis for agreeing to MC the celebration," announced Dave.

"We're absolutely delighted, Dave," replied Dr. Willis. "And I want to tell you, Dave, that you, Jim and everyone at DIL can be extremely proud of this accomplishment. Perhaps Mr. Taylor and the others might not be aware that DIL is unveiling the 25 millionth shell produced here. That's today. A superb accomplishment! I know that you'll all want to attend the celebration!"

"Amazing. Congratulations! Yes, of course," Taylor replied.

"That's wonderful. The festivities will begin mid-afternoon. We expect that several more dignitaries will be in attendance. Now, I think that you're going to find the tour quite interesting and informative, to say the least. Shall we get started?" prompted Jim enthusiastically.

"Jim, I think that since there are six of us, we should take two cars. Mr. Taylor, Doctor Willis, perhaps you would care to join me? Jim, you accompany Mr. Jelecanin and Mr. MacDonald," Dave directed. The two cars slowly rolled away from the main gate passing the five miles per hour sign on their right.

"Okay, the first building is the Community Hall on your left. We provide all kinds of social activities for our employees. We try very hard to encourage employees to stay inside the plant area as much as possible."

"Could you explain that a bit more, Dave?" Dr. Willis inquired.

"Sure, Doctor Willis. DIL is very much a family 'business', in the sense that sons, sisters, brothers, moms, dads, husbands and wives work side-by-side each day. So, it makes perfect sense to me that they should see their workplace as their social centre and we deliberately promote that," Dave stated proudly.

Celebrating DIL's production of the 25 millionth shell

"What sorts of activities, Dave?" Taylor queried.

"Everything from our most popular social event, the Saturday Night Dance, to Wednesday Night Bingo. That's a big draw all by itself! Tuesday nights, we feature a full-length movie. Every one is a new release from Hollywood. There's something going on nearly all the time. Every day and evening, week in, week out," explained Dave.

"That's impressive," Doctor Willis commented.

"Thanks. Now, over there is our post office. The building we're passing now is the Staff Hotel, specially built to house visiting dignitaries such as you gentlemen. Matter of fact, this is where you will be staying tonight. I'm sure you'll enjoy it. As you can see, it's two storeys. The lobby on the main floor, without being elaborate, is welcoming and comfortable, while the private rooms upstairs are tastefully furnished and quiet," said Caldwell.

"Dave, is there a specific reason why these buildings are on the main plant property?" asked Taylor.

"Yes, I'm glad that you asked that question, Sir. We have a limited number of guards here who have to be on duty around the clock, seven days a week. All of them are Veteran Guards, from the First War, as you likely know, Sir. Most are in their fifties and some, their sixties. They have a tough enough job just maintaining the entry gates for employees coming and going without piling on more inspections for them. This way, we keep as many activities as possible inside the plant grounds," explained Dave.

"Well, that certainly makes sense, especially in light of the fact that Ajax is such a crucial asset in the Allied scheme of things," Taylor commented approvingly.

Doctor Willis asked, "Have you had any major problems with security, Dave?"

"Nothing huge, knock on wood. A couple of people who just don't get it. Last week a woman was caught with cigarettes and matches while entering Line One. That cost her fifty dollars. A while ago a fellow was caught smoking behind one of the buildings; he spent fifteen days in the Whitby Jail. They just don't understand how many lives are at stake here."

"I've never seen that before!" exclaimed Taylor, pointing towards the west.

"What's that, Sir?" asked Dave.

"The banks of earth at each end of that building."

"Oh! Line Two. Yes, it's the pride of the plant. That's where we produce the Twenty-Five Pounders. Tens of thousands of them. You'll see those embankments at each end of Line One, Two, Three, and Four. See them?" said Dave as he pointed with his left hand at the plain looking, single story military huts.

Final assembly of 25 pounder shellls

“And the purpose?” queried Taylor.

“An ingenious idea, actually, Sir. If there should be an explosion from within the building, God forbid, the blast will go straight up into the sky without causing any further damage to any of the other buildings, virtually self-containing the problem. All of the buildings have been designed so that they are exactly the correct distance away from each other.”

“Brilliant, I must admit that when I was first briefed on this enterprise that I was highly sceptical of how one could maintain security not to mention the possibility of sabotage and its catastrophic effects," Taylor remarked.

"I can assure you, Sir, we've thought of everything."

Still travelling south towards Lake Ontario, Dave commented, "Oh, the steam chimney that you see to the west; that's our steam plant which is connected to all of the buildings."

"And does that really keep all of these buildings warm when it's five below zero?" asked Doctor Willis.

"Absolutely, Doctor," replied Dave. "Toasty and warm. At the back of the steam plant are the Maintenance and Stores buildings. The buildings on the other side are the Pellet and Tracer and Cap and Detonator."

"The plant is massive in size, Dave," remarked Taylor

"Hundreds of acres and we now employ nine thousand people," Dave recounted. "And here we are at the south end of the plant where we store the finished shells all ready to be put on rail cars headed for Halifax. Would you like to take a look?" asked Dave.

"Certainly, I find all of this very fascinating," replied Taylor.

The three men exited the staff car and walked the short distance to two large doors, which were blocked by Veteran Guards.

"May I see your passes please, gentlemen?" requested one.

"Certainly, Private," replied Dave, handing him Temporary Visitor Passes. "These men are my guests and I'm giving them a tour of our plant."

"Very well, Sir. These papers appear to be in order," replied the guard, returning the special entry passes that had been issued at the main gate by Charley.

Dave swung open the huge barn-like doors exposing thousands of boxes neatly stacked in rows. Walking over to one of the steel cases, he knelt down to open it. Pulling out a shell, Dave proudly held it up. "And this, gentlemen is what it's all about; the Canadian - made, twenty-five pounder shell. Ready to ship out. This baby along with the thousands of others here will be in the hands of our soldiers within five weeks time."

25 pounder (25pdr) artillery field piece

"Once again, Dave, I'm very impressed. Particularly in terms of the layout and how exceedingly well-organized the Plant is," commented Willis.

"It's simply amazing," Taylor declared. "It makes me extremely proud to be Canadian."

"I would like to echo that," reaffirmed Doctor Willis.

"Believe me, gentlemen, when I arrive back at The Hill, my first priority will be to advise, no, insist that the Minister arrange a visit at the first available opportunity," Taylor insisted.

"That would be grand, Mr. Taylor. The Minister is welcome. Anytime. I look forward to it," Caldwell stated. "Now, suppose we head up to the Staff Hotel? You can check in and then, after lunch, we'll take a tour through some of the lines before the celebration."

"I would love to have an opportunity to chat, briefly of course, with some of your employees, if that would be possible, Dave," commented Willis.

"Absolutely, Doctor Willis.

"Thank you, Private. You can lock it up now." Just as the three men got into the car and started to drive away, Jim pulled up in the second car. Dave gave him a friendly wave and thumbs up.

DIL Bomb Storage Depot

Arsenal of Democracy

Chapter 5 *Piece of cake!*

Camp-X

Fall 1943

"Right then. I'm off to Number 20, Betty."

"Who is duty officer this afternoon, Colonel Findlay?"

"I thought that I had already told you. Perhaps not. Michael Heaviside."

"Does Major Heaviside know that?"

"Yes, yes, of course. He also knows that Brian Jones is due to return from Camp Borden at 2300h, and that I'll be back in time for dinner, God willing!" Winking, Hamish gave her a snappy salute.

"Very well. Have a good flight, Colonel Findlay!" Betty remarked with a quiet sigh of resignation.

Stevenson Road, North Oshawa, Ontario

Bringing his Jeep to a rolling stop, Hamish Findlay paused, then accelerated in a cloud of dust as the guard simultaneously saluted and rushed to open the gate. Now entering Elementary Flying Training School No. 20, Findlay continued toward Hanger 2. Swerving to avoid hitting a pair of cyclists wearing Polish Air Force uniforms, he honked and gave a gallant V-for-victory sign as he roared around the two startled pilot-instructors.

John looked up from his workbench at the sound. "Here's your friend, Hamish, Al! I hope he flies better than he drives!"

Hamish strode into the hangar, looking incongruously like a WWI aviator, complete with leather greatcoat, flying helmet and goggles on his forehead. "Good morning, gentlemen! Is she prepped?"

"Good morning, Colonel," John and Albert replied in unison. "All set, Sir!" Albert continued. "There she is! Fuelled and checked out, purring like a kitten."

"Excellent, chaps! Great day for flying: CAVU[1]. I'll just nip up to the tower and file my flight plan, do my pre-flight, and then I'll be off!"

"Very good, Sir. If you need anything, John's your man, at your service, Colonel. Right, John?" Albert added innocently.

"Oh, sure. Anything at all, Sir!"

"Well, that's good of you, but I'm sure there won't be any need," Hamish replied jauntily. "Cheerio!"

"Pip, pip, old chap," John muttered when he judged Findlay was beyond earshot.

"Shut up, you idiot!" Albert hissed.

"Here's a little something extra for your trouble," Findlay called, returning with two fresh one-dollar bills fanned out in his outstretched hand.

"Gees, thanks, Colonel!" Albert answered, taking the money. "Much appreciated. Have a good flight, Sir!"

"Oh, I expect I will. Pip, pip!" Hamish's voice echoed off the hangar walls.

Albert glanced at John who gave a non-committal shrug as he turned away, intently wiping grease from a spark plug wrench.

"Oh, Colonel Findlay!"

Hamish paused and turned. "Yes, Albert?"

"Sir, could you mention to Darryl in the tower that I'll be taking up 9653 for a circuit? We've just tuned her and I want to make sure that she's up to spec."

"Roger. Wilco."

[1] *CAVU Ceiling And Visibility Unlimited*

Albert Cowan sat in the rear open cockpit of 9653 waiting until Hamish Findlay lifted off in 9666. By the time Hamish's wheels had cleared the tarmac and the Moth was banking eastward, Albert's pre-flight check was completed. Receiving a visual clearance signal for takeoff from Darryl, he waved back and then released the brakes and advanced the throttle. The Tiger Moth started rolling down the airstrip. As he taxied past John Billington, Albert gave him a 'thumbs up', and shouted, "She's sounding real good, eh? Be back in a jiff!"

Albert realized that he was taking an enormous risk. By common understanding, as a mechanic and a certified pilot, he was to make a circuit over Oshawa, perhaps two at the most. There was no provision for landing, unless forced by mechanical problems. The purpose of his flight was not only deceitful but illegal and almost certainly actionable by the Canadian Government, especially during wartime. He was taking advantage of Darryl's good nature and trust in the mechanics to do the right thing. At the very least he would be fined and perhaps his licence would be suspended: temporarily, he prayed. At the worst, his 'ticket' could be revoked and into the bargain, he would lose his job. Beyond those possibilities, he hadn't given much thought. Yet, he couldn't turn down his friend's request flatly. And if all went as expected, he'd be back on the ground within a half-hour, with no one the wiser, or so he hoped. As a precaution, he had concocted a story to explain the extra-long test flight.

Scanning the sky for a sign of Hamish in the distance, Albert levelled off to follow his plan, staying low, 1,000 feet, until he reached the area of Orono and was able to make out the barn. Approaching for a landing, he saw two figures standing, waving as though he might not see them. Touching down in a pasture, as arranged, he taxied, bringing the short take off and landing airplane to a stop just yards from the welcoming party.

"Hi, Rolf!" Albert called out as he throttled back the engine to low idle. "Who's your friend?" Upon setting the brakes, Albert climbed out of the Tiger Moth's cockpit.

"Hi, Albert!" Rolf Enders and Christoph Hartt replied in chorus. "Albert, I'd like you to meet my friend Christoph. Christoph, this is Albert, the guy from the model aircraft club I was telling you about," Rolf proclaimed.

"P, pleased to m, meet you, Albert," replied Christoph awkwardly.

"Likewise, Christoph." Albert grinned while offering his grease-stained hand.

"And so, Albert, can I go up solo?" asked Rolf.

"Nope, not today, Rolf. Sorry."

"Why not? You said I was ready after the last time we were up!"

"It's not that you're not ready, Rolf. I don't have enough time now. I just took this out for a short hop and I'm expected back right about now. I'm taking a big chance coming this far off the test circuit. If I'm late or spotted here, I could lose my licence and my job."

"Albert, you have to, please?" Rolf pleaded. "You promised."

"Damn it, Rolf, I don't have to do any such thing! There's a colonel up there right now and I have to be near my work station in case there's an emergency," retorted Albert.

"A colonel? From Number 20 EFTS? No wonder you need to get back," Christoph commented.

"That's right, boys; a real, in-the-flesh, Colonel. Actually, he's not from the school. He's from a military base nearby. I'm not at liberty to say anything more. Top secret and all that guff."

'I knew it. It's Colonel Findlay,' Rolf concluded silently. "Look, Albert, you've got to let me take her up. Just for five minutes, please? I'll take Christoph with me."

"Rolf, I said forget it. If you're going up with anyone it'll be me. Besides, you're not going today. Okay? We'll arrange another….."

"Christoph! *Gott in Himmel*! What are you doing?" screamed Rolf.

Albert lay on the ground beside the idling Tiger Moth, the back of his head lying in a rapidly spreading pool of blood. Behind him stood Christoph, a blood-stained shovel in his left hand.

"Why did you do that?" exclaimed Rolf, shaking his head in disbelief. "He's my friend! We're in big trouble now!"

"Will you kindly shut up and help me drag him into the barn? And get those registration numbers and the camera while you're there," ordered Christoph.

"Shut up? You said, 'shut up' to me?" You shut up, you oaf of an Austrian peasant. I'll teach you German manners…"

"I'm not listening to your insults, Rolf," Christoph replied in a child-like singsong lilt.

"Enough, Christoph. I'm sorry. I think I'm going to throw up!"

"No problem. Go right ahead. Not here! Over there." Christoph waited while Rolf composed himself. "Look, Rolf, this is our best, maybe our only chance for the reward. Just help me move him. Are you feeling better now, my friend? We must hurry. Please!" Reaching down, Christoph took hold of Albert's wrists. "Take his ankles. Go on. That's good. On three, lift."

"Do you think that he is dead, Christoph?"

"I doubt it very much. I only grazed him. Scalp wounds always bleed like that. Okay, let's set him down. Here."

"I hope you're right, for once," Rolf muttered.

"What?"

"I said, 'He's light. Lucky for us.'"

"Just get the damn numbers, Rolf, would you? Now! I'll get the camera."

Ascending to 1,800 feet, Hamish levelled off and banked east, headed for 8 Wing RCAF Base Trenton, Ontario. Flying conditions were ideal. His flight plan indicated that he intended to follow the Lake Ontario shoreline. Assisted by a twenty-knot tail wind, he and his biplane were approaching the Town of Bowmanville almost four minutes ahead of schedule. Keeping a regulation five nautical miles distance from Prisoner of War Camp 30, he remembered his recent mission there: to pluck his colleague, Colonel

Roger Stedman, out of the hands of an extremely aggravated mob of German PoWs.

'Dear old Roger,' Hamish mused. 'You almost bought it, didn't you, playing secret agent. Hope you're enjoying wherever you are, old chum.'

Officially, Hamish and Canadian Air Vice-Marshall Shearer were scheduled to meet at the Wing privately at 1100h, followed by lunch at 1215h, as guests of the Wing O. C. Unofficially, Hamish was hoping to convince the Commanding Officer to permit him a flight as co-pilot in one of the-first-off-the-line superb Canadian-made deHavilland 'Wooden Wonders', the Mosquito Mk 1V medium bomber.

"Cobourg in five minutes thirty seconds, by my reckoning," he shouted, glancing down at his lap map. "A slight deviation northward to Rice Lake would seem to be in order. Scads of time to get to Trenton." The site of wilderness survival exercises for Camp-X agents-in-training, or 'clients', Hamish had developed a strong affinity for the Rice Lake area. He particularly loved the excellent small mouth bass fly-fishing by canoe in the shoreline marsh grasses while the 'clients' struggled to endure, and, if fate and dogged persistence permitted, completed his ingenious and 'devilishly-challenging schemes'.

"Ah, there you are, my beauty!" he exclaimed delightedly as he gently banked the biplane to starboard, thereby affording himself an unobstructed view of the lake's glistening surface. Below, an angler waved a greeting. Hamish waggled his wings in acknowledgement. "Lucky devil!" Moments later, he rhapsodised, "And here's the Otonabee River! It's a month-long fishing jaunt on the Trent Waterway in this lad's next lifetime.

"Hello. What's this?" The deHavilland Gypsy four-cylinder engine missed a beat. "She's running a touch ragged. Slightly rich, possibly," he observed. "Must remember to let Albert and Johnny know," he added, adjusting the throttle setting. "Much better! Must get back on course." Consulting the compass, airspeed indicator, and his map, Hamish circled as he determined his heading. Seconds later, the engine coughed again, sputtered, and quit.

"Ruddy hell, what's going on here? The blinking oil pressure! It's non-existent!" He tapped the glass cover plate on the gauge. The needle sat flat against the pin, registering zero. Quick glances at the idly revolving propeller blades and at the dashboard tachometer confirmed the engine's state.

"You're losing altitude! Restart the blighter, Findlay!" The acrid odour of super-heated aircraft engine lubricant drifted into the cockpit. Leaning over the side, Hamish saw a whitish-grey trail emerging from the underside of the engine housing. "That caps it! She's blown the header, or it's a cracked oil line. Calm down, old man, or you're for the high jump!"

Checking the altimeter and the airspeed indicator, he made a rapid calculation. As a seasoned pilot, he was confident that the Tiger Moth's legendary airworthiness, inherent in the little biplane's dual-wing configuration, would carry him safely well beyond the shore. Her airframe was lightweight but sturdy, of wood and fabric construction. Spotting a familiar three hundred square foot clearing used as the assembly point for his infamous training schemes, Colonel Findlay felt a sudden surge of exhilaration. Deftly, he trimmed the aircraft's controls to prepare for a textbook dead-stick landing. "Piece of cake!" he shouted optimistically.

Somewhere Over Lake Ontario

"Rolf! Do you see it yet?" yelled Christoph.

"No, but we should be sighting it soon!"

"It's got to be close, no?"

Tiger Moth

"When we see the high antennas we'll have to go up to make sure we're clear of them. There, Christoph! Over there! On our right." Pointing downward, Rolf shouted over the spirited roar of the deHavilland Gypsy inverted inline engine. "Get the camera ready. I'll take us in right over the buildings."

"I dropped it on the floor. Wait a minute!"

Unable to hear Christoph, Rolf continued to steer directly toward Camp-X. "Are you ready? I'm going in. Here we go!"

"Ya, almost…" Fumbling, Christoph awkwardly cocked the shutter and then aimed the camera downward. "*Scheiss*! We passed it!" he muttered forlornly watching the buildings rapidly vanish into the distance.

"Did you get it, Christoph?"

"No, it was too fast, Rolf! Go around, and come back again, but slower," he yelled.

"Good work, knucklehead! Christoph, can't you do anything right?" screamed Rolf as he banked the aircraft to the left, heading back out over the lake. "You've probably killed Albert and now you're going to get us killed, too!"

"Just calm down and take us back. I'll do it this time!"

"Don't drop the camera!"

Camp-X SSW Aerial View (c. 1943)

Off-duty for the afternoon, Captain Hugh Mason lazed on the grass at a safe distance as Major Michael Heaviside instructed a class of Yugoslav clients in the fine art of firing a Tommy gun. At the sound of a single engine aircraft approaching directly overhead, Mason looked up. Cupping his hands, he shouted, “Hey, did you see that, Mike?”

“What?”

“Did you see the Colonel’s Tiger Moth?”

“See what?”

Mason loped toward Heaviside to announce, “The Colonel’s plane; he just buzzed us. You didn’t see him?”

“No. I was watching the lads firing into the lake,” shrugged Heaviside.

“Here he comes again,” shouted Hugh.

“I see it. How do you know that it’s Colonel Findlay?”

“His number is 9666. It’s him. I guess he decided to come back for a fly over. Watch out, though, he’s liable to drop some flour bags or worse, if I know the Colonel,” Hugh chuckled.

Grabbing a Tommy gun from a startled trainee, Heaviside began directing a stream of fire at the biplane.

“Hey, Mike! Are you nuts?” With a running leap, Hugh knocked Mike down and pinned him to the ground face first. “What the hell are you doing, Major? Can’t you see it’s the Colonel?”

“It’s not the Colonel, Captain. There are two people in that aircraft. Hamish Findlay always solos. No one flies with the Colonel. No one! Never! That is an intruder. Now let me up, please.”

“Damn! You’re right, Mike, you’re right,” replied Hugh, pulling Heaviside upright. The two men watched as the plane descended below their line of sight, a trail of black smoke billowing from the rear of its fuselage.

“I don’t think it’s going to make it!” Mike pronounced grimly. “I’ll dismiss the lads. Get a Jeep and a couple of guards, Hugh. Bring every fire extinguisher you can lay your hands on.”

"Christoph!" Rolf shouted. "We've been hit!"

"Ya, I know. I got one in my right foot! Are, are we…?"

"We're in trouble, Christoph! I can't use the rudder or the elevators. They're completely useless. I, I can't control the airplane."

"We're too low to jump with parachutes!" screamed Christoph. "Get us down, please, Rolf!"

"There are no parachutes, you fool! We're going down. Hold on. I'll try to make a soft landing!"

"Do you know how to do it, Rolf?"

"No, dammit, I don't! Oh, God, I can taste gasoline. The overhead fuel tank has been hit! It's pouring out… pooling at my feet!"

"Mine too! Stings like blazes! Oh, no! Now it's covering my goggles! It's in my eyes!" Christoph screamed.

"We're done for, Kamerad!" Rolf stated matter-of-factly.

"Please, God, please! I don't want to burn to death…."

"Mike; over there…!"

"Yes, I can see the smoke. It has to be less than a mile. Hang on, chaps! We're going a bit off the beaten path."

Bumping and bouncing across the furrows of a freshly ploughed field, they quickly came upon a grim scene of twisted, smoking debris.

"The Captain and I will take care of the plane. You men take the other two extinguishers and put out the grass fires before they get out of control," ordered Heaviside.

"What do you think, Mike? Safe to get closer?" Hugh panted.

"Another minute. Aim for the petrol tank. That's it, Hugh… atop the front cockpit, to be sure that it doesn't blow." Within a few minutes the fire had been extinguished. While the smoke was still being dissipated in the breeze, the four men cautiously approached the wreckage. “Oh, my God, Major! They’re burned to cinders!” exclaimed Doug, a guard. “I’m going to be sick!” Through the haze, Hugh was able to make out the charred remains of two contorted bodies strapped into the tandem cockpits. Each still wore the blackened, ragged, remnants of their flying helmets, the glass in the goggles crazed by the intensity of the flames.

“It’s as though they have been hit full blast by a flamethrower,” Heaviside commented.

Hugh nodded in agreement, adding nothing.

“I don’t know if we’ll ever be able to make out who these poor devils were. But someone will have to try,” Heaviside resumed. “We’ll need a forensic specialist. And a coroner. You two go back to the Camp. Have Miss Robertson contact Doc Miller and explain what has happened. Get him here soonest! And have her track down Colonel Findlay! He must have returned from his flight by now! If he’s not there, she is to contact Robert Brooks in Toronto for instructions. I want twenty-four hour security on the site. Bring three more guards... with their own jeep. No one comes within a mile. No, two miles. She will tell Motor Pool to have a couple of lorries on standby. We’ll need power and lights as well. I’ll require a field radio. Have the Hydra boys patch it in. What’s left here will have to be loaded and taken back to the Camp for detailed examination, when the Doc or HQ gives their say so. Captain Mason and I will remain to secure the area until you get back with the reinforcements. Let’s get a move on, Doug, Charlie.”

Michael and Hugh sat on a knoll looking down glumly at the rubble. The smell of gasoline, castor oil, hydraulics fluid, charred metal, and smouldering fabric was mixed with the nauseating stench of scorched flesh.

“Poor blighters. Do you think that they suffered, Mike?” asked Hugh.

“Well, the trip down would have been a hair-raiser, particularly if the fire started while they were still aloft. I’m not qualified to say. My guess is that they knew what was coming, unless I gunned them. If you look at the position of the arms and hands, they're in the typical 'protect myself' position. Once they hit the ground, I think they likely cashed in instantly. It appears, and I didn't get close enough to be certain, that they made no effort to take their harnesses off at all."

"What do you think they were up to, Mike? It's the Colonel's plane isn't it? They're his numbers for sure."

"Are they?" asked Mike.

"What do you mean?"

"Half of the planes' numbers at Oshawa EFTS start with 96. It would be an easy job to change two numbers. They're all painted an identical yellow and you can't tell one from the other," replied Heaviside.

"Wow, I never thought of that. You're right. That's damn clever of them, whoever they were."

"I'm not sure who they were but I think I know what they were up to," said Mike standing and walking over toward a tree. "Look. Up there, hanging from that long branch."

"That's a camera case!" Hugh exclaimed.

"Right you are and here's the camera." Reaching down, Mike picked up something off the ground.

"Well, I'll be… It's an expensive one. A Leica! German. Are you thinking what I'm thinking, Mike?"

"Exactly. It must have been thrown clear on impact, surviving the fire. We'll take it back to Camp and have the film developed. If my hunch is correct, we'll be seeing pictures of the Camp. Remember to have one of the guards shinny up and retrieve the case."

"Will do. Son of a bitch? Spies!" Hugh mused aloud. "What the hell…? Oh, great, it's the fire department."

A fire truck turned off the dirt road, and headed across the field toward them, dust flying as its sirens wailed.

"Stand fast. Polite, but NO information. I'll make it up as I go," Mike directed. "You smile and stay mum, okay?"

The fire truck came to a halt as Mike and Hugh looked on.

"Hi, fellas! Captain Gary Benson, Ajax Fire Department. We received an emergency call about a plane crash. Whoa, what happened?"

"Well, Captain, there's not much to see. In fact, there's not much left," Heaviside remarked.

"I can see that. Did you know them or what is your connection to this?"

"They belong to our military unit. In fact, I'm just waiting for some trucks to arrive so that we can take the remains back to our base where we can examine them more closely."

"I'm afraid you won't be moving anything, pal. At least, not until the coroner gets here."

"Captain Benson, I've already taken care of that," protested Heaviside firmly.

"Fred, radio in, you had better let the OPP know as well."

"One minute, Captain, this is my jurisdiction," stated Heaviside.

"Your jurisdiction? Putting it politely, Sir, bull roar. You're in Ajax. That's my jurisdiction. We'll see about it when the OPP get here."

"So you see, Inspector Swann, if you will kindly call the RCMP and relate this exact sequence: twenty-five dash one dash one, everything will be tickety-boo," said Mike as cheerily as he was able.

"Okay, Major, I'll call," replied Swann testily. "Back in a flash, I sincerely hope, for your sake."

"Doc, glad you made it! Any word on the Colonel's whereabouts, Doug?"

"No, Major. Not a sign. Miss Robertson is worried sick, Sir. Trenton Base has been calling frantically. The flying school too. On the plus side, Sir, Mr. Brooks is coming out with another party. The top Mountie, I was told to tell you."

"Good. Stand fast everyone. I'll do the talking," Heaviside asserted.

Inspector Swann returned from his car. "Major, my apology. Apparently RCMP Commissioner Reynolds is on his way. That more than satisfies me. Captain Benson, you and your boys can head back to Ajax, that is, unless the Major wants you to stay and make certain that there's no danger of a flare up. Major Heaviside, if you need anything, give my office a call. Here's my card."

"Thank you, Inspector Swann, I appreciate your cooperation," replied Mike. "You were doing your job. Cheerio!

"Things seem to have cooled down, Captain Benson. Thanks for your help."

Turning to Doc Miller and the guards, Heaviside remarked under his breath, "Thank the Lord for that code! We'll let Mr. Brooks and the Commissioner take over when they arrive. In the meantime, Doc, I'll need you to certify these two blokes are DOA. Okay? You three lads are to guard the perimeter. Here." With a stick, Heaviside traced out on the ground the roads they were to patrol. "Doug and Charlie, stay here on site with the Doctor and me."

"Did anyone think to bring something hot to drink?" Hugh inquired.

"Yes, Captain Mason. Coffee, hot chocolate, and a mountain of ham and lettuce sandwiches, Sir," piped up Sergeant Mac proudly. "Right here! It was actually Miss Robertson's brain wave," he added.

"Sergeant McDonald, I haven't offered my congratulations yet on your recent promotion. Well done! Remind me to treat both you and Miss Robertson to drinks in the Officers' Mess!" remarked Mason.

"Yes, Sir!"

"Now hit the road, boys. And for heaven's sake, don't shoot Mr. Brooks or the Commissioner!"

From the time Commissioner Reynolds was able to rouse the RCMP's chief forensic air crash specialist, Dr. Bruce R. Dodds, at his home in Toronto, until his arrival at the site, it was 0015h. By 0130h, the trucks had arrived, the portable generator running and the lights set up. By 0215h, the two bodies had been extricated and were on their way by ambulance to the morgue at Oshawa General Hospital for autopsy.

"Well, Doc, that about winds it up for you. You might as well head home," commented Robert Brooks to the Camp-X, 'Doctor'. "Thank you as always for your invaluable assistance."

"Glad I could be of help, Robert. I should have the autopsy results by tomorrow. What am I saying?" he laughed. "Late this afternoon. I'll forward my report to you and Commissioner Reynolds via the new facsimile transmission device Mr. Williamson wants us to use for, uh, sensitive documents, if that is satisfactory."

"Yes. Fine by me, Doc! You have one of Erik's machines, right Ted?" Brooks queried.

Nodding affirmatively, Reynolds shook Doc Miller's hand, bidding him thanks.

Dr. B. R. Dodds, having completed his solitary examination, after extensively photographing the wreckage, reported his preliminary findings to Reynolds, Brooks, Heaviside, and Mason.

"Alright, men. Following Dr. Dodd's direction, we are about ready to load the airplane onto a truck or trucks, as need be. Dr. Dodds, it's all yours, Sir," announced Major Heaviside.

"Gentlemen.... Hello, who in God's green earth is that fool?" Dodds asked angrily as a bobbing pair of partially blacked-out headlights approached the site. "Major Heaviside! I understood that this area was restricted!"

"Damn right it is, Doctor! Sergeant McDonald! Swing that light onto that vehicle. Now!" Heaviside demanded.

"For God's sake, Major, turn it off! You're blinding me!" returned a voice.

"Colonel Findlay?"

"One and the same!" replied Hamish jauntily, drawing up beside the cluster of men. "I say! Exactly what happened here?" Listening intently, he made no comment until Heaviside had finished.

"Poor sods," Hamish concluded. "As for me, I decided to hoof it back. Just as the clients have to. Piece of cake, actually. Entirely my fault. I deviated from my flight plan. My God, Heaviside," he continued, surveying the wreckage being loaded. "That could well have been me! What made you so sure that it wasn't?"

"I wasn't one hundred per cent certain, Colonel," Michael admitted, "that is, until Mason and I noted that there were two persons aboard. You always fly alone, correct, Colonel?"

"True, 'tis true. Well done, chaps. Now, let's get this hulk into the Barn. Fill me in on the details when we get there. Carry on, Major. You seem to have everything under control.

"Say, Robert, Ted, you'll never guess what I discovered when I was tramping around the shore of the lake. Look, an Indian flint arrowhead …. Yes, Michael? What's that you have?"

"A camera," Heaviside reported. "German manufacture. A Leica. Excellent optics; variable shutter speeds, solid body. Here, Sir, take it."

Examining the workmanship, Hamish commented, "A beautiful instrument isn't it, Michael? Where did you find it?"

"Over there," Heaviside commented, pointing to the tree. "Mason and I figure that it fell clear of the aircraft. There's no sign of either mechanical or fire damage. It's in mint condition. We'll retrieve the case and…"

"I want the film developed. Directly we're back at the Camp," Hamish ordered.

"Very good, Colonel."

Orono, Ontario

For Timothy and Alma White, the discovery of Albert's corpse in their barn on their return from a trip to visit Alma's ill sister in Lindsay was a dreadful shock. Almost as upsetting were the reporters camping on their doorstep, hounding them with ridiculous questions about their relationship with Albert Cowan every time they ventured out to do their chores. As Timothy had already explained to the police, he only knew Albert casually, from the model airplane flying club, and had given him permission to use the pasture as an emergency landing strip if he was ever in a pickle.

It wasn't until RCMP Commissioner Reynolds and OPP Inspector Swann ordered the newsmen off the property and had an around-the-clock detail of police officers assigned to keep the reporters at bay that the Whites could even think about trying to resume a normal life.

Alma remarked, "Those fellows are like a plague of locusts! They have no regard or respect for anyone's feelings, do they Timothy?"

"It's their job, Alma," Timothy replied quietly. "The price we pay for living in a free country. That's what this war is all about! Besides, it didn't help that you brought out cider and oatmeal cookies the first day," he chided her gently.

"I suppose you're right, Tim," she replied, picking up a framed photograph of a handsome youth in a Royal Canadian Naval Able Seaman's tunic. "That poor fellow, Mr. Cowan. His mother and father must be heartbroken. I should send them something. A card? At least our Tim Junior is alright!"

"Thank the good Lord for that, Alma."

"I do, dear: morning, noon, and night."

"Me too, me too. Alma..."

"Yes, Tim?"

"The coroner's inquest: remember Commissioner Reynolds said we'd have to sign some papers beforehand?"

"Yes."

"Well, I spoke privately with Jake Delaney, you know, the new criminal lawyer? He was at the Masonic meeting Tuesday night. He's joining, by the way."

"Oh, that nice, red-haired fellow with the pretty young wife from Scotland, and the twins? They are adorable. Hair just like their Dad's."

"Uh, huh. Well, according to Jake, it's to be a closed hearing and everyone who'll be attending has to sign some kind of official papers to keep the proceedings, he called them, secret. Sounds sort of frightening, don't it?"

"Well, I'm sure they know what they're doing. That Mr. Reynolds is a gentleman and wouldn't ask us to do something that would harm us. As you said, Tim, it's wartime and heaven knows what really went on out there. Could have been German spies for all we know. That's what the inquest is for, to find out once and for all, what or who is responsible for Mr. Cowan's death. Personally, I'll sleep a whole lot better just knowing. Or I think I will…"

"You're right, dear. I'm going out back to have a look at the combine. I think it needs a new belt."

"Well, be careful, Tim. That's a very powerful piece of machinery.

"Don't you worry, Alma. I'll be careful, you bet I will! If it needs replacing, I'll have to drive into the Massey Ferguson dealer to pick one up. I'll let you know. You can come, too, if you want to do a bit of shopping."

"Thanks, but I'll be starching your best white shirt for to wear to the inquest."

"Okay, then."

The Blue Swallow Inn

Whitby, Ontario

Private Conference Room

"In closing, I wish to express my sincere thanks to all who have attended this inquest and given testimony to the best of your ability. Your attentiveness and patience are greatly appreciated. Do you wish to add anything, Commissioner Reynolds?"

"No, General Constantine, except to remind you all of the provisions of the Official Secrets Act, to which we are all signatories… parties, that is."

"Thank you, Commissioner. Question, Mr. Brooks?" asked Constantine.

"Actually, General, just a reminder that dinner will be served in the main dining room at 1730h. Drinks in the bar, as soon as we can get there. That's all, thanks."

"I pronounce this hearing concluded. You are dismissed, with thanks."

Do you think we should take up on Mr. Brooks' invitation, Alma?" whispered Tim.

"It's very nice of him and all, but I'm exhausted after these past three days. Very, very intensive, didn't you find? Let's just thank him and take our leave."

"Whatever you say, Alma. Fine by me. Oh, they're the hotel's owners, Wes and Wilma Curtin out in the hallway. Come on and I'll introduce you."

"And how do you know them, Timothy?"

"Well, I don't really, but there was a lot in the paper about Mrs. Curtin in particular when she helped Commissioner Reynold's Mounties nab those Nazi spies in that church basement in Whitby. Remember?"

"Oh, my gosh, yes. So, that's her. She's no bigger than a minute! You go ahead, Tim."

"No, I want you to meet them, too. Real Canadian heroes. Come!"

Camp-X

Later That Evening

"Gentlemen, we narrowly avoided a major security bollix, to quote Major Findlay. Had it not been for the quick thinking of Michael and Hugh, the integrity of this base, STS 103, would have been severely compromised," stated Robert Brooks emphatically. "Let me assure you the entire matter is receiving the personal attention of Erik Williamson and his most senior advisors at BSO HQ's and SOE, London, as well."

"It was all Michael's doing, Mr. Brooks," Hugh Mason interjected.

"Hugh is being much too modest, Sir!" replied Heaviside. "I didn't even hear the aircraft until Captain Mason drew it to my attention."

"Come now, gentlemen. You are both to be commended and Mr. Williamson will hear of your resolute actions, both then and subsequently. That, I can promise you. Both. But to continue without going on all night," Brooks resumed, "It is apparent now that the two subjects, Enders and Hartt, were intending not only to photograph the Camp but the DIL manufacturing works in Ajax, as well. We need to consider the implications of that. Toronto HQ now has firm intelligence regarding the identity and location of their contact here, Günther, and his means of passing on the photos to Berlin, by submarine, we reckon.

"What we need to focus upon and resolve promptly is the 'why?' Is Berlin planning an attack on DIL? On Camp-X? Both? Ask yourselves this: If you were Adolf Hitler, wouldn't you? It follows then that the next questions must be- *how?* and *when*? Gentlemen, your comments, suggestions, please?"

Ajax DIL
Ajax DIL
Ajax DIL

Chapter 6
Case Fafner *will proceed*

Berlin, Germany

Office of The Chancellor, Adolf Hitler
Fall 1943

"So, tell me, Canaris, what exactly is the reason for this latest 'Most Urgent' request for a meeting? Party Secretary Bormann tells me that you were, in his words, 'quite relentless.' Very well. Here we are. However, I sincerely hope it's not another of your interminable and indecipherable disaster reports," Adolf Hitler commented acidly. "Sugar, Admiral? I know that you take it without milk. Much healthier. I can't stomach those pansy professors in Himmler's Race Research Bureau who insist upon adulterating an excellent Lapsang in that manner." While stirring a fourth heaping spoonful of sweetener into his tea, the German Chancellor pushed the Meisenware china bowl across the desk toward his frail and diminutive spymaster, Admiral Wilhelm Canaris, Chief of the Abwehr, Germany's respected military counterintelligence service.

"Thank you, as always for this opportunity, Mein Führer," Canaris replied graciously, delicately stirring in two teaspoonsful.

Brilliant, reserved, secretive, an acute observer and documenter of human character, Wilhelm Franz Canaris was a celebrated World War 1 U-boat commander, responsible for the sinking of as many as eighteen vessels in the Mediterranean. His many exploits before that included two daring escapes from the clutches of British Intelligence in Chile and in Spain, a hotbed of international intrigue. During the post-war turmoil of the Weimar Republic, he followed a traditional German Kriegsmarine [Navy] career path, serving in various posts. Rising to the rank of Captain of the ancient battleship *Schliesen*, the frail, unathletic son of a wealthy and privileged Dortmund family was attracted to the élite naval counter intelligence service. Here, able to pursue his boyhood love of tales of adventure and travel and an unusual flair for inventing sophisticated stratagems and schemes, the young Canaris son rose to become the troubled Weimar Republic's unacknowledged master of espionage.

Appointed Chief of the Abwehr in 1935 by Führer Adolf Hitler, he would become one of the most powerful men in Nazi Germany. Although credited as a founder of the anti-Nazi underground conspiracy known to the SS and Gestapo as the Schwarze Kapelle [Black Orchestra], Canaris, the consummate professional walked a dangerous tightrope. While an implacable and deadly enemy of the Allied secret services in the silent war, he and his trusted associate, Deputy Chief of the Abwehr, Hans Oster, played fast and loose with vital state intelligence, passing it along to London when they judged it would cripple Hitler's criminal plans for invading and enslaving European countries such as Czechoslovakia.

Admiral Canaris, anti-communist, German patriot, loathed both the Nazi Party, which he steadfastly refused to join, and the amoral megalomaniacs with whom he had to deal, while protecting his turf from their intrigues. Canaris shrewdly cultivated SS-Chief Heinrich Himmler, and his henchman, SS-Obergruppenführer (General) Reinhard Heydrich, head of the rival SS-Reich Security Service, a one time cadet-shipmate, and associate. Swiftly, Canaris appointed an SS-dupe, Rudolf Bamler, an old guard Nazi, as chief of Abwehr counterintelligence. An unwitting Bamler served as Canaris' eyes and ears at Reich Security Head Office, 8 Prinz-Albrecht-Strasse, providing the Admiral a window onto Heydrich's anti-Abwehr plots and schemes, while cementing Himmler's trust. Although enormously powerful, Germany's elusive master of intrigue kept his distance from the SS security apparatus, choosing to remain an outsider.

Following Heydrich's fatal wounding by SOE-trained Czech resistance fighters in Prague, 27 May 1942, Adolf Hitler appointed Party-faithful Dr. Ernst Kaltenbrunner, head of SS-Reich Security Service, 30 January 1943. Kaltenbrunner's unbridled lust for power coupled with a deep distrust of Canaris in particular, and the Abwehr in general, would eventually prove the Admiral's, and the Abwehr's undoing.

Canaris tensed involuntarily. Based upon 'reliable sources', he knew it was common knowledge within Berlin's inner circles that the current surge in reports detailing the disasters being inflicted upon the Atlantic U-boat fleet, were routinely met with stinging rebukes by the German dictator. These outbursts were routinely followed by vitriolic harangues against: the unlucky messengers, the Reich Admiralty, the British, particularly Winston Churchill, or any number of persons, military and political, whom he deemed unfit to command or unworthy to wear the uniform of Nazi Party officialdom.

"I, I believe you will be pleased with this information, Mein Führer." Canaris remarked cautiously. Swiftly regaining his customary poise, he continued. "However, these are matters of unusual sensitivity, Sir. Perhaps the Führer…"

"Perhaps what, Admiral?" snapped Adolf Hitler in exasperation. "Perhaps what?"

Leaning forward, Canaris whispered conspiratorially, "Perhaps the Führer, um, would wish to dismiss the guards…." The wily, white-haired master of intrigue sat back, awaiting the Führer's reaction.

"Becoming a trifle paranoid, are we, Canaris?"

Wilhelm Canaris silently contemplated the richly detailed Turko-Persian carpet on which his immaculately-buffed black Oxfords rested. 'Adolf Alois Hitler, the crown prince of paranoia, is accusing me of obsession?' Looking up, with a virtuous smile, he added, "Simply precautions, if you will, Mein Führer."

"Very well. The guards did conduct a thorough search for concealed weapons when you arrived. No?" Hitler queried, smiling faintly. Pressing an intercom switch beneath his desk, he issued an order, concluding curtly, "… and no interruptions. Understood?" Within seconds, an impossibly perfect specimen of Aryan maleness, a captain of the Führer's personal SS- Liebstandarte (Lifeguards) entered. Saluting his Führer in the approved Roman manner, the SS man turned smartly and exited silently, the two SS-Liebstandarte sentries at heel.

"Now, Wilhelm. Satisfied?"

"Thank you. Yes, Mein Führer."

"Very well, proceed. Are you now going to announce that the Allies are about to launch a second front in Italy, perhaps? More tea? I must confess that I've grown quite fond of this blend. It is specially imported from Venezuela: The Caracas Tea Company. Are you quite sure?"

Gracefully declining, "Thank you, no," Canaris plunged ahead. "Mein Führer, the issue at hand is…"

"There is something that troubles me," interjected Hitler. Removing his breast pocket handkerchief, he proceeded to swab a few miniscule droplets of tea from the top of his desk. Satisfied, he continued. "I find it most upsetting."

"Mein Führer?" His heart pounding, Canaris waited for the announcement that Kaltenbrunner had discovered his most recent peace overtures to the Swiss authorities.

"Your interference with the SS in the performance of their duties!" Hitler bellowed, standing.

"Sir?" inquired Canaris, leaning forward.

Stalking back and forth behind his desk, the Führer railed, "Be quiet! Quiet! Listen, damn you! You know very well what I mean! Reichsführer Himmler tells me that you were caught red-handed." His hands clasped behind his back, Hitler paused, his body visibly shaking. Turning, he confronted Canaris, forefinger wagging accusingly. "Admit your treachery!"

Dumfounded and terrified, yet having no idea to what Hitler was referring, Canaris averted his gaze and waited for the next volley. It was not long in coming.

"The seven SOE criminals!" Hitler screamed. "You, Canaris," he sputtered, his mouth foam-flecked, "Yes you! You, Canaris, actually had the gall to lie straight-faced to SS-Lieutenant-Colonel Eichmann that all seven of them were Abwehr agents. Unbelievable!"

Without looking up, fearing that his face would reveal his lie, Canaris responded evenly, "Begging the Führer's pardon, but in fact that there were, er, are!"

"And so you demanded their release?"

"I did, Sir. It was all quite legal. I was only protecting my people, as I believed you would have expected of a diligent and responsible head of a department, Sir!"

"And where are these so-called 'agents' now, pray tell? In Washington?"

Regaining his capacity to invent fiction on-the-fly, Canaris continued convincingly. "Washington, yes. Two. Correct, Sir. The other five are serving undercover in New York City, and Toronto, Canada, I'm pleased to report. Much useful intelligence comes down the wires from them, almost daily," he stated assuringly. In fact, the seven prisoners bore no connection whatsoever to the Abwehr. Bound by cattle car for execution at Buchenwald Concentration Camp from Gestapo HQ in Berlin, Canaris had brazenly claimed them from SS custody, over strenuous objections and threats, taught them a few outdated German codes, and then spirited them off to the obscurity and relative safety of Portugal. As a future bargaining chip, Canaris had ensured that London was informed promptly, "through the usual channels."

"Good lord! Will wonders never cease? British Intelligence agents of the Third Reich!" Hitler fumed. To Canaris, as Hitler looked skyward, hands clenched, his mouth now rimmed with spittle, the Führer had the appearance of the mad Russian monk, Rasputin. "I would order you shot in a minute for insubordination, treason, and God knows what else, Wilhelm, if I had even the slightest suspicion that this was another of your double-dealing schemes!" he raged. "Be advised, you are on very shaky ground. Be assured that I will pursue this matter all the way with Kaltenbrunner and Himmler. Count on it!" he concluded grimly. Sitting down again in his armchair, composed, Hitler steepled his fingers and calmly asked, "You were saying, Admiral?"

His heart pounding like a trip hammer, Canaris carefully measured his next words. "Thank you, Sir. This intelligence is closely associated with the Allies' long-term strategic objectives. It concerns a disturbing development at their major armaments production facility, in Ontario, Canada, to be precise..."

"Yes, near Oshawa, Ontario, site of the Canadian General Motors factory.

Very close, I might add, to, what is his name? Yes, Erik Williamson; Erik Williamson's pathetic excuse for an SOE espionage-kindergarten at… Whitby. Is that how it's pronounced? Do continue, Admiral."

Stunned, Canaris nodded and struggled to maintain his composure.

"Come, come. Surely you of all people are aware that the SD [Sicherheitsdienst-SS State Security Service] is not without a number of well placed and, I should say, extremely successful agents strategically placed throughout North America," remarked Hitler, drumming his fingertips on the desk blotter. "Your late protégé, Obergruppenführer (General) Heydrich, was well-known as a man of limitless creativity and unparalleled resourcefulness." Hitler paused to allow the slight to register fully. "Gruppenführer (Lieutenant General) Kaltenbrunner, I am delighted to say, is cut from the same cloth. Now, what about the DIL facility, Wilhelm?"

'And ruthlessness', reflected Canaris on his former friend, Reinhard Tristan Heydrich, the naval officer-cadet, whose unusual talent as a violinist had first drawn them together in the 1920's. Dismissed from the German Navy in 1931 by Admiral Raeder, for 'conduct unbecoming an officer', following a court-martial regarding an affair with a female minor, not to mention a spate of dalliances with the wives and daughters of senior officers, an unfazed Heydrich shrewdly sought his salvation in politics by attaching his star to the new and thriving Nazi Party.

Impressing the party hierarchy not only with his keen intellect and an obsessive fascination with administrative detail, the somewhat effete young entrepreneur immediately displayed a Machiavellian grasp of the Nazi principle of rule by fear, freely using bullying and intimidation, even murder, and, what would become his trademark tactic as military governor of Czechoslovakia, a callous and brutal 'stick and carrot' policy that was intended to terrorize, control, or eliminate, personal rivals and enemies of the Reich, who, in Heydrich's narrow view, were identical. Thus, the destruction of these real or imagined foes took on the 'respectable' quality of state-sanctioned executions.

Persistent rumours of Heydrich's father's Jewish ancestry notwithstanding, evidence for which, Canaris maintained a secret dossier in a safe,

Heydrich's rapid rise to Chief of the Abwehr's rival agency, the SD, had been accomplished with a cold-blooded, calculated ambition, rivalled by few of his contemporaries, even the arch-schemer Hermann Göring, founder of the Gestapo, the Reich secret police, His successor, SS-Gruppenführer (Lieutenant General) Dr. Ernst Kaltenbrunner, Austrian by birth, a fanatical Nazi, and a Doctor of Laws, was proving himself a worthy successor to Heydrich, so much so, it was rumoured that even SS-chief Himmler feared him.

"Quite so, Mein Führer. Gruppenführer Kaltenbrunner is that. Assuredly so. Only yesterday, I have learned that the Canadian Government's Minister of Defence issued a *diktat* ordering that the production of war materiel at Defence Industries Limited must be increased by twenty percent, effective immediately or heads will roll."

"I rather admire the Minister's style," Hitler commented wryly. "And so, Canaris, tell me. You will be taking precisely what actions to prevent this from happening?"

"As always, the foreign branch of the Abwehr is two steps ahead…of the enemy, Mein Führer." 'God help me. I have no idea,' Canaris reflected privately.

"Yes, yes, of course, Admiral. But I want to hear the basic elements of an operational plan, not hare-brained theories concocted by your backroom *wunderkinder* academics. God knows, Canaris…"

"Of course, Mein Führer." He paused to clear his throat. "It is my intention to nip this initiative in the bud completely and ultimately destroy DIL," he bluffed.

"How so? With dynamite or have we a new long-range secret vengeance weapon at Peenemünde on which I have not been briefed?"

Ignoring Hitler's sarcasm, Canaris continued, "Begging the Führer's indulgence, may I outline the steps which I have already undertaken? The initial phase of **Case Fafner**, as it is named, was put into play two weeks before the official announcement came down from Ottawa," he lied. "And, incidentally, Herr Williamson's espionage base STS 103 is targeted for obliteration, as well."

"Really? Now that would be a most welcome bonus. Perhaps we could remove the Kommandant, Findlayson, at the same time and bring him here for interrogation. The man for the job is Himmler's favourite SS-Sturmbannführer, Otto Skorzeny. Skorzeny has proven to be an accomplished 'removal agent'. I'm sure Herr General Findlayson has a considerable store of interesting insights to spill regarding the inner plots and schemes of that gang of SOE and BSO hoodlums. However, those cretins can wait for the moment!

"Our U-boat fleet is being decimated, Admiral, as if you, a navy man, don't know. The Allied convoy escorts are creating havoc. Their merchant ship convoys slip through our nets with impunity. It's as though they can anticipate our Wolf packs' every movement." Hitler rose from his chair, pounding his desk in rage. "I demand that they be stopped!" Sitting down he resumed, calmly. "**Case Fafner**. Very good, very good indeed. The fire-breathing dragon of Wagner's glorious *Ring Cycle*. Perhaps Dr. Kaltenbrunner still has a lesson or two to learn from you, Canaris.

"A sweet biscuit, perhaps? With the slightest hint of bitter almond, for balance. My favourite. Here. Continue. And spare me no detail, Wilhelm."

"Thank you, Mein Führer. With my plan, the convoys' destroyer escorts will be reduced to useless, floating hulks of metal."

"Do tell. How?"

"Mein Führer, what good are a Spitfire's cannons without shells, or a Lancaster without bombs? Similarly, Sir, what good are the Allies' naval guns, torpedoes, and depth charges without explosive charges?"

"And you say your **Case Fafner** can accomplish this miracle?" demanded Hitler sceptically.

"Yes, Mein Führer, it can and it will," Canaris responded earnestly. 'Or God help me and the Abwehr!' He shuddered at the thought of the gigantic, brutal alcoholic, Dr. Ernst Kaltenbrunner, usurping the reins of his beloved Service.

"For how long can this be extended, Wilhelm?"

"Six months definite, perhaps more, Mein Führer." Canaris waited as

Hitler leaned back, fingertips steepled, eyes closed. Silently, Canaris started counting to ten, in anticipation of a torrent of abuse.

On 'nine', Hitler leaned forward, hands gripping the arms of his chair, his eyes ablaze. "**Case Fafner** will proceed, Canaris. Take note that I will not accept failure, lame excuses, or administrative obstructionism," he snarled. "Moreover, I will expect reports, from you personally, written or verbal, as I decide. They will be concise and to the point. Daily. No questions?" he asked rhetorically. "That is all, Admiral! You may see yourself out. Send in the guards." Hitler indicated the door with a dismissive wave of his hand.

"Thank you, Mein Führer. All will be carried out as you have ordered."

"See that it is, Canaris. See that it is. You alone will be held accountable."

Two Weeks Later

Against his better judgement, Canaris had taken home a thick file indexed, **Foreign Agent Günther**. Having excused himself immediately after dinner he now sat in his study, riffling through the contents. Suddenly he froze. His eye had caught 'STS 103' and, 'Defence Industries Limited' in the same paragraph. "Good God! What if Bamler has read this!" With mounting apprehension, Canaris read on. Flipping back to the inside of the front cover, he scanned the **Signature i.e. Read** insert slip. With a sigh of relief, he noted that his name was the only one initialled. If true, no one other than his Executive Secretary, Marthe, whose responsibility it was to manage and update all Top Secret files, had seen this.

Although his initial reaction was to telephone his Chief of Staff, General Hans Oster, Canaris quickly rejected the impulse. Since taking office, he had assumed that Kaltenbrunner's SD, Sicherheitsdienst, security police, constantly monitored his 'secure' telephone line. Hans Oster, an urbane, well-educated and devout Protestant, was also a decorated WW1 veteran who shared the Admiral's view of the Nazi's as criminals and was a leading member of the major anti-Hitler conspiracy. Taking a calculated gamble, Canaris and Oster had hand-picked a Nazi, Major Rudolf Bamler, as the Abwehr's head of counterintelligence. Canaris' ploy had worked, up until the present. With Bamler unknowingly acting as Canaris' puppet, Himmler and Kaltenbrunner were satisfied that they had 'one of their own' at the very heart of the Abwehr. In reality, Canaris and Oster fed him only information which they deemed 'neutral' or misleading, while they directed day-to-day counterespionage operations.

Canaris realized that if **Günther** were to fall into Bamler's hands, it could be potentially fatal to the Abwehr. At its worst, he reasoned, Bamler would see that the most damaging excerpts were on Kaltenbrunner's desk by the following morning. Then, by Führer Decree, the SD would take over **Case Fafner** that afternoon. Or, Bamler might choose to keep it to himself for the present, to use when most advantageous to himself. Pacing, Canaris weighed his options. 'First: those two fools, Hartt and Enders, and their so-called spy airplane, have compromised my phantom **Case Fafner**, alerting the Canadian authorities with their ridiculously amateurish scheme. Everybody and everything within ten kilometres will be turned upside down and inside out.

'Second: I have no idea how to accomplish this and keep those SD and Gestapo clowns from meddling.' Standing at the parlour room window, he watched the raindrops coursing down the glass, the Führer's final words still echoing. "'See that it is, Canaris. See that it is. You alone will be held accountable." Time for a walk in the rain,' Canaris muttered.

"I'm going out for a little while, dear," he called up the stairs from the bottom landing.

"In this weather? But why?"

"To clear my head. I'll be fine. Don't worry!"

"Don't be long, Wilhelm, and wear your rubbers!"

"Will you make some hot chocolate when I get back, dear?"

"Yes, of course. It will be ready in half an hour."

"Just let it simmer. I might be a little longer, alright?"

"Very well, dear. Where's Heinzl?

"Oh, there you are." The dachshund had positioned himself between his master and the door expectantly. "Not tonight, my little friend. You'd catch a chill. Be a good boy, Heinzl. Look after Mother."

Seemingly unconvinced, Heinzl wagged his tail as Canaris gently edged his way past and exited. With an accusatory look, a thoroughly dejected Heinzl slunk to his cushion beside the stove.

Glancing quickly up and down the thoroughfare before he stepped into the darkened entranceway, Canaris knocked on the weathered wooden door with the ivory handle of his umbrella. "Go away!" muttered a husky voice.

Knocking once again, Canaris uttered two words, "Ingrid? Willy."

"Why didn't you say so? Coming, coming."

He waited patiently while deadbolts were unlocked and chains unfastened. The door opened a crack, revealing a wisp of blonde hair and a heavily mascaraed eye. "You look like a drowned wharf rat, darling! Come in! Drink?"

"I think not, Ingrid. I am supposed to be out alone. Just walking to gather my thoughts."

"Who is that?" called a feeble voice from up the stairs.

"It's alright, Mother. It's Willy. He is paying me a visit." She paused. "Willy! You remember him. Go back to sleep, dear," she called back.

"Out alone are you? Hmm, I see. Being a bad boy, are we? Here, I'll take that." She smiled knowingly as she offered Canaris a wooden hanger after he had removed his greatcoat. "Now, take off those horrible, ugly boots, Willy. Come into the parlour, sit beside me, and tell me all about the nefarious schemes that you're plotting," she encouraged seductively. "I have a little fire going that will keep us warm and dry you out, poor darling."

Taking her bird-like hand, Canaris did as invited. To the casual observer, Ingrid was a faded femme fatale, a relic of the decadent Weimar Republic era when too much French perfume, rouge, eye shadow, outrageously red nail lacquer, and peroxided, bobbed hairdos were *de rigueur* for the ultra-sophisticated set, not all of them female, who frequented Berlin's more scandalous night spots.

Wilhelm knew well that Fraulein Ingrid Holtzbrinck was anything but the caricature of a tragically out-of-date cabaret goodtime girl that she presented. Brilliant, fanatically devoted to the Fatherland, and more than a little unconventional in her methodology, she had ruled the Abwehr's notorious, efficient, and highly successful school for spies with an iron fist between 1910 and 1914, where she was revered and feared in equal measure. A perfectionist, she habitually washed out candidates by the dozens for a perceived 'lack of spiritual resolve', at the least infraction of the academy code of conduct, or the slightest sign of academic slackening.

When Germany declared war on France, August 3, 1914, she was promoted overnight to Chief of the Abwehr's 'French' counterintelligence bureau. With unlimited funds and resources at her disposal and a bloody-minded determination to outwit, demoralize, and defeat her French and British adversaries, she pushed, cajoled and literally drove her agents to achieve results that were the bane and the envy of every counter-intelligence service, friendly and hostile. Early on, she perfected 'the sacrifice', the Okhrana [Czarist Russia's secret police] tactic, in which a field agent of lesser importance was 'given up', betrayed to the enemy, in order to protect the identity of a more valued operative.

Despite wild speculation and backroom gossip that linked her romantically with the royal family, including Wilhelm II, the Kaiser, assorted grand dukes and lesser nobility, as well as a certain arms and munitions industrialist robber baron, details, whether titillating or humdrum about her private life, were sparse to non-existent. Nicknamed 'The Devil's Mother Superior' by the few bureaucrats and staff officers who were either careless of their careers or dim, or both, she had abruptly vanished at the war's end.

Determined to mine her intimate working knowledge of the French, British, and Russian intelligence services, and capitalize on her unrivalled expertise, Canaris had spent months following dead-end leads until at last he tracked her down in Barcelona, Spain.

Giving gilt-edged assurances of anonymity and financial assistance, he convinced her to return to Berlin, where she lived frugally under an assumed identity in an Abwehr 'safe house', with her aged mother as her sole companion. Gradually, as Admiral Canaris earned her trust, she brought him into her confidence.

Their bond of friendship and mutual understanding was cemented by her opinion of the Nazis in general and Chancellor Adolf Hitler in particular, whom she detested, referring to him as, "That mentally deranged, impotent little Bohemian upstart." Both she and Canaris agreed that Hitler's wilful disregard of common sense and the reasoned counter-arguments put forth by the nation's foremost military thinkers had plunged their beloved homeland into a war with both Great Britain and Russia, and now America, which would reap catastrophic consequences. They agreed that the new world order, which would follow upon the heels of Germany's certain defeat would be far different from that glorious vision trumpeted by Adolf Hitler.

While a prostrate Germany lay in ruins, the victorious Allies would be squabbling and shouldering one another aside like ravenous jackals picking her bones, until the Soviets and the Americans, in their drive for world domination, tore apart and claimed the remains of the carcass. Unlike Wilhelm Canaris, Ingrid had no association with any shadow group of dissidents such as the 'Black Orchestra', [Schwarze Kapell] a band of high-level military conspirators who were devoted to ending the Führer's folly through constitutional means, however unlikely, or in all probability, a coup that would lead to Hitler's arrest and timely execution.

"Now what is bothering you, Willy?"

"I have been given an impossible assignment, Ingrid. If I fail, the Führer will throw me to Heinrich's SS wolves. They will rip me apart and devour our Abwehr," he confessed. "And that is what matters."

"Tut, tut. We can't have that, can we? The chinless chicken farmer [Himmler] is a throwback, a barbarian. No, that is an insult to Atilla," she smiled wistfully. "Beware little men, darling! They are always much too ambitious."

"On the other hand, if I succeed too well, Ingrid, it may well prolong Germany's agony for heaven knows how many more months… or years. The same can be said if the SS…"

"You know, Willy, you surprise me!" she interjected. "You, undoubtedly one of the cleverest men in Germany, know that there is no such thing as an impossible assignment," she lectured, patting his arm consolingly. "Difficult, demanding, formidably complicated, yes; all part of our business. Tell Ingrid all the spicy details, from the beginning, darling, and together we'll find the middle way. Come with me into the kitchen. I'll boil the kettle and make some tea."

"I see," Ingrid continued. "And so you lied your way through the entire meeting. Do you have a plan and do you have a man… an agent... man or woman in Canada?"

"A plan? No, Ingrid. That is why I'm here."

"Sorry, pet. I meant do you have a blueprint, diagram, or an outline of the facility? You'll need one."

"No."

"Can you get one?"

"If I had an agent."

"Well, do you?"

"Mmm, yes. His code name is, '**Günther**'."

"Well, that is a beginning. Is he smart or is he lucky?"

"Both, but I'd say, but unquestionably lucky. He managed to go to ground after the Italian SIM [Secret Intelligence Service] agent who he was running, operational name of 'Marco', was exposed at the BSO base, Camp-X. Marco was murdered in a hotel room by their pet assassin, Robert Samson."

"As Napoleon Bonaparte said, "Give me lucky generals every time," she smiled. "Does Günther have a network?"

"Not any more, so far as I'm aware. The Canadian Mounted Police force rounded them up in Toronto. Kaltenbrunner, on the other hand, claims to have several ‘sleepers’: ready, willing, and able.”

“Hmm. I see. That may not be a problem, Willy. It may well work to our advantage. In your opinion, is Kaltenbrunner serious, or is he playing power games?”

“I’m not sure. However, he certainly has the Führer convinced.”

“Find out where and who they are, that is, if they do exist.”

“I will.”

“Good. Can you still reach ‘**Günther**’? Sorry, darling, I have neither milk nor sugar.”

“If you mean, radio contact, yes. Dangerous, but possible. We do employ our U-boats in the St. Lawrence River not only as couriers and electronic eavesdroppers but as trans-Atlantic signals relays. Our encoding/decoding measures are absolutely fiddle-proof. The problem is, fewer and fewer vessels are making it here and back home. The war at sea is lost, to all intents and purposes. Oh, my, look what I found in my pocket!” he exclaimed, holding up a small, sealed white envelope. “Here, sweets for the sweet.”

“Sugar! You are an old darling!’ she exclaimed, throwing her arms around the little admiral, kissing him soundly.

“No, none for me thanks,” he replied, leaning back in embarrassment. “I brought it for you. Oh, look at the time! I said I’d be back within an hour.”

“Far be it for this old gal to start a new career as home wrecker. Why are you looking at me that way, Wilhelm?” she giggled.

“Oh, no reason,” he replied, shifting uncomfortably in his straight-backed chair.

‘To finish,” Ingrid continued, “You must somehow reach out to ‘**Günther**’ to secure the plans. We can do nothing without that piece of intelligence. I assume that it is quite massive, this DIL? When we have that information, we can begin to plot our strategy. I suggest you do some quiet but quick investigations into Kaltenbrunner’s claim of sleeper agents in Canada.

Find out everything you can about them, in your usual manner. And one other thing. Have your Special Means people look into thermite as a possible fire starter for sabotage."

"Why thermite?"

"Because aluminium and iron oxide are all that are required, in the correct proportions of course, and heat in excess of 2500 degrees Celsius is produced. It must be at hand in a munitions plant. Safe crackers and welders swear by it," she chortled. "Strategically placed, if we had the plans, it can cause an inferno that would be well-nigh impossible to contain, which would send the entire plant sky-high. If on the other hand, you simply want to do significant damage but not disable it entirely, in order to keep up appearances, that too can be worked out."

"Yes, of course. Hand grenades, incendiary bombs, armour-piercing shells. I'll get on it first thing tomorrow," Canaris replied excitedly. "Thank you for everything, Ingrid. I really must run," he commented rising from the kitchen table.

"Must you? Yes, how silly of me. Of course you must. I do enjoy our little times together, so much. Promise me you'll let me know how you make out with '**Günther**', and the phantom SD agents, etcetera. Etcetera?"

"Count on it, my dear friend; within the week."

As she assisted him by holding out his greatcoat, he inserted his right arm into the sleeve. Then taking her hand, he kissed it.

"My, you are a romantic, Willy. From another era. Well, so am I."

"Good night, Ingrid. Please give my kindest regards to your mother."

"Is that you, Wilhelm?"

"Yes, so sorry I'm late, Katherine. I ran into an old colleague." He bent down to pet his dachshund, Heinzl. "What's the matter old fellow? You seem skittish."

"I put your mug of chocolate in the refrigerator," his wife called down.

"You'll have to reheat it."

"I'm fine. I rather like it cool." Removing his coat and footwear, he walked carefully in the darkness through the kitchen into his study as Heinzl followed him. 'Where is that '**Günther**' file? I could have sworn I left it there, on the end table. That is peculiar.' Getting down on his hands and knees he felt around under the table and beneath his easy chair. 'Huh! Not there. I wonder if Katherine put it away?' he murmured. Threading his way back into the front hallway, he called up to his wife. "Katherine, did you happen to see a file lying about in the study?"

"A file? No, dear. I wasn't in your study this evening. I went to bed to read just after you left. Why?"

"It's not there and it is very important. Do you think I dare turn on the light to check?"

"If it's that important, yes, I suppose you might, but only for a moment, so long as the Block Captain doesn't catch you. The blackout curtains are drawn. No bombers tonight. At least, not yet."

"Very well," he responded, padding back into the study. 'Damn.... Nothing. It's not here.' "Katherine!" 'She can't hear me. Of course no one came in the house. Or did they?' He sat down in the darkened study. 'Someone has been in here. I can definitely sense it. But who? Damn! The SD! Now all Kaltenbrunner has to do is show it to Reichsführer Himmler. He'll show it to Hitler, of course, and convince the Führer that it was an Abwehr foul-up from start to finish. And in one stroke, there goes my control of **Case Fafne**r and farewell to the Abwehr. My God! I cannot let this happen.'

Picking up the handset of his 'secure' line, he dialled a number and waited impatiently for an answer. "Franz, this is Admiral Canaris. Heil Hitler and good evening to you, Lieutenant. Would you please have a car sent around to my house? Ten minutes? Very good. I'll be waiting out front. Headquarters. Yes. Thank you.

"Katherine, I must go to the office. Yes, the office! Don't worry. Good night, my dearest."

Arsenal of Democracy

Chapter 7
Hans, we have a problem

Ajax-DIL, Coles Cafeteria

November 1943

Lunch Break

Grease!" Val grimaced theatrically, as she popped another French fry into her mouth. "But the best kind, eh, kids? May, pass the salt please, Hon?"

"Go on, June. Tell us more," continued Val.

"Well, I told her that if she isn't going to do a thorough job of cleaning the shells, there's no way that I'm going to pass them. I'll just keep putting them off to the side with a red tag on them until she gets it right," June explained.

"Good for you, June! Give that prima donna what for," Val exclaimed. "She probably thinks the solvent will ruin her nails. She'd be right, too."

"Bonnie, what are you knitting now?" June asked, hastily changing the subject.

"Mittens," Bonnie replied.

"Mittens for kittens," June rhymed. "And for whom are they, Sis?"

"Our men in New Brunswick," Bonnie replied matter-of-factly. "I've heard that all of the supplies in our depots have been depleted. Sent overseas. The Red Cross is asking for whatever we can give," she replied, accompanied by the busy click of her knitting needles.

"My, you are dedicated, Bonnie. Here you are on your lunch break and you're still giving," June commented.

"That's what it's all about, June. Everyone has to do their part and I feel good that I'm doing mine. I could teach you to knit in no time."

"I suppose so, Bonnie," June replied to her sister, unenthusiastically.

"Look! Out the caf window!" Carole exclaimed, "It's snowing out!"

"Yes, so it is. It's a little early, but according to the Farmers' Almanac, it's going to be colder than our usual winter," explained Lil. "A good sign for a white Christmas."

"Oh, I hope so. Don't you hope so, June?" asked Bonnie.

"No. And you know how I hate winter," June replied, making a face. "It's only good for three things: the 'flu, flannel underwear and frostbite!"

"Oh, come on, June. It's as Canadian as maple syrup. Deep down inside, we all hope that we'll have a white Christmas. Admit it, June," countered May.

"Look, I don't mind snow on Christmas Eve, but that's it. After that, no more snow."

"I'm not a big fan, either," chimed in Val. "And you forgot figure skating-falling flat on your…face. Is everyone giving blood this afternoon?"

They all nodded their heads.

"What are you reading, May?" inquired Lil Montgomery.

"***Commando***. Listen to this. According to this reporter, J. H. Wright of the Transportation Department, displaying a safety-conscious mind and with no thought for his own personal safety, drove his burning truck away from the magazine area near the lake and thereby averted a possible serious explosion. He was approaching Magazine 2261, when the hose connection to the heater broke, spraying alcohol over the engine. Fire broke out immediately. I didn't hear a thing about this. Did any of you? Lil?"

Lil shook her head in silence. Ever since Jim had been promoted to Supervisor, they had an iron-clad agreement: no company talk outside of the home.

Sensing the tension, Carole interjected, "My goodness gracious! Just when you think that you're safe so far away from the war zone."

"Read on, May. What happened?" Val prompted.

"With the motor blazing furiously and only fifty feet from the magazines, he quickly turned and drove to a point of safety about a quarter of a mile away," May continued. "It was only then that he jumped from the vehicle and stood watching as it burned to complete destruction. Had Mr. Wright allowed the truck to remain in the magazine area, there is little doubt but that an explosion would have occurred, which may have resulted in the loss of many lives. Mr. Wright has been working here since May, 1942."

"I sure hope the company does the right thing for Mr. Wright," May commented quietly.

"I'm sure it will, May," stated Carole. "That was a very brave thing to do, but with all of these explosives so close by, I can see why he didn't hesitate. He surely wouldn't have wanted that guilt on his mind if something terrible had happened."

"Okay, girls! Lunch is over. Back to work. Here, I'll take your plate for you, Sis," said June. Then, pausing thoughtfully, she stated. "You know what?"

"No…" Bonnie commented somewhat suspiciously.

"I think we should all take it up!"

"Take what up, June?"

"Knitting. What say, girls!"

"I'm for it!" Val exclaimed.

"Count me in!" added May.

"Me too!" offered Carole. "First lesson tomorrow. Lunchtime. Okay, Bonnie? What do we bring?"

"Nothing. I'll bring needles and enough wool to get everyone started."

78 Tirpitzufer Strasse, Berlin

Fall 1943

Slipping his personal journal back into his briefcase, Canaris switched off the overhead dome light. Reaching forward, he grasped the door handle. "You may let me out here, please, Ensign."

"Very good, Admiral." The massive black Mercedes 770 Grosser glided silently to the curb. Opening his door, Wilhelm Canaris alighted, then courteously bidding the driver, "Good morning," set out for Abwehr Headquarters. As the limousine pulled away, the pale blue haze from its exhaust pipes drifted upward, mingling with the veil of fog that all but enshrouded the beautiful chestnut and lime trees of the Tiergarten, Berlin's largest public park.

Customarily, Canaris looked forward to a brisk two-block walk to his office at 76-78 Tirpitzufer Strasse, Abwehr Headquarters. This morning was different. Slowing down, he needed time to plan his strategy so that he could involve his Deputy, Hans Oster, without tipping off Bamler, the Nazi informant. For a moment, Canaris considered taking a detour and crossing into the Tiergarten, on the chance that, if he waited, he might intercept Oster who routinely cut through the park on his daily five-thirty a.m. stroll to the office. 'No, not a good idea. Risky. Much too obvious,' he decided. Fastening the top button of his greatcoat, he picked up his pace, muttering, "Much too chilly, and damp for this old sea dog to sit around waiting for hours on a cold, hard park bench."

His thoughts were interrupted by squealing tires accompanied by a blaring car horn. Looking back, he saw a small brown form bounding toward him from across the road. "Heinzl?" The dachshund leapt toward Canaris, causing him to drop his briefcase as the dog jumped joyfully into his arms. As the car that had narrowly avoided hitting Heinzl passed by, a child in the passenger seat craned her neck, watching the sight with a smile of pure delight.

"You are a little scamp," he whispered affectionately. "Thought I'd forgotten about you, eh? How did you get out?" He was answered with a very wet, enthusiastic kiss. "Come then. Off to work we go. Remind me to call Mother and tell her to lock the door."

At the entrance to 78 Tirpitzufer, Canaris set down the dog. While the Admiral signed the logbook, the security guard at the desk smiled, remarking, as he did almost every morning, "Good morning, Admiral. Biscuit, Heinzl?"

"Good morning, Lieutenant. Yes, I'm sure that would be in order."

Together, Canaris and his dog ascended to the fourth floor in the squeaky, swaying old elevator. When Canaris unlocked and pushed open his office door, Heinzl trotted to the farthest corner. Upon circling his nest three times, the dachshund settled down contentedly on a cot piled with old army blankets, his chosen vantage point.

Visitors to the Abwehr Chief's office often remarked that it more closely resembled the cluttered inner sanctum of a preoccupied and slightly eccentric academic than the lair of Germany's spy master who controlled the Third Reich's immense military espionage organization. The walls were adorned with pictures of historic ships of the line, including his first command, the battleship *Schlesien*, Adolf Hitler, the avowed landlubber, boarding the cruiser *Dresden* on which Canaris had been first officer, and the Admiral's beloved U-boat. His desk, ink stained, brass bound but unpolished, was a relic from the nineteenth century, as was the tattered Persian carpet. The shelves and bookcases were jammed with books and journals, with miniature brass anchors and other naval bric-a-brac serving as makeshift bookends.

Sitting down, Canaris remembered to telephone his wife with whom he had a brief chat. At 0550h, a young naval attaché knocked and entered to deliver the night's MOST SECRET decoded Enigma radio traffic. The ancient naval clock on the wall facing his desk registered 0600h as Colonel Oster poked his head in the door.

"Good morning, Chief. Anything significant on the wires?"

"Good morning, General Oster. Be my guest," he commented, motioning toward the mound of dispatches on his desktop, which had arrived minutes earlier from the Signals Room. "Come in, Hans. Close and lock the door, if you would, please."

"Yes, of course. What's…?"

Hearing Oster's voice, Heinzl looked up. Upon deciding that the Deputy was an approved visitor, he went back to sleep.

"When was the last time you had the building swept?" asked Canaris, mindful of the SD's practice of electronic eavesdropping on all departments and services, including the Gestapo.

"Mm, Tuesday last. It was clean. Why, Wilhelm?"

"Hans, we have a problem. A very serious problem."

"Go on, Sir."

"Last night my home was infiltrated and the **Günther** file was removed."

"Good, Lord. Any idea who?"

"Someone near and dear, I fear," replied Canaris with a meaningful shrug.

"Bamler. I see. But why would he want that file in particular, Wilhelm?"

"Let me give you the background. It's not a pretty tale."

Oster sat bolt upright, his face draining of colour. Admiral Canaris had swung his chair around to afford himself a view of the majestic Brandenburg Gate in the distance. At length, Canaris broke the silence. "Well, Hans, what do you advise?" he asked.

"Excuse me if I speak plainly, but that bastard Kaltenbrunner has us by the… well, our throats. It's a classical dilemma, a damn near impossible situation. If we go ahead with Case Fafner, we risk the Führer's wrath if it's only a token strike. If we go full bore, then the Allies' munitions supplies will be so drastically affected that this bloody war is certain to drag on for God knows how much longer."

"What's more, Hans, our London contacts will not be at all pleased," continued Canaris. "The Allies rely heavily on this facility. It is crucial to their efforts, although, God knows, we don't want to spill any more blood, German or theirs. And if we fail, or in any way fall short of our glorious leader's expectations, he'll hand our heads to the SS on a plate."

"And 'au revoir' to the Abwehr, as well," Oster added sadly," together with any hope of a negotiated end to the war. Who else has the means and credibility to speak for decent Germans?"

"Precisely," Canaris concluded. They sat wordlessly, until at last Canaris pushed his chair away from his desk and began to pace. "I spoke with a friend last night. You might remember her, Ingrid Holtzbrinck. Does the name ring any bells?"

"Ingrid Holtzbrinck! The Devil's Mother Superior? Only by reputation," he smiled. "That is very interesting, Wilhelm. I didn't realize that she is still alive."

"Living, breathing and at the top of her game."

"Am I correct in assuming that you wanted her opinion, Wilhelm?"

Canaris turned to face Oster. "Correct."

"And?" Oster looked at his Chief expectantly.

"I'll tell you later. First though, I need you to retrieve the **Günther** file. This morning. Before it goes anywhere or Bamler has the opportunity to make copies of the most sensitive documents. I am assuming that he'll be keeping it to himself for the time being, as insurance, a bargaining chip for future consideration."

"Very well." Oster hesitated, and then queried, "How do you propose I do it?"

"I am calling a staff meeting of all Department Heads for 1000h to announce my plan. Colonel Bamler is usually in his office by 0800h. I suggest you go in and calmly announce that I want him in here immediately, with the file in hand. If he plays the 'Who, me?' innocence card or resists in any way, inform him that he will be arrested and court-martialled."

"On what charges? It's a bluff, no, Wilhelm?"

"To some degree, yes. But, if needed I'll think of something. Mm, we'll start with Break and Enter, theft and unlawful possession of classified government documents, and breach of the Reich State Secrets Act. If need be, I can arrange for an 'accomplice' who will swear on a copy of *Mein Kampf* that Bamler's intention was to hawk the file to SIS. Even his so-called friends in the SD will abandon him, or do the fellow in."

"I like it, Wilhelm. Very well, I'll do it."

"Oh, and one other thing, Hans, you can inform him that if he cooperates, there will be no record of this on his dossier. No recriminations, no reprisals, no after-the fact Board of Inquiry. He has my word as a German officer that it will never be brought up again, without cause."

"Very good. Well, I'd best get to my office and wait for Herr Bamler to arrive." Standing up, the elegantly-uniformed Deputy Chief began walking towards the door, then stopped, and turned to Canaris. "Staff meeting at 1000h did you say? Do you want me to have Marthe get the word out?"

"No, I'll have Bamler attend to that when he delivers the goods. In that way, he can salvage a shred of self-respect. I feel that if I am too hard on the fellow, he is more than capable of doing the Service lasting harm."

"Agreed. Wisely said, Wilhelm."

Abwehr Headquarters

The Boardroom

"And so," Canaris concluded, "In order to bring Case Fafner to fruition, our various tasks are, and I emphasize, time bound and multifold. Let us run down our list of responsibilities once more. Would you begin please, Colonel Bamler?"

Enthused, Bamler sprang smartly to attention. "Certainly, Admiral Canaris. I am to make wireless contact with Special Agent Günther. He will be ordered to obtain the drawings for Defence Industries Limited. In addition, Sir, I will liaise directly with Naval Intelligence to arrange that a U-boat be waiting at a location to be designated by General Oster and there to pick up the documents on the date specified. The means by which Günther secures the drawings from DIL or conveys them to the rendezvous are at his discretion but subject to yours and the General's approval."

"Excellent, Colonel.

"And now, Lieutenant Rudner, your role as Colonel Bamler's radio… "

Canaris paused. "Yes, Colonel Bamler, did I overlook something?" There was a nervous shuffling of feet.

Oster studied the minute cracks and fissures on the surface of the massive, ancient oak table that Canaris had requisitioned from Admiralty Headquarters, citing its historic significance. "Do you realize, Hans, that at this grand table, in May of 1916, Admiral Reinhard Scheer plotted his brilliant 'hit and hide' strategy against the British blockade in The Battle of the Skagerrak [Jutland]?" Wisely, Oster had solemnly responded that, as an Army man, he had not been aware of its illustrious past until that very moment, nor did he inquire into the tactical manoeuvres that had led to its relocation.

"Begging the Admiral's pardon, Sir, but I do have something…er, additional, to say," Bamler stumbled.

Oster shot to his feet. "Excuse me, Admiral.

"Colonel Bamler, do you feel that this is the most appropriate forum in which to bring this matter to the Admiral's attention?"

"Yes, I do believe it is. General Oster if I may, I believe that I may have unwittingly compromised this mission, although with the best of intentions."

The room was deathly silent.

Oster could not believe what he was hearing. Less than two hours earlier, in Oster's office, Bamler had acknowledged the theft of **Günther** and had then complied with Canaris' demand that it be returned immediately. Further, he had voluntarily signed a sworn statement in which he testified that no copies had been made, or existed, to the best of his knowledge, on his word of honour as a German officer. 'What in God's name is this idiot about to say? Is he going to confess his sins to the world?'

"Approach, Colonel," Oster ordered brusquely. "What is this about,

Rudolf?" he whispered. "I swear that if you are playing games, the Admiral will have you arrested and summarily court-martialled. Well? Explain and be damn quick about it, Colonel!"

"No, Sir, I am not playing games. I swear that this bears no direct relationship to the **Günther** incident."

"You so swear?"

"I do, General."

"Very well, you may proceed, Colonel," Oster announced quietly.

"Thank you, General. Admiral, colleagues, as you are all aware, one of my principal areas of responsibility is North America, and in particular, the unfortunately now illegal German American Bund. Despite repressive measures taken by the government of the United States, a few of the organization's key operatives have managed to elude the FBI and continue to pursue the Bund's noble aims."

Glancing at Canaris, Oster commanded icily, "Colonel, please. We don't have time for political speeches. Get to the point!"

"Yes, General. In a nutshell, if you will, I had an agent shadowing one of the Canadian special agents, known as 3525. Without my authorization, this German American patriot pursued 3525 and attempted to shoot him while aboard a train bound from Montréal, Canada, to New York City."

"Interesting. And this means exactly what?" questioned Oster, impatiently.

"I'll take over from here, General Oster," Canaris asserted. "The Canadian agent 3525 is Blake Grey, of BSO. Grey is their top man, a senior officer at STS 103 and in all probability, likely to be our chief obstacle to the successful completion of Case Fafner. He is still alive and now thanks to this rogue agent's miscalculation and poor aim, his organization is fully alerted to our existence," uttered Canaris with uncharacteristic harshness.

Bamler hung his head.

"This is not your fault, Colonel, inasmuch as you had no prior knowledge of the agent's intentions and they were not a member of our organization. Such arms-length events are beyond our control. I can personally testify to that," he smiled thinly. "We must do whatever we can to neutralize Grey.

Thank you for your candour, Colonel. You may be seated. Now, where was I?" Turning to a hastily-drawn flow chart that was pinned to his map board, Canaris continued, "Ah, yes, Lieutenant Rudner, please."

Taking a cue from Canaris, Oster stood up and took control of the agenda. "Thank you all for your contributions. The final and most critical element to be discussed this morning is the nature and make-up of the Task Force, which will go into Canada and complete the assignment. As the Admiral and I have had precious little time to draw up the criteria, I invite your submissions, following which a Task Force Readiness Group will be formed to finalize personnel selection, preparation, and specific operational details. First, some non-negotiable assumptions or 'givens'." As he spoke, he wrote rapidly on a fresh sheet of chart paper.

"1. All Task Force team members must be fluent English-speakers, familiar with and fully capable of speaking idiomatic local Canadian English. The reason, I believe, is obvious," he added dryly.

"2. All team members must be expert in the nature, handling, and use of high explosives and, as well, thoroughly trained in industrial sabotage;

3. All members must have had extensive training and must currently belong to a Special Forces unit of either the army, Luftwaffe, navy, or a non-political Waffen-SS detachment. Thus, as an example, *Einzatgruppen* [special action mobile extermination squads] would be excluded.

"Finally, each man must be prepared to assume the role of any other team mate, interchangeably, at a moment's notice, in the event of death, injury, or capture. Which brings to mind; all men will be provided with false identities, papers, and Canadian services uniforms. Now, comments or questions, briefly, please. Captain König?"

"Are cyanide capsules to be supplied as a last resort in the event of capture and torture, General?"

Oster looked at Canaris for a signal, then responded, "No. Next question. None? Very well, gentlemen, I will now assign the Task Force Readiness Group Leaders who will select their subordinates."

Office of Admiral Canaris

"I'm pleased, Hans, very pleased indeed that it went so well. Thank you," Canaris beamed. "Although for a moment, I have to confess to thinking that Colonel Bamler was about to spill the beans. You handled him firmly but with diplomacy and tact."

"Thank you, Wilhelm. I too was horrified to think that he might be so imprudent as to risk his career and the integrity of the Service, all in one breath."

"You know, Hans, and I'm sorry that there wasn't an opportunity to share this before the Staff Meeting, but a very amusing thing happened when Colonel Bamler entered my office following your instructive 'one-on-one' with him."

"Sir?"

"Tell me, how does Heinzl usually react to visitors?"

"Well, he usually looks up, gives them the 'once over' and then goes back to sleep."

"Exactly! Not this time, though," Canaris exclaimed. "Can you guess?"

"Not really," Oster replied, politely feigning interest.

"He growled! Not only once, but twice. What's more, he sat up and was about to leap off the cot to attack him!" Canaris explained delightedly. "He has never done that in my recollection, not here, not even when Himmler, who hates dogs and makes no bones about it, so to speak, was here last month! Bamler was noticeably shaken. I think that if he had the means and the opportunity, he would have gladly strangled or shot him. Heinzl, that is."

Struggling to grasp the significance of this revelation, Oster merely uttered, "Oh?"

"Don't you see, Hans? This alone confirms that Bamler himself was the thief. Dachshunds possess a keen sense of smell and a highly-developed instinct for territory. Heinzl had picked up his odour during Bamler's presence when he was skulking around my house last night. Even though Heinzl was up in my wife's bedroom with the door closed, he recognized

Bamler's scent immediately. Amazing!"

"Tried and convicted by Judge Heinzl," Oster replied, halfheartedly.

"You know, Hans, he's listening to us. See the eye? Good boy, Heinzl!"

"I always thought that Dachshunds were specially bred to hunt badgers, but from Heinzl at least, they're also expert at smelling a rat!" Oster offered.

"Very good!" Canaris laughed. "I must remember to tell that to Katherine. Now, would you care for a light lunch, Hans? I'll ask Marthe to have something nice sent up.

"And for you, also, Heinzl," he added.

Canaris continued, "I want to talk over with you some possible candidates to serve as the Task Force Kommandant. I've made a list while you were leading the meeting. Here, take a look while I order."

I didn't have to read very far to see, 'SS-Sturmbannführer [Major] Otto Skorzeny'," remarked Oster enthusiastically. "Do you think there'd be a chance of snagging him from Himmler, Wilhelm? He is a living legend, a personal favourite of not only our SS-Reichsführer Himmler, but the Führer himself."

"Anything is possible, even, or particularly, in this Nazi madhouse," Canaris replied, smiling cryptically. "Tell me, beyond the legend and all that, why do you think he's the most suitable person? I need to hear your arguments if I'm going to make a convincing pitch to Heinrich for his star commando."

"Whew, where to begin? Well, I suppose I would cite his exemplary, or as some would say, reckless courage, and his indisputable sterling leadership qualities."

"Also noted for his disdain for 'going through the channels'. In other words, a rebel," Canaris counter argued. "That could lead to serious problems for Case Fafner. I want a leader who will make every effort to stick to the plan. If our planning and preparation are fully worked out, including every imaginable 'what if' contingency, the need for individual initiative and creativity are minimized, thereby reducing 'chance' mishaps and potentially fatal foul-ups."

"Agreed. But his rebellious phase is now behind him, or so he says. It was due to a lack of sufficiently exciting challenges. Take any of his recent exploits in Russia."

"Name one example."

"Very well. Leading a group of four SS commandos on a daring night raid behind enemy lines, they knocked out six T-34 tanks in less than thirty minutes and captured three tank commanders. He, his men, and the PoW's returned without incident. Although he was later injured, he was awarded the Knight's Cross of the Iron Cross for Bravery."

"In the Russian campaign, he fought with the Führer's favourite regiment, the SS Leibstandarte [Life Guard]-Adolf Hitler. Is he not therefore, a virulent Nazi?" queried Canaris. "Not the sort of chap we want to be associated with. I'd say that makes him undependable in terms of his loyalty and obedience to an Abwehr-directed mission."

"Yes and no. He's a career adventurer, an opportunist, more than anything," asserted Oster. "Skorzeny lives for challenges and the riskier the better. He would be just as happy as a British Commando. To him, it's all about the derring-do, the adrenalin, the thrill of action. It's his reason for being."

"Sounds like the classic profile of a psychopath," Canaris countered. "Is he a psychopath?"

"No."

"Would you care to qualify that?"

"I can't. Not clinically, at least. I'm not a psychiatrist. However, I have met him twice and he seemed quite the opposite: charming, intelligent, a good listener, extremely amusing, a ladies' man, quite like a Renaissance gentleman in the way he treats them: respectfully and with courtesy."

"No, that doesn't convince me. Those traits are also the earmarks of a full-blown psychopath. The reason they are dangerous is that they appear to be so charming, and normal."

"Just because he is a risk-taker, doesn't mean he's psychotic, Wilhelm!"

Oster stated emphatically. “He may be surrounded by psychopaths, but he’s not a member of the club!”

“Very well, I hear you,” Canaris responded soothingly. “Now, talk about his qualifications for this assignment.”

“I would say that his training as a civil engineer more than qualifies him as suitable to lead a mission whose purpose is to sabotage highly-sophisticated machinery. Oh, and by the way, Wilhelm, he holds an Instructor-level rating in terms of his knowledge of, and handling of high explosives.”

“Hmm, good. That’s very good,” agreed Canaris.

“With respect, Wilhelm, we could sit here all afternoon and into the small hours, debating his suitability…” Oster stated, his voice rising in frustration.

“Very well, Hans. I’ll have Marthe set up a meeting with Reichsführer Himmler to ask for his permission to meet with Major Skorzeny. I have a feeling that if I quietly inform Himmler that Hitler has personally endorsed Case Fafner, as if he doesn’t know that already, we’ll get to interview our man. Himmler loves the glory, the more the better. He’ll likely claim the mission as his own idea, if it turns out well. If not, it’s ours. I will reserve the right to make the final decision though, after we interview Major Skorzeny. Do you agree?”

“Yes, of course, Admiral!” Oster replied with scarcely concealed relief.

The Afternoon of the Next Day

Abwehr HQ 78 Tirpitzufer Strasse, Berlin

Office of Admiral Canaris

“Sturmbannführer Skorzeny, I believe that you have met General Hans Oster!” Canaris announced cordially.

Rising, Oster extended his hand to the 183 cm [six ft. 4 in.] national idol, who, in his immaculate black and silver-trimmed Sturmbannführer’s uniform, dwarfed the diminutive Admiral. Indeed to Oster, the Austrian giant seemed to fill the entire room. “Yes, it’s indeed a great pleasure to meet you again, Major Skorzeny!”

With courtly grace, Major Skorzeny leaned forward to take Oster’s hand. Then, saluting him in the Roman manner, his right arm parallel to the floor, thumb and index finger barely touching his breastbone, he clicked his heels while replying, “Herr General. An honour, Sir.” Now standing at attention, cap under his arm, he waited for his hosts to speak.

“Stand easy, Major Skorzeny,” advised Canaris in a kindly manner.

”Thank you, Herr Admiral.”

“Please be seated.” Canaris pressed a button on his desk telephone. Seconds later, a young female attendant wearing a white jacket and black trousers entered the room carrying an ornate silver tray. Silently, she set down the tray on the sideboard where she stood at attention, awaiting instructions. Oster noted that in spite of her apparent efforts to resist, her dark eyes darted over several times to dwell split seconds longer than mere curiosity or her training required, or permitted. Mildly amused, he reflected, ‘One millisecond longer next time, your ladyship, and its outright flirtation.’ Oster could only imagine the heated rivalry and spats that flared amongst the female cadets in the kitchen when it became known that their revered ‘Boss,’ Admiral Canaris, would be entertaining the towering, dashing and ruggedly handsome, scar-faced hero of the Belgian, Yugoslavian, and most recently, Russian campaigns, Sturmbannführer Otto Skorzeny.

Seemingly unconscious of her appraising glances, Skorzeny, a model of decorum, earnestly studied the Admiral’s historic photographs and exquisitely detailed ships’ models.

While Skorzeny gazed intently at the memorabilia, Oster could not help observing that the Major’s famous *Schmiss* [smite], duelling scar, was considerably deeper and more pronounced than it appeared in newspaper photos. Running from the centre of his prominent chin, and then curving like a crescent moon across his left cheek it ended only millimetres from his ear. ‘In an earlier time, he’d be the perfect, swashbuckling buccaneer, a charming, heartthrob rogue of the sort portrayed by the English actor,

Fairbanks. The Knight's Cross for Bravery glinting left mid-chest, added an almost supernatural aura to the man's undeniably charismatic persona, thought Oster. 'Devilishly attractive, I admit, but I wonder how it would play out if this attention-getter were to saunter down the main street of Toronto?'

After serving tea and superb Bavarian cream pastries, the slim blonde cadet quietly dispensed white linen serviettes to Canaris and Oster. All went well until she approached Major Skorzeny. Nervously, she fumbled the napkin, letting it fall onto the rug. With a barely audible expression of apology, she was about to curtsy in order to retrieve it when Sturmbannführer Skorzeny took her hand. Kissing it lightly, he then assisted her by sweeping both her and it up and placed the serviette upon his lap. Blushing, she collected the tray and withdrew to relate her impressions of this chivalrous knight, a latter day Lohengrin, to an envious claque below stairs.

Following an exchange of pleasantries and expressions of delight about the sweets, and after Canaris had politely inquired about the Major's health in relation to the injuries that he sustained in Russia, Wilhelm then commenced the interview with a direct question. "Major Skorzeny, we are searching for the right man to lead a highly risky mission overseas. It will involve him taking a group of four comrades by U-boat into New Brunswick, Canada. From there, he will lead the men, using false identities as Canadian servicemen, to Central Ontario where they will destroy a major munitions factory. Tell us frankly, Sir, knowing only this much, are you interested?"

Without hesitation, Skorzeny responded, "Yes, extremely interested indeed, Admiral Canaris. I am deeply honoured to have been asked, gentlemen!"

"Is that an acceptance?"

"Yes, Sir. Permission to ask one question?"

"Permission is not required, Major. Fire away."

"Regarding the Task Force, will I be involved in the selection of its members?"

"You will. Anything else?"

"No, Sir."

"Excellent! This interview is concluded." Canaris smiled, reaching out his hand to grasp Skorzeny's. "Thank you and welcome to Case Fafner, Major.

"General Oster, would you accompany Major Skorzeny into the boardroom to show him the material that has been prepared by the Task Force Readiness Group?"

"Yes, of course. But first, perhaps I should explain that, as the planning and preparations are evolving daily, it is critically important that you be involved in each phase and every detail. Are you prepared to see it through?" questioned Oster. "It will be time-consuming and exhausting."

"Without hesitation, General! Promises are cheap. The proof is in the performance."

Early evening

Office of Admiral Canaris

"Sit down and relax, Hans. Loosen your tie, man."

"Thanks, I will."

"So? Did I do the right thing?"

"No question, Wilhelm. He is the right man for this assignment, perhaps the only one. Of that I am absolutely certain. I do have one nagging reservation, though. It has nothing at all to do with either his competence or his commitment, or anything remotely like that."

Slowly twirling a pencil between the fingers of both of his hands, Canaris gazed out his window. Nodding his head, he remarked, "As do I. This should be interesting. Tell me yours."

"Perhaps you'll think I'm being overly cautious…"

"Hans, please. Say it!"

"Major Skorzeny is too, well…"

"Too well known?"

"Exactly. I cannot imagine how we can pass him off as a run of the mill, small town Canadian farm boy-soldier. There is nothing average about the man!" exclaimed Oster, now pacing rapidly. "His picture appears in newspapers and newsreels all around the world, thanks to Propaganda Minister Goebbels. Young people, women, pin his photo up in their kitchens and bedrooms. He's one of the few Germans, as well as Field Marshall Rommel, who is universally admired. He'd be recognized anywhere, even in a Canadian backwater town."

"I know. I know," Canaris replied quietly. "You are right. What do you suggest we do? We can't run the risk of souring him on the mission at this point. As you said, he's damn near irreplaceable. Correction, he is irreplaceable."

"I think I have it!" stated Oster excitedly. "We can have our cake and eat it too!"

"How so?"

"Simple, Wilhelm. He is our chosen Mission Fafner Kommandant. Agreed? Very well, he will train and then lead his quartet of saboteurs to Canada. But once there, and this is the brilliant part, if I may say so, he will direct and control the team by short wave radio, from the U-boat!" grinned Oster. "Of necessity of course, one of the team members on the ground will be the designated tactical commander."

"For heaven's sake, man, pour us each a brandy! And make them doubles! I will recommend an immediate rise in your pay grade, Oster. Ein Toast zur Mission Fafner. Prost!"

"Prost!"

The Cherbourg Peninsula, Normandy, Northern France

Benno, Franz, Hermann, Tristan, and Otto

"Stand easy, men. Let me tell you, I am impressed, very impressed, with your performances over the past five days. Not only have you endured and mastered these rigorous exercises and daunting tasks, I want you to know that your superiors chose each of you, not at random, but for the reason that you are first among equals. Gentlemen, you are the finest examples of the great brotherhood of German warriors that our Führer, Adolf Hitler, so generously and rightfully honours.

"However, although each of you has demonstrated the skills, stamina, intelligence, courage, and attitude that we are seeking, operational guidelines dictate that only four of the twelve finalists can be selected for this special duty." Striving to be heard above the furiously driving rain and hail which pelted the parade ground, Major Skorzeny continued, forcefully.

"I am pleased therefore to announce the following list. You will take one step forward when your name is called: Naval Signalman First Class, Lieutenant Benno Farber; Flight Lieutenant Franz Haldemann, mission second officer; Wehrmacht Technical Specialist Master Sergeant Hermann Klein, and, Mission Fafner tactical Kommandant, SS-Hauptsturmführer [Captain] Tristan Zeiss.

My sincere congratulations, gentlemen. I invite you to join me for a celebratory dinner in the Mess at 1800h. Now, don't get the notion into your heads that your training is finished. We have yet to get started!" joked Skorzeny. "Tomorrow at 0500h, we will be testing out your sea legs and stomachs!

"The remaining eight men will return to their units." Pausing, Skorzeny smiled, and then announced jovially, "Following a two-day furlough in Paris, in appreciation of your splendid service to the Fatherland! I should add that in the event of accident or unforeseen mishap, each of you is deemed eligible to be recalled to replace a team member. Staff Sergeant, dismiss the detail."

Aboard *U-4720*

Barely able to speak, much less stand upright, Hermann moaned, "The stink, the rolling, the pitching, Benno! How do you stand it?"

"The stink as you call it is *Miese*, which is comprised of sweat, diesel fumes and human waste, plus cooking odours and what have you. Get used to it. The rolling and pitching are a fact of life above or undersea. Like stale biscuits and cold tea." Softening his tone, the U-boat radioman inquired, "Now, what's the matter, Hermann? A bit seasick are you?"

"A lot seasick, Benno," gasped Hermann. "Where do I go to throw up?"

"The Head. Five metres along the passageway. But step on it! We're set to undergo a mock depth charging in just a few minutes."

"Oh, God!" Hermann's voice trailed off, as he surrendered to the insistent crackling of a close by loudspeaker.

"Attention! Attention! This is Kapitänleutnant Kettling. Welcome on board U-4720, gentlemen. As part of your training, our vessel will undergo a simulated depth charging. This is an exercise. I repeat, an exercise! Be assured that at no time will U-4720 be under enemy attack. Apart from that, it will be as realistic as our friends in the surface vessels above can possibly make it, without inflicting damage to our ship. Your Kommandant, Major Skorzeny, has something to say to you."

Before Skorzeny could utter a word, all hell broke loose on board. The first explosion threw Hermann violently against a bulkhead, knocking him onto the steel deck, unconscious. Despite the Captain's assurances, the force of the percussion briefly knocked out the lighting and caused a breach of the double-hull in the engine room, creating a leak.

"Attention! Attention! Battle stations," barked Kapitänleutnant Kettling. "Silent running. Mark now!"

Skorzeny and the U-boat's first officer quickly and quietly gathered the members of Team Fafner together in the aft torpedo room. "Hold onto anything you can get your hands on. Not the hot water pipes, mind. Hug a torpedo if nothing else is available," advised the officer as another explosion blew out the lighting, leaving only the red emergency system glowing dimly.

“Lord, some simulation!” croaked Flight Lieutenant Franz Haldemann, wide-eyed. “I’d hate to be in the middle of the real thing!”

“Where is Hermann?” asked Tristan, SS-Captain Tristan Zeiss. “Anybody see him?”

“I did. Just a few seconds before the first blast,” offered Benno. “He was heading to the Head. Sick as a dog.”

“I’ll go and find him,” stated Major Skorzeny. “Which…?” A high-frequency, ear-piercing pinging that threatened to penetrate and sauté his brain’s neurons, cut him off.

“Echo sounding: sonar,” commented the first officer tersely. “They’re ranging our depth in order to re-calibrate the fuse detonation point of the charges. We use it to find underwater targets. By its frequency, I’d say that it’s coming from an aircraft.”

“Sit tight. I’m going for Hermann. Tristan, take over,” whispered Skorzeny, as another explosive’s intense concussion made the hull plates ring ominously.

The pervasive stench of *Miese* combined with the signature scent of ozone emanating from the U-boat’s batteries reminded Franz of the scent of a thunder and lightning storm, but even more irritating. An asthmatic, he began to choke uncontrollably.

“Shut it down, Lieutenant. They can hear you,” the ship’s officer warned, gesturing meaningfully upwards.

I, I can’t.”

“Dammit, when I tell you to stuff it, soldier…!”

“That will do,” ordered Tristan, Hauptsturmführer Zeiss. “Here, Franz. Take my handkerchief. Cough into it to muffle the sound.”

‘Thanks, Tristan.” Nodding in appreciation, Franz was reaching out to take the Kommandant’s hankie when a thunderous blast seemed about to tear the U-boat asunder. The emergency lighting dimmed, flickered, and died. The sound of something being dragged across a steel grating made Tristan call out softly, “*Wer ist das*?

"It's me, Otto. I have Hermann. He's okay. Shaken, but he's conscious."

"What's that? My ass is soaking. Water! It's flooding!" Franz croaked.

"Water! We're done for!"

"That will do! Stop it. Now!" thundered Skorzeny. "It's from a small leak in the engine room that is already plugged," he stated calmly. "We're going to be fine. This is almost over."

A final shock wave and a fierce sonar lashing reverberated from bow to stern, drowning out Franz's muttered, "Sorry, Otto."

The lights came on. As one, the Fafner Team members looked up, tentatively, unsure. "Attention. Attention. All clear! Surfacing. All hands and officers will report to surface running stations. Bo'sun, take the con."

A loud cheer arose from the aft torpedo room. Within minutes, a purifying surge of fresh North Sea salt air had all but driven the *Miese* and fear from their consciousness.

Skorzeny stood up, the top of his head brushing the caged overhead light fixture. "Tristan, go and fetch the ship's doctor for Hermann.

"Well, men, this was your baptism of fire. Literally. The next time it won't be a game, that, I can promise you. However, you did bear up remarkably well, for landlubbers, eh, Benno?"

"Quite well, Otto, considering," Benno confirmed.

"Kapitänleutnant Kettling has kindly invited us to his wardroom for a tipple of rum. Let's show the Captain our appreciation for his outstanding hospitality," urged Skorzeny.

His announcement was met with dead silence.

"And any man who disagrees with my sentiments will be summarily transferred from Fafner to the U-boat service," he chided. "In perpetuity."

"Hip, hip, hooray for Kapitänleutnant Kettling!" uttered Hermann weakly. "I'll be stuffed if…if I'm going to be c, condemned to a lifetime of…p, peeing my drawers while I'm lying conked out… on the cold, wet floor…er, deck of one of these bloody sardine cans! C'mon boys. Let's hear it!" His plea was met with barely-muted chuckles from his comrades.

Following an inordinately long silence, they responded feebly, in a ragged chorus. "Hip, hip, hooray for Kapitänleutnant Kettling!"

"Two fingers. Not a drop more! You're in training, remember!" lectured Skorzeny. "All but me, that is!"

"How's that, Otto?" asked Tristan, hesitantly.

"Compensation, Tristan. *Standardized Universal Code of Military Conduct and Deportment of Officers and Ranks*, Sec.xii, Sub Sec. ii. In plain German, it is because I have to put up with you lot of insubordinate, supermen heroes! Any rebuttals?" he challenged, grinning broadly. As was to be expected, there were none. "Now, stand up and look sharp, like the Reich's Special Action commandos that you are reputed to be, not like those two ridiculous, sad-sack, weary-assed American GI's, Willie and Joe, in their silly *Stars and Stripes* pulp magazine. A-tten-tion!"

Normandy, France

Special Forces Operational HQ

One Week Later

With a deafening roar, the turret of the rusted, battle-worn British Matilda tank tilted upward, separating from the main body. Lurching sideways, it then crashed drunkenly, upside-down, two metres away.

"Excellent demonstration, Hermann. Well done! Thank you.

"*Plastikexplosivstoff*. One hundred times more powerful than an equivalent amount of TNT," Skorzeny announced. "And so, gentlemen, there can be no question of the choice between traditional and non-traditional explosive charges. If the express purpose of the mission were to create maximum destruction while inflicting as many casualties as possible, thermite, or one of its variants would be the preferred substance. However, my superiors have expressly directed that the intent of Case Fafner is to put this particular manufacturing facility out of operation, not to wage war upon civilians, the workers. That is their prerogative.

“Naturally, you will also make every effort to destroy the main storage depot, which will have a profound impact on the local population. But, more about that later.

“While the British and their Allies had a head start in refining the chemistry of this remarkable compound, which, by the way, was likely first made practical by the so called ‘father of dynamite’, the Swede, Alfred Nobel, it’s not surprising that our German scientists have taken it from its fairly primitive stage, known as **Nipolit,** made from leftover cannon propellant to new levels of sophistication. Here catch it!” For dramatic effect, Skorzeny threw a lump of the whitish-green substance at Benno, who cringed, drawing back. It landed harmlessly at his feet.

“The advantages of this new *Plastikexplosivstoff,* or more commonly, plastik, are self-evident. It is pliable, unless it is cold, and readily mouldable to take the shape and adhere directly to almost anything: a tank’s tracks, a ship’s propeller and hull, a bridge girder, or items of heavy machinery. It is also excellent for breaching a concrete hydroelectric dam, a use to which my little group of commandos put to effective use in Russia.” He paused as the squad chuckled politely in appreciation.

Without warning, he reached for his holster, withdrew his Luger Parabellum pistol, and fired a 9-mm round into the inert greenish mass at Benno’s feet. There was no reaction. “Without the proper means of ignition, perhaps a blasting cap, a time-delay fuse, or an electrical current, it is almost completely inert. One caution: it does have the scent of almonds which can be a detected by a canine especially trained to sniff it out. I seriously doubt if the operation at DIL is that advanced, but all factors must be taken into consideration.

“Are you alright, Benno?” Skorzeny inquired of the somewhat shaken Signals Lieutenant. “I promise not to make you the guinea pig again.”

“I’m fine, Otto. No worries. Thanks.”

“Good. Above all, it easily transportable, readily disguised, hidden and if handled with reasonable care and caution, exceptionally stable.

“Now, I am going to ask our technical specialist, Hermann, to talk about the various methods, and specific means by which it can be detonated. Give Hermann your full attention. Your life and that of your comrades may depend upon it, Hermann."

Special Forces Operational HQ

The Map Room

The four men of the Reich Special Action Squad came to attention, saluting Major Skorzeny when he strode into the room. Returning their salute, he announced, "Good morning, gentlemen. Please be seated. I am pleased to tell you that our training is progressing slightly ahead of schedule. I fully expect that by this time on Friday, you will be ready to commence the simulation exercises that make up the final stages in your readiness preparation.

"Today, however, let me begin in saying that my superiors have achieved not one but three extraordinary coups. By what means, I am under oath to the Führer not to divulge.

"What you are seeing on the left, as I draw back this curtain, is a detailed schematic outline diagram of the target. While, over here, on your right, is an official Canadian Government aerial survey map of the area in the factory's immediate vicinity. On your far, right, Tristan, if you would please, thank you, once again is a Government topographical map showing in detail the St. Lawrence River and the coastline of the Province of New Brunswick. Cartographic and other Intelligence specialists from the U-boat Naval Base at St. Nazaire will conduct the required briefings.

"I can see from your expressions that you are surprised. If that name, New Brunswick, has a familiar ring, the Province owes its name to the Duchy of Brunswick in Germany, which was a possession of the English King George III at the time the Province was established. Need I say that although George was born in England, his roots were decidedly German, being a direct descendant of the Royal House of Hanover.

"Now to the pièce de résistance. Join me at the table, please." In one motion, as though he were a conjurer, Skorzeny pulled away a cover sheet to reveal a three-dimensional model of Defence Industries Limited. "Beautiful, isn't it?" he commented rhetorically. "Examine the detail. Before you ship out for Canada, each one of you will be expected to have committed this plan to memory. You will know it as intimately as you know the back of your hand, or your sweetheart's …hand." Skorzeny paused briefly waiting for the manly chuckling to subside. "Tristan has been quietly working around the clock with the Abwehr's superb Artistic Rendering Unit and with me, also. He is now fully knowledgeable and capable of leading us through the actual raid, systematically. However, to better orient you, we will begin with photographs of the plant's surroundings and exterior features. Tristan."

"Thank you, Otto. Lights down. Slide one, please," began Tristan, as the overhead lighting dimmed. "Adjust the focus, please. Much better. This first picture shows DIL from the perspective of the main gate at Plant Road, looking southeast. Plant Road can be accessed back here at the King's Highway No. 2. As you can see, the buildings are wood construction and not much else, as is typical of these pop-up by night operations. Next slide. Here we have a close-up shot of the main gate and front entrance of the Administrative building. The security man visible here is a Mr. Charles Brown. Brown, a superannuated veteran of the Great War, would present no threat to us. Next.

"Ah, now this is more interesting. The two men in their shirtsleeves who are obviously enjoying themselves at a company outing are, on the left, the Plant Manager, Mr. David Caldwell, and one of his production Foremen, Mr. James Montgomery. Like Mr. Brown, neither of these men poses a serious threat. In fact, our intelligence sources inform us that the facility is 'ripe for the picking'. For the most part, it's guarded by people of Mr. Brown's calibre, with weak security overall. A remarkably amateur enterprise in that respect. I'll stop there for questions. Franz?"

"How much do we know regarding law enforcement and military in the locality?"

"Otto, would you care to respond?"

"Yes. Concerning the local police agency, Franz, the Ontario Provincial Police, are well-trained and equipped. The closest military base is an SOE school, approximately sixteen kilometres away. However, if we rehearse fully and then follow our plan exactly, we will go inside on Christmas Eve, when we can expect plant security to be minimal, set the charges, and then be well away before either the police or the military are alerted, much less able to get to the site. Tristan."

"Thank you, Otto. The next series of photos are what you have been anxiously waiting to see. The production lines at DIL; in other words, gentlemen, our targets. First slide, please."

The Next Morning

Standing in the aisle of a military bus, Skorzeny addressed Team Fafner. "I know how eager you are to get down to the operational 'nuts and bolts,' so to speak. Yesterday, you saw photographs of the machinery, which were obtained at great risk by Abwehr Intelligence. Today, you will experience the real thing, on a reduced scale, courtesy of the Reich Ministry of Armaments. I mention the scale as this factory is of course in France and so, it is not truly representative of our munitions works in The Fatherland. However, it will more than suffice. Your task today is twofold. One: you will study the equipment and listen carefully as the shop officials describe the function of the selected items. Two: you will absorb and memorize every detail of the plant's layout, and in particular the location and deployment of any and all personnel. Then, when we return to base, you will plan a clandestine raid, which will be executed using mock explosives, naturally, to test your readiness. Factory security will not be forewarned. Clear? Any questions? Good. Our traveling time will be one hour and fifteen minutes. I urge you to concentrate upon your upcoming tasks. Failure to succeed in the second part might necessitate your replacement and reassignment. At worst, you may be shot." Seeing a look of stunned disbelief on the men's faces, Skorzeny's tone softened, explaining, "No, not by me! By plant security, if you're careless. Enjoy the journey, gentlemen, but not too much. That is all."

Arsenal of Democracy

Ajax DIL
Ajax DIL
Ajax DIL
Ajax DIL

Chapter 8

In the name of the Führer

**Bay of Chaleur off Maisonette Point
New Brunswick, Canada
Monday December 13 to Wednesday December 15 1943**

Periscope depth, Herr Kaleu!"

"Up periscope! Oberleutnant, battle stations. Standby!" ordered Kapitänleutnant Kettling, matter-of-factly.

"Immediately, Herr Kaleu," replied First Officer Oberleutnant Krafft, relaying the Captain's command into the intercom mouthpiece, "All hands to battle stations. Standby!"

When the U-boat's periscope pierced the surface, Kapitänleutnant Kettling commenced scanning the rocky coastline of Maisonette Point. "Hurry, hurry! Damn it!" Drawing away from the eyepiece, he waited impatiently as the waves' washing over the lens subsided. "Better," he muttered, resuming the search. "Good! That's it, Oberleutnant!" Slapping the hand grips upward into the instrument's shaft, Kettling ordered, "Steady, steady! Stop engines!"

"Stop engines." Oberleutnant Krafft relayed the Captain's command to the Chief Engineer in the Engine Room.

"Success, Kapitänleutnant?" inquired Major Skorzeny.

Turning to Skorzeny, Kettling nodded affirmatively. "They have signalled, *All is ready*. It is your show, now, Sturmbannführer. You have exactly fifteen minutes to get your team topside and launched on their way."

"Very good, Kapitänleutnant. Thank you. I will prepare my men to disembark." Skorzeny made his way aft of the Control Room to where his four specialists were huddled. At his approach, they struggled to rise to their feet in their cramped quarters. Signalling that they remain seated, he crouched, speaking quickly. "Gentlemen, it is time. Need I repeat that the successful execution of **Case Fafner** is of crucial importance to the

Fatherland? No. I have the utmost faith in your dedication to duty. You are, each of you, courageous, virtuous Siegfried's, who will plunge your warriors' daggers into the heart of the dragon, Fafner. Your heroic deeds will strike a decisive blow for our beloved Deutschland. As German soldiers, you have obediently accepted that your safe return is, at best, uncertain. I pray that the gods of war will protect you. I am deeply honoured to be your commanding officer." Pausing, Skorzeny stood up. "Questions? Briefly, please. Hauptsturmführer Zeiss?"

"Sturmbannführer Skorzeny, if I may speak for the others, it is a great honour to serve under your command. We will not let you down. Heil Hitler!"

"Well said!" "We will not fail!" "*Ehrenwort*!" [My word of honour].

"Heil Hitler! Thank you. Hermann, Benno, Franz, and Tristan: you have rehearsed and memorized your cover stories thoroughly. I have purposely withheld your full code names until now. Why, you might ask yourselves? Doesn't Skorzeny trust us?"

"In order to protect the mission and to ensure there was no possibility that our Canadian identities could slip out by mistake?" volunteered Hermann.

"Precisely. Hermann, your nom de guerre is Wilf Johnson. Benno, you are Ben Anderson. Franz, you are Ernest Dixon. Tristan, you will become Tom or Tommy Fralick. These are your papers verifying your identities and backgrounds. Treat them with the utmost care. As you can see, they are flawless: watermarked, perfectly aged and creased, the handiwork of the world's most brilliant document reproduction craftsmen. The leather billfolds are known as 'wallets', not 'v allets' in English. Drivers' licences, military ID and other essentials except money are enclosed. A 1936 Chevrolet automobile similar to the model that you have been testing will be provided once you have made contact with our man in New Brunswick. Suitcases for each of you will be in the auto's trunk. He will supply a certificate of motor vehicle insurance, gasoline ration cards, etcetera. Very well. Put the documents away: inside jacket pocket.

"Ben, as radio operator, you will communicate with home base only using your code name, **Reindeer**."

"Tommy, make sure that the maps sewn inside your jacket are kept dry. Give me your wristwatch." As ordered, Tommy unfastened the tan leather strap and handed the **Bulova** timepiece to Skorzeny. With an upward flick of his thumbnail on the winding stem, Skorzeny flipped up the crystal and internal works to reveal a miniature compass mounted on the base plate. "You didn't know about this, did you?" he smiled. Tommy looked on admiringly. "Now you do. Here," Skorzeny continued, handing the timepiece back to Tom. "Close it; press down, not too forcefully, and put it back on. Oh, one other detail. Pull out the winding stem."

"Pull it, Sir?"

"Thumb and index finger nails." Skorzeny waited as Tom complied. By this time, the three other men had gathered around, watching closely. To their astonishment, Tom extracted a sixty-centimetre length of fine gauge wire.

"A, a garrotte!" Tom exclaimed.

"A beauty. Be damned careful if you are in a situation requiring its use. Wear gloves! It will not only kill your adversary, it can bloody near decapitate the poor bastard and make short work of your fingers at the same time. All right, give it a quick tug and let it recoil. En garde, or it will whip you in the face."

"Oh! Damn!" Tom shouted. The stainless steel wire glanced off his right cheek, drawing blood.

"See what I mean? Once more, lad, and you'll be looking like me!" Skorzeny joked, pointing to the jagged fencing scar on his left cheek. "It's just a scratch. You'll be fine. Moreover, women will love it! Speaking of the ladies, it is time for your makeup. One tube apiece."

As each man applied the greenish-black facial camouflage, Skorzeny watched closely, occasionally offering his professional advice. "Backs of the hands, gentlemen! Good. At the same time as you are making your way to Ajax, we will be out in the Atlantic, staying clear of the Canadian Navy," he explained. "We will return exactly two weeks from today. That is how long you have to complete the mission: in and out. No dallying, no romances, no alcoholic drink except beer and no more than two at any time. We cannot afford boneheaded blunders of any kind. The mission and your lives depend upon your common sense and discretion. But it's all been said many times before." Skorzeny paused, smiling broadly. "Your contact on the ground is an SS-Sturmbannführer, Johann Binder: Allgemeine, not Waffen SS, Tom. Nice enough fellow, but somewhat, ah, peculiar. Still, Johann is all that we have left there. He'll look after you." Inspecting their blackened faces, he gave his approval. "My, you are a fierce-looking band of desperados! Ready?"

"Yes, sir. Ready," replied Tom, grinning self-consciously.

"Good. In the name of the Führer, Godspeed. Four minutes to departure. Follow me forward.

"Herr Kapitänleutnant, please open the hatch."

"Oberleutnant! Open the hatch and prepare to deploy the life raft," ordered Kapitänleutnant Kettling. "Good hunting, gentlemen. Heil Hitler!"

U-boat

Climbing the conning tower's steel treads toward the open hatch, each man breathed in the refreshing night air while trying not to think of the mission ahead. Arriving first on deck, Skorzeny reached down to assist Tom, and then each of the others in turn.

Seated at the bow of the small landing craft, Tom tucked his kit securely between his knees, waiting with his comrades while the two submariners unshipped their paddles. As the raft slipped silently away from the side of the U-boat, a single shaft of moonlight emerged, reflecting brilliantly off the gently lapping waters of the Bay of Chaleur, eerily silhouetting the receding figure of Major Skorzeny. Incongruously, a half-forgotten Christmas carol, *Silent Night*, entered Tom's mind: "All is calm. All is bright." A cloud rolled over the moon. Otto Skorzeny and the now distant U-boat had faded into the darkness.

We're at the rendezvous point, Sir," whispered the Chief Petty Officer. "You'll have to get out now. It's only knee-deep. Have an eye for the boulders underfoot. Here is a small package for your contact. Good luck, Sir!"

"Thank you, Bo'sun. The same to you," Tom replied, tucking an oilcloth-wrapped parcel inside his jacket. As he was about to swing his legs over the side of the dinghy, he paused, and took a breath. Hoping to sound as coolly decisive as Major Skorzeny, he ordered, "After me! Silently!"

Stepping into the chillingly icy water, each man fought to suppress gasps of shock. "I thought *chaleur* was French for warmth!" muttered Ben as Ernest choked back a chuckle.

"I said silently, damn it!" Tom cautioned.

Emerging from the frigid bay, the four Germans fell into single file behind Tom, picking their way stealthily over the stony beach. Suddenly, with a downward swoop of his hand, Tom hissed, "Down!" Lying motionless, their eyes strained to see into the void. In the near distance, a light flashed once.

Raising his head, Tom called softly, "*Kamel. Kamel.*"

As prearranged, the light flashed twice. 'Careful, might be a trick,' Tom reminded himself. 'Wait for it.' Counting silently to five, he was about to repeat the code word when a dark figure stepped out from behind a natural fortress of boulders.

"Hauptsturmführer Tristan Zeiss? I am Sturmbannführer Johann Binder. We are quite alone here, Hauptsturmführer. It's safe to get up. Tell me, did everything go well?" he inquired breezily.

As he and his men rose to their feet, Tom replied, "Yes, just fine, thank you, Sturmbannführer Binder." Saluting stiffly, Tom continued, "With respect, Sir, for the purpose of this assignment, I am 'Tom'. Allow me to introduce my squad."

"Yes, of course. Tom. How careless of me." After greeting each man amiably, the Sturmbannführer added, "Forgive my lack of a uniform. As you can see, I am becoming quite accustomed to wearing the garb of a Norwegian/Canadian fisherman. A scallop man, actually. Jon Jansen. Delicious, world famous for their exquisite taste and texture, the fishies are," he remarked in an aside.

"Fishies?" laughed Tom inwardly. Catching sight of his men's smirking faces, he frowned, shaking his head in disapproval.

"Life could be worse," continued Binder blithely. "Hospitable people, remarkably similar to our good Baltic Sea fisher folk, you might be surprised to know: hard-working, generous to a fault, damn clever, fine-looking women, hearty beers and excellent wines to boot. The French contingent, Acadians they call themselves, proud Breton, Norman stock and others, historically, they have no great love for England, which is good, but the races do seem to get along quite well. This entire area could be a fascinating site for the study of racial harmonization and future resettlement by our Aryan *volk*. I have dispatched several reports to Berlin to that effect, earlier. Alas, no acknowledgement, no replies. *Nichts*. Ah, well, c'est la guerre, one supposes. All in good time," he concluded philosophically, while blowing his nose vigorously on a large red and white polka dot handkerchief.

"Damn cold out here. You will all be down with pneumonia. Not in the plan book. Heads would roll. Mine, to be precise. HQ is not very forgiving these days. Very well, are we ready? Come with me, gentlemen. I have a small chalet, more of a cabin actually. I use it for storing my fishing gear. Must keep up appearances, you know. We will have you kitted out and on your way in no time. Mind your step; damned treacherous, this terrain. Why, only last week a local lad and his sweetheart were…"

As they followed the rambling, rotund Major Binder around the boulders and traversed the sand dunes, Tom tried to reconcile this garrulous relic with the legendary Otto Skorzeny, the dashing, and heroic SS-Sturmbannführer, whose description of their host, Tom now recalled. '"Your contact on the ground is a certain Sturmbannführer Binder. Allgemeine, not Waffen SS…peculiar..." 'Of course,' reasoned Tom, 'the fellow is an honorary SS-Man, and not a member of my and Major Skorzeny's fighting Waffen section. Good God, he would never even pass the physical! Likely a professor or writer or a shore bird fancier or perhaps Daddy is bloody well enough off to have bought his dear boy, Johann, a nice, safe, unmerited commission. Why in God's name was he sent here? Nonetheless, here he is and at this moment, we need him.'

After ten minutes, they arrived at what appeared in the flashlight's beam to be Binder's 'cabin', in actuality a ramshackle wooden hut. "Enter, gentlemen. Close the door, please. Allow me to throw a little light on the subject." Lighting a kerosene lamp, he carefully blew out the wooden match. "As tightly shuttered as a drum, old man," he smiled, noting Tom's evident unease. "One moment." Humming off-key while he rummaged in a battered chest of drawers, each one overflowing with fishing line, pieces of net, assorted sinkers, cork bobbers and floaters along with various other pieces and remnants of fishing paraphernalia and tools, he at last produced what appeared to be a rusted automobile jack handle. "Seen better days," he commented, "but it does the job. Care for a drink? Scotch whiskey's up there, left side," he commented without waiting for a response, gesturing vaguely to a cupboard. "Clean glasses are on the right side. Pour me a small one too, if you would be so kind. Prost!"

Tom, mindful of Skorzeny's warning, having poured each of his men and himself a thimbleful, replied in kind, then watched as Binder walked to the far side of the cabin and pried up two wide floor planks. "Ha, here we are!" Binder exclaimed to no one in particular, bending down to retrieve two small suitcases and a cardboard carton stamped, ***Fresh Scallops Rush***. "This one is my shortwave radio and in this one, I have everything that HQ asked for. Your maps, ration cards and money, Tom. I have taken special care to make sure that you have bills and coins in small denominations…well worn. A suitcase for each of you is already in the trunk of the car. I believe that you have everything else. Is there anything that I've missed?"

"I don't believe so, Sir," replied Tom. "Oh, I have a package for you. Here, Sir." Tom held out the oilskin parcel to Binder.

"Wunderbar! New dry cells. And components!" he exclaimed excitedly, upon opening the package.

"I hesitate to ask, Sir, but what is in that carton?"

"Take a look for yourself, lads."

Tom and the three men gathered around Binder while he pulled apart the cardboard flaps to expose a jumble of vacuum tubes, condensers, dials, batteries, wires, rheostats, rolls of solder, flux, a Morse key, earphones, pliers, a propane torch, soldering iron and assorted apparatus.

"Spare radio parts?" Tom asked.

"Yes and no. You see, old man, I build them from scratch. This one here I made in about a week. What the U-boats don't drop off, and they don't come here much anymore, I used to scrounge or find in town in the hardware shop. Amateur radio has been my love since my boyhood. And so, the higher-ups found a use for me. I was writing scholarly treatises on African Zulus as the descendants of a long-lost tribe of Aryan warriors, pure claptrap, that no one in Berlin HQ ever read or elsewhere, for that matter. I asked to be transferred to do something even remotely useful. They certainly got the remote part correct," he chuckled. "By the way, I'm the last remaining shore-to-ship high frequency relay base station on this coast. Code name, *Avalanche*. Which of you is **Reindeer**?"

"I am, Sir!" declared Ben, the Naval Signalman. "You have a high-gain antenna, Sir?" "Yes. The antenna is strung up there in the rafters. Quite well concealed in that tangle of broken lobster traps, nets and such, if I say so myself. With any luck at all, Ben, you should be able to contact me on the 30m band at night. But be bloody careful, young man. Keep your signals brief and timed strictly according to the schedule. Government eavesdroppers, and by that I mean highly sophisticated RCMP and military static and mobile listening posts are the equal of anything the SD and Gestapo have."

"You can count on it, Sir," Tom replied.

"Wait, down here at the bottom. Ah, here it is," Binder proclaimed, holding up a Walther PPK pistol and two 9-mm clips of ammunition. "Never have used it. The RCMP are not on to old Jon Jansen yet, but that day will come, eventually. Not planning a Wild West shoot out, though. I'll go quietly, hands up, and pray for the best. I hear that the Canadian Prisoner of War camps are quite civilized, if I am lucky enough to escape the noose, that is. The Allies, Tom, do not hold the SS in high regard. We are all branded as criminals. The fine folks here would likely gladly lynch me, if they knew or suspected the truth about harmless old Jansen." His voice trailed off.

"On the brighter side, I've packed some lunch for your trip tomorrow: cheddar cheese, bologna sandwiches, hard boiled eggs and apples. First, though. Let us get that camouflage paint off. Very dramatic and all, but it won't do to have you running around the countryside like players in a minstrel show, will it? I am heating a pot of water to wash with and the kettle is already boiling on the naphtha stove. Soap and cloths are on the counter. How would you feel if I were to make a fresh pot of tea? Good. We'll have tea and sweet biscuits and then you can kip out on the floor for a few hours. Die Toilette is outside, set back about 20 metres."

December 14 1943

With a start, Tom awoke to the unmistakeable, familiar hissing of a gas field stove, accompanied by the sounds and smells of breakfast being prepared. Peering at his watch in the semi-darkness, he growled, "0545h. Get up, men!

"Good morning, Sturmbannführer!"

"Good morning, Tom! Johann will do," answered the plaid-shirt and overalls-clad Sturmbannführer Binder. "Thought you wouldn't mind, so I'm cooking bacon and eggs."

"Mind? You are far too good to us, Johann," Tom commented, stepping from man to man, prodding each one with the toe of his shoe. "Get up! *Aber, aber*! Now!

"I'll just pop out the back door to the latrine; be back in a moment," Tom remarked.

Re-entering, his blonde head partially covered with snow, Tom called, "Next! It's snowing, Johann. Quite heavily, too."

"Yes. I was up early, listening to the CBC News Service at 0500h on my crystal set. That could be problematic. However, the snow will likely continue for several hours and should cover your tracks. Besides that, we are quite out-of-the-way here. Coffee? I've poured four mugs. Hope you lads can stomach it black. Over there, on the counter," Binder gestured with his spatula. "Sorry that it's so damn cold in here, but I thought it best not to light a fire in the wood stove."

"Thank you. It's just fine." Tom replied, as the men jostled one another good-naturedly in their bid to get the hot coffee, before heading to the outhouse.

"You can each take a plate and a slice of bread. There's not much to go around, but it should get you on the road to Moncton."

0635h

"Thank you for your help in tidying up. You and I must be on our way, gentlemen," Binder announced, then continued, "0635h. Sunrise is at 0720h, less than an hour away. Tom, before I forget: the keys to a car. All of the necessary papers are in the glove compartment. You will find it parked five hundred metres from here on a gravel road. Go out the door, and walk due north. You do have a compass, no? If not, I…"

"Yes, I do; thanks, Johann," Tom asserted, tapping the face of his wristwatch, "complete with a garrotte," he remarked, laughing.

"Elegant, aren't they? Good, then you cannot miss it. It is a wooded area well away from any habitation or military installation, so you should be safe. The tires are relatively new. It's unlikely that the roads will be ploughed, so be careful not to skid into a ditch. Canadians drive on the right hand side of the road, as we do. This is not England. Do not travel at night. The RCMP is pulling over cars at random, so it is better during the day when there is more traffic. Drive straight to Moncton. I have marked the best route on this map with red pencil. From Moncton, I would suggest that two of you take the train to Whitby, Ontario while the other two drive.

The two men taking the train should not travel together. In the same coach, that is. I suggest that the other two alternate driving. It is a long trip. The passenger would be well advised to lie down on the back seat, to rest, and to stay out of sight.

"You will link up again just east of DIL. There is a house on the hill overlooking a racetrack on the north side of the King's Highway Number 2. Look, here. It is marked on the map. The ironic thing is that the pitch of the roof of this house points directly towards DIL, your target. And not by mere coincidence, or so I have been informed. Any questions?"

"No. Johann, the men and I want to thank you for all of your help," Tom declared. "Take care of yourself, Sir!"

"Oh, don't worry. I'll be fine," shrugged Binder, "or my name isn't Jon Jansen! *Lykke til*! Sssh!" Cocking his head, Binder paused, listening intently, then whispered, "Someone's outside!"

The other men stopped breathing, when a hoarse female voice demanded loudly, "Jon? Es-tu là dedans?" followed by three rapid knocks on the door. "Jon, chéri?"

Grimacing, Binder shook his head.

"Jon! Es-tu là?" Several knocks followed. "C'est moi. Bernice, ta bonne amie. Ouvrez la porte!"

Carefully, Tom pulled out the Bulova's winding stem, unlocking it.

Detecting the slight click of the mechanism, Binder frowned, while Ernest looked on.

Accusingly now, the pitch escalated, "Jon, damn you, do you have another woman in there?"

Glancing at the obviously embarrassed Binder, Tom flashed a grin. Shrugging, Binder tapped his right temple with his forefinger.

"Alright, you salaud (bastard)! I'll drink these mickey's by myself and you can go straight to hell!" This declaration was punctuated by the sound of the door receiving several vigorous kicks, accompanied by muttered curses. Then, silence. They held their breath as Binder crept stealthily to the shuttered window. "That's a relief. She's gone," he reported after what seemed to Tom a lifetime.

Anticipating their questions, Binder explained, “Bernice Boudreau fancies herself a trapper. She’s a local legend, a character. A harmless soul, except when she drinks too much, she becomes a little bit bekloppt-crazy, cuckoo. She will come by with a couple of bottles of rum, get thoroughly soused and it’s all I can do to get rid of her. She hasn’t been around since the summer. Most times, I let her stay and sleep it off. They say she lost her husband and two children in a house fire in ’32, somewhere in Quebec. She babbles about it occasionally. From all that I have been able to gather, she blames herself, saying that she was responsible, although accidentally. Poor woman never recovered from it, I suppose. But, as I said, she’s harmless.”

“Where’s Ernest?” interjected Ben. “He isn’t here, Tom. He’s disappeared.”

“Maybe he went to the latrine,” suggested Wilf.

“What? When? Did you see him go out the back way?” Tom demanded. Without waiting for Wilf to respond, Tom strode to the rear door, throwing it open. “Dammit all, Ernest! What have you done? You brainless bastard!” he shouted, running outside.

Hurrying to the door to see what had happened, Binder, Wilf and Ben were confronted by the sight of Tom striking Ernest in the face with his fist. Reeling from the blow, Ernest slipped, toppling heavily onto the snow-covered ground where lay the inert body of a woman, face down. Her head was tilted at an unusual angle, resting on her right shoulder, as if her neck were contorted. Her jacket, which had apparently been ripped open, was spread out on either side of her body.

“Oh, my God! It’s Bernice!” Binder exclaimed. Rushing out, he knelt in the snow beside the body. Feeling a limp left wrist and then her neck for a pulse, he announced, “She’s dead. Her neck is broken: snapped between cervical vertebrae four and five. Why did you do it?” He turned her over gently, revealing a woman of surprising beauty: slightly built, olive complexioned with delicate features and wavy, albeit stringy, raven-black hair. Tom estimated her age to be between forty and forty-five. Binder looked up, his face streaming tears. Tom now knew what he and the others had intuitively: suspected that she, Bernice Boudreau, and he, Johann Binder, were far more than drinking companions or casual acquaintances.

In anger and frustration, Tom walked in circles, while Ernest, now standing, stared fixedly at the woman's body, muttering as though in shock. "She was listening. She knew we were in there. She was coming back. I caught her coming around the corner at the back. She was listening. Look at these...!"

"Shut the hell up!" screamed Binder. "She was not coming back, you cretin. She was going home to her own shanty. That way," he emphasized, pointing. "I would shoot you here and now if I had my gun! Bloody murderer!" he snarled. Rising, Binder approached Ernest threateningly. Ernest backed away, cringing.

"Wait, Johann, let me handle this, please," Tom interjected. "Flight Lieutenant Haldemann. Front and centre. Attention," Tom barked.

Hastening to obey, Ernest slipped and stumbled in the snow. "S, sir?" he inquired shakily, approaching Tom and Johann warily.

"Silence. I am speaking now as your commanding officer. Listen well! If we had the time, I would request that Sturmbannführer Binder convene a court martial. As we do not have that luxury, it will have to wait upon our return to Germany. In the meantime, I am relieving you of your rank as mission 2IC and appointing Master Sergeant Klein, Wilf, in your place. Have you anything to say?"

"Sir, on what grounds? She was the enemy, Sir, and in my professional judgement, she presented a threat to the mission! Major Skorzeny would back me up, Tom! He emphasized individual initiative throughout our training. Please, Tom, have a look…!"

"Believe me, Haldemann, as an officer and a gentleman, Sturmbannführer Skorzeny would neither condone nor order the cold-blooded murder of a harmless, non-combatant female civilian. There is no time for further discussion," Tom replied icily.

"Oh! Then what about these?" shouted Ernest, brandishing papers in Tom's face. "She's no trapper…! She's a spy!"

Ignoring Ernest, and taking a step back, Tom turned to Johann. "Pardon him, Sturmbannführer Binder. What would you suggest be done with the, er, Miss Boudreau's remains?"

Unable to speak, Binder shrugged and stepped aside.

"Tom! Look! Proof!" Ernest's voice, normally high-pitched, was almost screaming.

"For God's sake, Ernest! Keep it down! What is this spy business all about? Let me see those papers! I said, give them to me. Thank you," Tom commented as he proceeded to examine them in silence, finally uttering, "Damn! Damn!" Looking at Ernest, he queried, "These were sewn inside the lining of her jacket?"

"Yes, Tom. Sewn into the lining of her jacket."

"You are right, Ernest. I apologise. Let me tell Johann," Tom muttered under his breath.

"Johann, I am afraid your lady-friend is not a harmless, homeless trapper. She *is* a spy!"

"A spy! Wha, what? That's preposterous!" shouted Johann. "You, you're both making this up! It cannot be."

"Come, have a look, please, Johann," Tom stated calmly. "No question: Canadian security service identity papers. How careless. Here, see for yourself."

His hands trembling, Binder took the documents from Tom. "Good Lord. What an old fool I've been! Why, she, is, wasn't even French-Canadian!"

"So it would seem. Name, Alice Larkin. Certainly sounds Anglo to me." Folding the documents, Tom placed them in his jacket's inner pocket. "Gentlemen, this presents several problems. Sturmbannführer Binder, with due respect, it appears that Ernest's suspicion was correct. However, Ernest, I will not rescind my decision and reinstate you to the rank of 2IC. Your action, however timely and urgent you thought it to be, was ill considered, and insubordinate. I simply cannot overlook the fact that you took this measure without my knowledge or approval. Had you followed standing orders, you would have waited, concealed in the latrine, for her to depart and then reported your observations to me. Tell me truthfully, had she seen you?"

"I don't think so, Tom," interjected Ernest. "I spotted her at the back door of the cabin as I came out of the outhouse. She was not looking in my direction."

"Thank you for your frankness. It will be taken into consideration. Now, we must move on, and quickly. Suggestions, Johann?"

"She'll be missed by someone, eventually. And, inevitably, there will be questions. RCMP security service men will be all over the area like maggots on a dead mackerel. Burying her is out of the question at this time of year. I very much doubt that we could break the ground much less dig down five or six feet. Besides that, I cannot have a mound of fresh earth on my property. You will have to take her with you. I am sorry if I can't give you a hand to put her in the trunk. You'll have to find a place…somewhere along the way," Johann stated dejectedly, walking into the cabin.

"Wilf, Ben, help me carry Mata Hari to the automobile," Tom muttered.

0755h

"Anybody know what he said?" Wilf asked quietly when they were several metres distant from the cabin. "Before the …incident. It sounded like lyyk…"

"*Lykke til.* It means, 'Good luck'. My granddad is half Norwegian," Ben explained.

"What's the other half, Ben?" Ernest asked.

"Reindeer," Ben replied without breaking stride. "A big, stag reindeer! Horns like that!"

"That explains it," chortled Ernest. "I knew it wasn't your dashing good looks that had the girls in Dieppe all hot and flustered."

"Wouldn't you like to know!" Ben retorted.

"Knock it off," Tom interjected gruffly. "This isn't a Berlin nightclub. It's a mission!"

"Sorry, Sir, er, Tom." Minutes later, pointing at the profile of a car on the top of a ridge, Ben whispered excitedly, "Over there. I think I see it."

After they had finished clearing the accumulated snow from the car's windows, Tom declared, "Well, men, what do you think? Binder is certainly a perfectionist. We trained in a 1936 Chevrolet, the most popular car in North America, Major Skorzeny said, and that is exactly what the man has delivered. Get in. Let's hope she starts. Wunderbar! Gasoline tank's full, as well," Tom commented approvingly as the Chevrolet's motor caught on the first try. "Alright, Wilf, up front with me. Keep low. You two in the back will have to stay down as well. Ready?"

"It's going to be crowded back here. I hope you don't get car sick, Ben," Ernest griped.

Turning abruptly, Tom stated, "Maybe you would prefer to ride in the trunk with Mata Hari?"

"Or walk?" Wilf added.

"Alright, alright. I get your point," Ernest replied sulkily. "Listen, I'm sorry for what happened back there. I really am."

"If I was Sturmbannführer Binder, you'd be wearing your guts for garters about now," murmured Ben. "She was his girlfriend, for God's sake! You had no bloody idea…"

"What? Is that a threat?" countered Ernest, "Just remember who the hell you're talking to, Farber!"

"Don't give me that 'rank' crap! You're just one of us now, like Wilf and me, *Leutnant* Haldemann," Ben retorted, spitting out the term.

"Leave it alone, Ben. And shut the hell up, both of you!" fumed Tom, "or I'll call off the bloody mission and leave you on the roadside with Mata Hari to explain yourselves to the RCMP. And stop using your German names! Understood?"

"Understood," replied Ben and Ernest.

"Then do exactly as I say! Button it, unless you would prefer that we end up in a ditch. I can't drive in this snow and crap with your stupid arguing."

14 December 1943

1250h

"Tom, according to this map, we're halfway to Moncton," Wilf explained, pointing to the road map. "Want some lunch now, men?"

"Sure! Okay!" Ben and Ernest responded.

"Whew, halfway. That's good to know," Tom commented. "Yes, a bite and a leak would be excellent. Is that a cross road just ahead on our right, Wilf?"

Leaning forward in his seat in an attempt to see, Wilf nodded, adding, "Yes, I think so."

"I must say that this car's heater and defroster are first rate. Otherwise, I would have driven off the highway half a dozen times, at least. Even so, the windshield wipers are useless. Completely clogged with ice. Frozen. When we pull over, do you suppose that you can clean them? *Ach, was zum teuffel*? Black ice! Hold on tight!" Encountering a patch of ice at thirty miles an hour, the rear end of the Chevy abruptly fishtailed wildly.

Summoning up his training on a 7,000 pound, Daimler armoured reconnaissance vehicle as an SS cadet officer, Tom relaxed his grip on the steering wheel and lifted his foot off the accelerator, and gently shifted down to second gear. Then, delicately 'blipping' the gas, and alternately touching the brake pedal with his toe in a skilful effort to let the vehicle 'find' its course, he attempted to 'nurse' the car's right rear wheel back onto the shoulder. Just as it was stabilizing, Tom was suddenly forced to swerve to avoid smashing head on into a snow bank. The rear end careened sideways and slithered unceremoniously off the shoulder into the ditch. Using the transmission to rock the vehicle back and forth only caused the rear wheels to spin frantically, until both were hopelessly buried axle-deep in the snow. "Everyone lift and push when I give the command! Lift and push like hell!"

Piling out, the three men bent down, taking hold of the rear bumper.

Rolling down his window, Tom called out instructions. "Okay boys. I'll try to get some momentum by rocking it. On three! One! Two! Three! Wait!

"Again. One! Two! Three!"

Wilf came around to the open window. "It's no use, Tom. The wheels are just spinning. Like they are on glass. It is in too deep and only getting deeper! You'll burn out the clutch if we keep this up!"

"Well, can't the three of you lift it?" Tom asked impatiently.

"We're trying, believe me," Wilf protested. "It seems to be pinned midway on something. Likely snow. Maybe…"

"Okay, tell them to take a leak or whatever over there and then come back inside before you freeze. We have to think. Damn!" muttered Tom, hitting the steering wheel with his fist, while Wilf, Ben and Ernest trudged toward a grove of pines. 'Calm down, Tristan. Think, think! That is why you are mission commander. How's the gas tank? Over half full. Good, keep the engine running with the two side windows partly opened to be safe, and we'll have lunch. Maybe that and a little rest will give them the energy they need to do it. If not, we're…'

"Hello there! Stuck are we?"

Feeling a sudden surge of panic, Tom turned to his left to see a burly, bearded, parka and snow-booted shape approaching the car. 'Where the hell did he come from? Oh, God, is he the Mounted Police?'

Replying politely, "Yes, I'm afraid so, Sir," Tom bit his lower lip. 'Get a grip on yourself, Zeiss!'

"Hi, I'm Gil." Removing a glove, the smiling, bear-like stranger offered his massive hand through the open window. "Ya know, ya oughta have chains on a day like this. No wonder ya ditched her. Some treacherous, this stretch. No windbreak so she drifts like billy-ho. Yes, Sir! The Province should be shot for not putting up snow fence all along here.

"Hello, I'm Tom," replied Tom shaking Gil's massive hand. Given his literal understanding of English, the notion of 'chains', 'snow fences' and most improbably, that of 'the Province' being shot, were beyond his understanding, bringing to mind Major Skorzeny's advice, "When in doubt, smile, und Halt den Mund! Shut up!"

"Mind if I take a look-see?" Gil asked, reaching for the handle of the trunk.

Seeing what was about to happen, his eyes transfixed on the handle, Tom lunged toward the car trunk. "Wait! What are you looking for?" Tom's hand blocked Gil's.

"I was just going to see if there's anythin' we can use in the trunk for traction, you know, to put under the back wheel," Gil replied.

"There isn't anything. It, it's locked anyway. I, I don't carry anything in the trunk. I know that I should." Rushing to explain, he continued. "In fact when I get back to the base, I'm going to put a twenty pound bag of sand in there." Tom smiled with as much bravado as he could manage.

"Or rock salt, if you can find any. Good thinkin'. I'd sure advise doin' it, Tom. Say, those your buddies?"

Looking to his right, Tom saw that Wilf, Ben and Ernest were less than twenty-five metres from the car. "Yes," Tom gulped. Deciding to take the initiative, do or die, he continued, "We're Norwegian airmen with the RCAF, on the way back to our base. Unless we get there soon, we'll be in a lot of trouble."

"Norwegian lads, eh? Very good people. The girls and I'll have you fellows back on the road in no time, Tom," Gil stated assuringly, indicating with his thumb a wagon with two massive, steaming, stamping, grey and black-dappled Percheron draft horses patiently waiting.

Anticipating Gil, Tom opened the car door. "Thank you, Gil, that's wunder, wonderful. I'll introduce you to them." Taken by surprise, but quickly picking up on Tom's cue to be silent, the three Germans found themselves shaking hands with Gil Barrows, a kindly, New Brunswick pig and potato farmer. Gil then proudly introduced his two 'girls', Maude and Martha. Raised on a farm, Tom did not doubt that the two could easily tow the wagon *and* the Chevrolet to Moncton, if necessary.

As Gil was unhooking the length of chain from the Chevrolet's undercarriage, Tom took out his wallet, extracting a suitably worn five-dollar bill. "Here, Gil, please take it. We're very grateful to you and your girls."

"No, no. Put that away. I'm glad to be able to help you out. You Norwegian lads are doing a great service for Canada. My son, Gil Junior, would be green with envy. He's eighteen, in the Army, a Lance Corporal. Young Gil was crazy to fly a Spitfire, but his eyesight's a bit on the weak side for that, apparently. Good enough to handle a rifle and shoot some Nazi's though.

"Are you sure you have to be back today?" he inquired earnestly. "What with the bad driving and all, you're more than welcome to come to my place. It's not far! You can follow us. Have some nice hot dinner, a good warm bath and then hit the road first thing in the morning. What do you say? The wife and I'd be honoured to have you."

'Oh, yes!' "Oh, Gil, that is a very kind offer, but you know, our *Schwad*, squadron, is flying out tomorrow. We cannot be late. But, thank you very much. Right boys?"

'Right," they replied unenthusiastically.

"Well, if you're ever back this way, even after the war, the door is open. Just ask anyone in these parts for Gil's place. Okay then, on your way, boys, and God bless. Get lots of Germans! And watch the speed, Tom!" he called, waving.

"Makes you wonder, doesn't it?" Ben commented at length.

"Yes, I'd like to be a fly at his dining room table tonight," Tom commented quietly, adding, "A fine gentleman."

Wilf passed around the food. They ate and drove the rest of the way to Moncton in silence.

Carefully manoeuvring the Chevy around a pillar at the entrance of the old train station, Tom slowly brought the car to a stop.

"There you go, Wilf, Ben. You know what to do from here. Do not forget your suitcases! Wilf, the darkest brown, battered one. Ben, yours has Imperial Luggage stamped on the handle. Make it fast, please, for obvious reasons. Remember. Do nothing to draw attention to yourselves. No cologne, no after-shave, nothing out of the ordinary for meals. No arguments with staff or travellers and stay away from the women! Ben, you in particular. That is all. Now go. Good luck and we'll see you in Ajax."

"Thanks for the ride, Tom. See you there!" Ben and Wilf exited the back seat of the car, and walked around to the trunk. Opening it, Wilf reached inside. As he was about to remove his luggage, he recoiled, muttering under his breath, "Damn, Ben! I forgot she was in here." Extracting the two suitcases and slamming down the lid, Wilf and Ben then began walking to the entrance of the station as Tom and Ernest drove around to the rear parking lot.

"What are you doing?" asked Ernest.

"Saying goodbye to Mata Hari. There, that one!" Tom whispered.

"I'm confused. One what?"

"Just do as I say: Get out, open the trunk, grab our suitcases, and then close it. I will be waiting in that dark blue car parked by the laneway. Got it?"

"Ya, but…"

"Listen to me, Ernest. We are leaving this car and the woman's body here. By the time anyone bothers to check, we will be in Ajax. Do it, dammit!"

"But what about the blue car, Tom? Won't it be reported as stolen?"

"It's a '35 Oldsmobile. If you notice the amount of snow on it, it has been here awhile. I'm thinking that the owner's not about to return to claim it."

"Do you know how to get inside and start it?" asked Ernest skeptically.

"Yes! Go! Now!"

"Okay, then!"

"Ben, go buy your ticket to Whitby while I go to the washroom. I will purchase mine when I come out. Get on a car as close to the end as you can and stay there. I'll be at the front of the train. Good luck. See you in Whitby."

"Okay, Wilf. Thanks. Good luck," Ben replied.

Wednesday December 15 1943

As Tom and Ernest continued towards Ajax along King's Highway Number Two, a light dusting of snow was falling.

"My rear end is asleep," Ernest announced, squirming in the back seat.

"Really? Mine too," Tom commented.

"Ever since we passed the Quebec and Ontario border. I had no idea how big this Canada is. Can we stop soon?"

"Yes, soon. I saw a sign that said Kingston two miles. We should be coming up on it any time now. When we get there, we will stop for something to eat. Are you hungry?" asked Tom, glancing down at the road map on the seat. "Look for an exit sign that says Division Street to take us into the city."

"Look, over there. What about that place, **The Hotel Bel…ve…dere**?"

"No, be sensible, Ernest," Tom shook his head, "It's too… extravagant."

"Meaning what?"

"Meaning we certainly can't afford it and besides that, we couldn't get past the doorman. He would send us around to the Tradesmen's Entrance. Have you noticed recently how we are dressed?"

"Like vagrants?" Ernest suggested, smiling.

"*Ja, die Landstreicher.* That's us, for sure. Keep looking," Tom directed, stopping at a red light. "Don't look now, but there's a police car on my tail. Oh, damn, is he signalling me to pull over? Hold on. No, thank God, he wanted to get past us. Goodbye, officer!"

"I've never seen so many buildings made out of limestone, have you?" Ernest remarked. "There, **The Kingston Arms**. That should be a good place to eat. Not too extrava…"

"Extravagant...costly, excessive," Tom corrected him smugly. "You might be right. We'll park and have a closer look."

"Have you noticed that just about everything around here is named the Kingston - something or other? I wonder why?"

"Perhaps it's because we're not in Montreal?"

"Seriously, Tom, do you think it means the 'King of England's ton... town'?"

"Quite likely, just like Königsberg back home. Here read this, on the right hand side of the map. I didn't think of it until you mentioned it."

"So much for my idea. There's a university here named Queen's."

"Queen's University at Kings town," Tom reflected. "Very fair minded of them."

"Something else. There's an old military fort here called Henry. It says that it was built to keep the Americans out."

"Seems that it didn't work as well as they hoped. I have seen at least ten New York State and Ohio license plates so far and we have been here less than ten minutes. The hotel looks just fine. Alright, my good man, hop out."

They looked admiringly at the old hotel's stark grey granite stone front onto which had been added a graciously curving, white wooden porch that encircled the front and left side of the building. A swinging chair situated close to the entrance swayed back and forth forlornly in the bitterly cold, damp wind. Entering the foyer, they were met, or rather received with disdain by the haughty grey and black hotel cat.

"Tom, I must go to the washroom. Could you find us a table? I'll be right back."

"I'll order two cups of coffee. What do you want to eat?"

"A chicken sandwich with vegetable soup," Ernest replied, hurrying down the hallway.

Catching the eye of a waitress setting tables, Tom asked, "Any table in particular, Ma'am?"

"Nope. Anywhere your little heart desires, hon," she replied.

''Your little heart desires,' and 'hon'?' Again, his textbook English had stymied Tom. 'Is this place a brothel, a bordello, I wonder?' Feeling uncomfortable, he wondered if his face was flushed. 'As soon as Ernest comes back, we're leaving.'

"Hi, hon. I'm Megan. Menus. Take your time."

The waitress, or whatever she might be, was undeniably attractive, thought Tom, in the decadent Hollywood-starlet blonde, brazen manner. Her uniform, while not quite indecent, gave the impression that it was two sizes smaller than her voluptuous figure allowed.

"Was that other gent with youse?" she queried.

"Ah, yes. He will be back shortly. Tell me, if you would please, ah, Meg, this *is* a hotel and restaurant, isn't it?"

For an instant, she stared at Tom in disbelief. "Why, yes, dear. Did you think it was something else?"

"I, I wasn't quite sure," he stammered, looking down at his triangular red napkin. "Perhaps a private club, of some sort?" he ventured weakly.

"Oh, aren't you the limit!" she laughed. "Like a Wild West house of ill repute?"

"No, no," he stumbled, searching desperately in his mental dictionary of English phrases for le mot juste.

"Bet you did. Isn't that a hoot! It must be the red and gold-flocked wallpaper and fancy light fixtures. Hope it's not me! Wait 'til I tell Marv. He's the owner! Marv'll have a royal conniption fit!"

"Do not draw attention to yourself'. Zeiss, you are a certified idiot!' "May I order, please?"

"Will youse be having breakfast or lunch?"

He watched with morbid fascination as she chewed the metal and rubber-capped tip of her pencil. Nevertheless, her front teeth were flawless to all appearances. "I think that we'll each have a, a fried egg sandwich, to take away, if you don't mind. We're in a bit of a hurry." Tom's eyes darted back and forth between the girl and the hallway.

"White or brown?"

"Whatever's easiest, thank you, Meg. Could you please hurry up as we have to leave now."

"Okay, mister, one on white, one on brown. That way, you and your pal can have a sharesy. Hope you don't mind me askin', but what's the big hurry? You two rob a bank or something?" With a flirtatious grin, she reached forward with a water jug, exposing more of two well-proportioned breasts than Tristan could remember seeing in several weeks. 'Stop it! I do not have time for this! What the hell is keeping Ernest? Did he fall in or murder someone, again?'

"Going to the kitchen to place your orders right now, hon. Back in a flash. Don't start without me!"

Tom started down the hallway looking for the **Men's** washroom door. '**Gent's**, that's close enough,' he muttered, trying the handle. The door would not open. Damn it. It's jammed. Ernest, Ernest! Are you in there? Ernest?"

Wiggling the doorknob, Tom concluded that the door was locked and not simply jammed shut. Taking a metal toothpick from his inside pocket, he jimmied the lock in three and one half seconds and then cautiously pushed the door open. It was standard issue: white and black tile walls and floor, a urinal on the left, a sink and mirror on the right. It was very, very cold. And dismal. He flicked the brass light switch without response from the single overhead light fixture. He walked quickly toward the stall at the far end of the room, looking up. "That's why it's so damn cold!" A horizontally hinged window over the stall was wide open. 'No, that's at least one metre overhead. Not possible.' "Ernest, it's Tom! Come on out! We have to leave!"

"Ernest, is that you in there? Are you sick?" There was no reply. "Come on, man! I can see your skinny legs. Stop playing games!" In exasperation, Tom pounded on the stall door.

"Game time is up, Ernest! Look out!" Tom warned, placing a well-aimed kick at the point where he estimated the wood door's hasp to be. Hearing the 'zing' of metal hitting tile, he pushed open the door, exposing Ernest, head sagging sideways, seated on the toilet.

"Ernest, what's wrong man? Wake up," Tom pleaded in desperation, as he reached out in the semi-darkness cautiously to touch Ernest's face. "Oh, Mother!" Drawing in his breath sharply, Tom saw the thin wire running upward from Ernest's neck to the steel window frame one metre above. "SOE! Their trademark," Tom sighed, recognizing the telltale garrotte of the Special Operations Executive. "Bastards!" Turning, Tom ran from the washroom, down the hallway, into the foyer, almost tripping over an indignant cat, and out the front door.

"Hey, cutie, where're ya going? Your sandwiches are ready," called Meg. "Cheapskates. Men! I shoulda known. Always the good lookin' ones are the biggest creeps. Mind if I eat the white one, Joe? The brown one's all yours. Ya, I won't tell Marv, if you don't. Deal?"

Tom jammed his foot to the floor, spraying rock salt, ice and dirty snow over the porch steps. 'Keep calm, get a grip Zeiss; you can't blow the mission now. Just drive the speed limit. Remember the cop!' Tom muttered. "Got to get rid of this car! How did they do it? Why? What if it wasn't SOE goons? Who else would have a reason? Binder?"

A Day in the Life
Wednesday December 15 1943

DIL A Women's Residence

"What time is it, Big Sis?" asked a voice groggily.

"Five minutes past."

"Seven"?

"Uh huh!" replied Bonnie, glancing in the mirror at the large Westclox alarm clock on the night table, while fastening her bright yellow bandana firmly in place with hairpins.

"I'm going back to sleep. Wake me in ten..." Turning over, June placed a pillow on her face to shield her eyes from the overhead light fixture.

"I'll be long gone by then," Bonnie stated. "Have you seen my lipstick?"

"In my purse. You loaned it to me in the Blue Swallow Ladies' Room after church. Remember?"

"So I did. Here it is. C'mon, up and at 'em. We have a war to win!"

"Okay." Replying with a yawn, June sat up and swung her slim legs over the edge of the bed. "Is today really Wednesday the fifteenth?" Yawning, she examined her bright red-painted toenails.

"All day. Are you coming for breakfast?"

"Absolutely. We're off Christmas Eve at 4:00 o'clock. Just nine more days, Bon! Wow! Can't wait! Hey, can you hold on, Bonnie?" Energized, June leapt into action. "I'll be ready in, um, five minutes. I promise," June vowed, on her way to the bathroom.

"Make it four, dear, and I will!"

"Great. Hope you left some hot water!" June called through the bathroom door.

"When was the last time you ever remember DIL running out?"

"What? I can't hear you..."

Women's residences; each housed 100 persons. (Note boardwalk).

Bonnie smiled despite herself. Of the two sisters, she, the 'lark', was an early riser while June, at eighteen, and three years younger, was the eternal 'owl'. Roommates since their childhood at home, Big Sis, Bonnie, had resigned herself to accepting June's concept of time that was, to put it mildly, elastic, depending upon the day and the prospect for 'fun and games', of any forthcoming event. Although a hard and conscientious worker, June, like many of DIL's teenaged female employees, lived for the company's social life: dances, bowling, curling bonspiels, softball, wiener roasts and twice-weekly movie nights as opportunities to meet and mix with the few remaining young, eligible males at the plant, or, for that matter, anywhere in Ontario County. For Bonnie, the pursuit of male company was a non-issue. Her high school sweetheart, Bill Davies, now her fiancé, a Master Sergeant and Gunner with The Ontario Regiment Armoured, at the last time of his writing, was somewhere in Italy, killing Nazis, in his big Sherman tank.

For that reason alone, her job as an Inspector on the Cleaning Line at DIL, the British Commonwealth's largest munitions manufacturing facility, was particularly meaningful for Bonnie, as it was for most of the workforce, who each had a direct personal stake in producing shells and other armaments to the highest possible quality standards. It was quite simple, she reasoned: 'The Axis powers, or at least their leaders, Mussolini, Tojo, and Hitler, were evil. Even the Reverend Peebles, a charitable Christian man if ever there was one, had said so again in yesterday's sermon. And everyone had heard or read Mr. Churchill's opinion of Adolf Hitler. With every shell coming off the line, another blow could be delivered against Hitler and his ilk by an Allied dad, husband, brother, son, boyfriend or neighbour's kid.

'Sure, the German, Italian and Japanese armed forces were made up of kids too: brothers, dads and so on. And they were doing what their leaders were making them do, for their own gain and glory, but their leaders were in the wrong and it was Canada's job to stop them once and for all and send them packing, preferably six feet under and this was war. Better their boys than ours. Talk does not stop tyrants, we've learned the hard way, but our boys with the proper ammunition and equipment can.' "June! Hurry or we'll miss breakfast!"

"Almost ready!" June announced, rushing past Bonnie, her head swathed turban-like in a towel. "How'm I doing, Sis?"

"Fine. Dry your hair. You'll catch your death!"

"I didn't wash it. Not enough time. I used your shower cap. What's it like out?" June asked, as she fastened her favourite blue and white bandanna over her short blonde hair. What's it like out?"

"Bitter! Three above. Bundle up!"

"*Get your coat and get your hat,*" June warbled, reaching into the hall closet. "Okay, let's go, kiddo.

"Honestly now. You don't like my hair this short do you. I look a mess, don't I?" June remarked as they made their way cautiously, arm in arm, down the icy wooden steps of the residence and along the snow-covered boardwalk.

"It's not you, June. I like it the way you had it. It suits you better, longer."

"Oh, well," June shrugged, "thank goodness it grows fast. Hey, Sis, next week we're on C Shift, graveyard, so you and I can take a bus into Whitby to have our hair and nails done at Marcel's for the Christmas Dance. Can't wait. It's Mart Kenney and His Western Gentlemen Orchestra! Monday okay with you?"

"Sounds fine. You're not getting yours cut, though, I hope."

"Just a wash and set. Could you call and book us? But pu-lease, Bonnie, not first thing in the morning," she pleaded. "Let's say, around one o'clock."

"Okay. I'll look after it," agreed Bonnie, stamping her feet while holding open the door of the Coles Cafeteria. "I'll get into the line-up, June. You get a table. Over there, with Lil Montgomery and Valerie Cole."

"Wow! Looks good! I could eat a horse," June remarked approvingly when Bonnie set down the tray. "Half a grapefruit, scrambled eggs, toast, jam and coffee. Not bad for ten cents, eh, girls?"

"Yep, a good deal, for sure," replied Valerie. "Wow, do I need a smoke! You know, I still can't get over seeing Mary Pickford in the flesh at the Community Hall last May. Here it is December, and I'm still dazzled. My gosh! She is one beautiful babe."

"I agree, Val. She's radiant and even lovelier than she is on-screen and in the movie magazines at the hairdresser's," Bonnie added enthusiastically.

"Compare her to Marie Dressler, and, well…But they're both big Hollywood stars in their own ways, and they're Canadian."

"If only Mary had brought along Douglas Fairbanks. Now, wouldn't that have been the capper! He's so dreamy…" whispered June.

"Amen to that, June, kiddo. By the way, did you hear about that new guy on Line 2? Harold, something or other?"

"A new guy? Do tell." June exclaimed excitedly. "Is he cute?"

"June!" Bonnie interjected. "Be a lady."

"Not unless you like geezers. Wait. Hold on 'til I finish, kiddo. We're not talkin' Einstein here. Charley, the Security Guard caught him goin' in on the B Shift with a full package of matches and a flat fifty of Sweet Caps tucked in his trousers waistband last Thursday. Can you believe it? What a dim bulb!"

"So, tell us what happened," Lil asked.

"Well, according to my Gus, management not only suspended his ass, the JP gave him ten days in the Whitby hoosegow."

"JP? Whazzat?" queried June.

"That's what cops and crooks call a Justice of the Peace, doll."

"About this Harold man, Val," Bonnie remarked, "I hadn't heard a word!"

"Nor me," agreed Lil.

"As true as I'm sitting here, girls. So, are you three going to hitch a ride on the company cattle truck?" Valerie asked nonchalantly, standing up to return her tray to the counter.

"Why in the world would we, Val?" queried Bonnie. "The plant's just a three minute walk. Besides that, I can't imagine that it would stop here. It's for folks who live outside of the grounds. Why would it even stop here?"

"Oh, shucks, Bon, I do it all the time. Drive and arrive in style's my motto. It stops here, because, when I'm on shift, I always have a takeout cup of java for Stu. You know, Stu. The older-but-not-dead company driver. He picks me up after his last run. He'll be at the front door in three, four minutes. Hurry, if you're coming. I can charm Stu into waiting for a minute," she remarked, with a wink. Her above –average height, statuesque figure, striking features, red hair and easy-going warmth made her the subject of plant rumours, none of which had ever been shown to bear the slightest resemblance to the truth. Although by nature flirtatious, Val, as she preferred, was devoted to her husband, Gus Linton, an OPP Constable, and former linebacker with the second-place 1939 Toronto Argonauts, and to their three-year old daughter, Sherrie.

It was Bonnie's opinion, shared by DIL middle and senior management, that Valerie was an exemplary worker: a dedicated, smart and self-motivated employee whose job skills and whose recommendations had produced improved efficiencies in terms of shortened maintenance downtime and significant cost-saving measures in the Cleaning Room. Soon after her hiring, she had gained the attention of the Plant Manager, Mr. Caldwell, and the Shop Foreman, Jim Montgomery. Valerie was the first female recipient of the prestigious DIL Muskoka Summer Vacation Awards.

"It's too darn frigid to walk even three hundred yards! Freeze your keyster off," Valerie called back. "Just going to get Stu's coffee. Hey, do you know what they call those guys in the Arctic? You know…"

"I've heard it: frigid midgets with rigid digits! Sorry, Sis!" June giggled.

Ignoring June's feeble apology, Bonnie stated firmly, "I'm walking. You two go ahead, if you want to."

"This is downright silly. I'm walking too, Bonnie," Lil confirmed.

"June? What are you doing?"

"I'm goin' for a ride, Sis.

"Tell your pal, Stu, that I'm taking him up on his offer, Val!" June called, laughing.

Bonnie did not let on that she was amused by her sister's occasional forays into Hollywood film slang, in imitation of her idol, Val, as long as it was not vulgar.

Outside the Cafeteria, as Valerie had predicted, the ‘cattle truck’, an open GMC stake truck, was waiting, running on high idle, spewing a mist of blue exhaust under the entrance canopy. Waving to Bonnie and Lil, paper coffee cup in hand, Val stepped up onto the running board and entered the cab’s passenger side. As soon as June had climbed onto the back, Stu revved the engine, dropped the clutch, forcing her to lunge in desperation at the wooden sides so as not to be thrown over the tailgate. Looking back through the cab’s rear window, Valerie gave her a ‘thumbs up’ and a grin, as Stu briefly gunned the engine before he swung the truck around and braked fifty feet from the building.

Stepping down, Val commented, “Wasn’t that a hoot, Junie? Short, but sweet. More fun than the Dodgem bumper cars at Sunnyside and the Crystal Beach ‘Cyclone’ roller coaster, combined, eh?”

“A real barrel of laughs, Val. If you ask me, he’s loonie tunes and a big show-off. I think I sprained my wrist, too. Remind me to walk next time, thanks all the same,” confessed June, shaken but wiser.

“There won’t be a next time, June. That was Stu’s swan song. He’s being let go. Today.”

“No wonder!”

All this fun and $21.00 bucks a week, too!

“Morning ladies!

“Morning, Charley!” replied a scattering of voices.

“Got anything I should know about? Any old iron…rings, bracelets, belt buckles, cigarette lighters? Matches?”

“Nope, sorry, ” replied Val on everyone’s behalf. “Still want to search me?” she teased.

“Only if you promise not to tell Gus this time, Val,” bantered the security guard, good-naturedly, pretending to have a broken arm. “Move along please, ladies. ‘A’ Shift starts in seven minutes. Have a good one!” he called encouragingly.

Val opened the door to the building as Charley, the guard, kept a close watch on each worker passing through. "You too, Charley! Don't take any wooden nickels!" Valerie called, as she sauntered in the entrance way.

Passing unchallenged past two female security guards whose random body searches were felt to add another layer of protection from catastrophe, Bonnie, June, Lil and Val, along with many of their 'A' Shift mates, arrived in the crowded Change/Locker Room, greeting one another and the remaining outgoing 'C' Shift workers. "Hi, Connie, Ethel, Linda. Hi, Marg, how's the hand?"

"Getting better thanks, Val. Doc says I won't lose my index finger after all. The nail's going to grow back eventually, thank heavens," Marg replied, carefully scrubbing her partly bandaged right hand with a homemade mixture of salt and sand to remove the orange discolouration that resulted from handling copper shell casings without gloves. Although it was against company regulations, many of the women had quickly discarded the heavy cotton gloves provided by DIL as too thick and awkward to be useful on the lines. Some brought substitutes from home, which although less clumsy, were too thin to prevent the chemicals from leaching through. Thus, for the majority of workers, the resulting tint of their hands served to identify her or his specific job: blackened fingertips being common as the result of handling the sacks of high explosive gunpowder. As the washroom soap was incapable of completely removing the tarnish, many workers kept small bristle brushes and containers of salt and sand or **Snap**, a popular, gritty, commercial hand-cleaning compound in their lockers for end-of-shift cleanup.

As they chatted, Mildred, an attractive, partially clad woman of June's approximate age walked by. Her white undergarments were tinged with a distinct, bright pinkish hue, a sure sign that her workstation was close by the TNT Storage Room. Val whistled, and with a throaty laugh, called, "Hubba, hubba!" to which Mildred responded with a smile and a universal hand gesture of defiance, before going to the sink and rinsing her mouth. She and many of her colleagues customarily packed a quantity of salt on their gums before going on shift to counteract the bitter odour of the fumes emanating continuously from the chemical soup of nitrites, nitrates, fulminate of mercury, saltpetre, nitro-glycerine, toluene …

"Really glad to hear that, Marg," June chimed in. Marg was only one of several workers who had suffered an injury. Her's was relatively minor, far less severe than were some of the other's, who, either by mischance or carelessness, or both, had suffered the loss of one or more finger tips, or fingers or albeit rarely, a partial or an entire hand. Only senior management and the families of the unfortunate victims knew of cases of severe maimings or fatalities, if any. Although the company took aggressive steps to continually educate and train the workers in order to prevent such incidents, with a workforce of 9,000 persons, they occasionally occurred nonetheless, in the production of 1,700 or more shells, six days per week, excluding Sundays. Though medical care at DIL was first rate, it was decided by Head Office that no injuries would be reported in the weekly staff newsletter, ***Commando***, for reasons, it was stated, of employee morale.

After pulling on and fastening their dark coveralls, June and Val sat down on the wooden bench beside their Cleaning Room Supervisor, Bonnie, to put on their special rubber-soled safety shoes, lacing them through the non-metallic eyelets, then tying them up to a comfortably snug fit.

As they hurried along the corridor, Bonnie glanced at her watch. "One minute, girls." Just as they stepped into the Cleaning Room, the ear-splitting DIL works whistle sounded eight o'clock. "Hot damn, we made it again! All this fun and twenty-one bucks a week, too!" Val exclaimed.

Harwood and King, looking SE (c. 1941)

The Cleaning Room

Bonnie's thirty workers were responsible for 'cleaning' out the gelatinous anti-corrosion 'gunk' with which the 40 mm shell casings were packed before shipping by railcars to DIL. Once they had each been dipped in solvent, then scrubbed and dried, Bonnie, Val, Lil, June and others inserted a metal washer into the base of each one, tapping it in place with a wooden mallet to ensure that the ring was properly seated before sending the shell out of the room and down the assembly line. Later, after filling with the explosive powder and 'capping', the 'det', detonation cap, would be fitted into the open centre of the washer, thereby arming the artillery shell.

It was Bonnie's responsibility to certify each empty 40 mm shell's quality and readiness for 'Filling', 'Cap' and 'Det,' operations. After careful inspection, she manually stamped her approval code, including the date and the time on the side of each casing. Bonnie loved her work. Val, June, Lil and the rest of the crew loved working with her. They frequently sang, often joked and sometimes worked through their regulation ten minute, twice per shift breaks. Their production figures and safety record were always among the top three in the entire plant.

'Best of all', thought June, 'in a bit more than a week, it'll be Christmas Eve.' The plant would shut down at four o'clock sharp and not reopen until December twenty-seventh. 'I'll use some of my Christmas bonus to get Bonnie some nice stationery and a good pen. Lucky her, having Bill to write to. Oh well, lucky me. I can sleep 'til noon on the 26th, Boxing Day!'

Arsenal of Democracy

Ajax DIL
Ajax DIL
Ajax DIL
Ajax DIL

Chapter 9
Apple Pie, Zombies, and Fafner

Wednesday December 15 to Thursday December 16 1943

"Tickets, tickets, please. Belleville next stop. Belleville. Belleville station in five miles."

Awakening with a start, temporarily disoriented by the conductor's singsong announcement, Wilf was about to reach into his jacket to retrieve his wallet, when he realized that it would be a 'bone headed mistake'. He was accustomed to the Nazi regime's boundless zeal for frequent inspections of passengers' papers either by the Reichsbaun (railway) police, the Kripo (Criminal Police), Gestapo and increasingly, the Military Field Police, who were on the lookout for deserters. Wilf was grateful for the Canadian wartime authorities' evident acceptance of a traveler's bona fides at the ticket booth, barring unusual circumstances, such as paranoid lunatic passengers. Following the example of his fellow travellers, Wilf had attached his ticket stub to the metal clasp of the window shade in Moncton. 'And yet,' he pondered, 'even though my documents are first-class forgeries, it is always possible to be caught.'

With a cursory sideway glance in Wilf's direction, the plump conductor continued his rolling gait down the aisle, intoning, "Belleville, Belleville."

Wilf breathed a mental sigh of relief, recalling the incident that had occurred somewhere in Quebec, when a passenger created a disturbance by repeatedly insulting and then threatening a French-speaking porter, accusing the elderly gentleman of deliberately poisoning him with cyanide in his egg salad sandwich. Following a brief struggle, the Sûreté-Provincial Police arrived and forcibly removed him from the train. The train was held up on a siding for several hours as six gendarmes checked the passenger manifest against the ID of every person on board. Wilf did not want to go through that again. Afterward, his seat mate informed Wilf that the troublemaker was on a restricted day pass from a mental institution. "How'd ya like to be the chump that sold that wing nut the ticket?" asked the man known as, "Ralph, Ralph Gordon, Taronta, farm implements. The big fellas: tractors, combines, harvesters. What's your name and your game, son?"

"Wilf Johnson. Insurance. Halifax," Wilf had replied, as rehearsed. 'Game? What does he mean by game? *Fussball*? Ice Hockey? When in doubt shut up.' Hoping that he had accurately interpreted Ralph's current question by its tone, Wilf shook his head in sympathy.

Although Wilf and Ben had not been in contact since they had boarded the train in New Brunswick, Wilf was confident that his companion's documents and cover story had passed muster. As a strategy to avoid idle chitchat with Ralph, Wilf made himself as comfortable as possible in the upright chair seat and closed his eyes. Having a fleeting vision of the trunk's contents, he hoped that Tommy and Ernest were able to dispose of Bernice-Alice without trouble.

"Oshawa. Next stop Oshawa."

Wilf stood up. Removing his suitcase from the overhead rack, he was about to make his way to the exit at the far end of the coach, when Ralph, who had been fixated on a farm equipment catalogue, looked up quizzically at his departing travel companion. "Going so soon, Wilf?"

"Yes. My Home Defence Unit has been ordered to report to the Armouries in Oshawa. More training," Wilf smiled.

"Well, that's the spirit. Good for you, lad. I'm too darn useless for even that. A word of advice: Keep an eye out for the active service boys. Some of them have it in for Zombies. Sorry, that's not a word I like to use. I suppose they're thinking that while they're overseas, their wives and girlfriends are being squired around and well, you know all that guff about keeping the home fires burning."

Baffled, Wilf had a vision of the Home Defence as a roving band of double-crossing arsonists. 'Perhaps that is why they're referred to as 'Zombies'?'

Ralph carried on enthusiastically. “Me? I’m a vet of the First World War and I sure don’t have a problem with it. Mind you,” he confided, “I’d be back doing something or other if it weren’t for this trick right knee,” which he emphasized by clasping his shattered kneecap. “Caught some Hun shrapnel at Passchendaele in ’17. That got me a ticket home, and a lifetime of sleepless nights. To be honest, I wasn’t about to say, ‘No thanks, Doc. I like the mud and misery.’” He grinned. “But I’m not complaining. My biggest regret is that I left so many of my pals there. Most of them never did return, poor beggars.” Brightening, he inquired, “What’s your deferment, if you don’t mind me asking, Wilf?”

“No, not at all, Ralph. I contracted rheumatic fever when I was nine years old. My mitral valve…” Wilf replied, tapping his chest, thankful that this cover story had been drilled into his head.

“Nasty business for a kid. I had scarlet fever, but luckily for me, it didn’t turn into the rheumatic. I look at it this way, son: I figure that anyone who does his duty as he sees fit and the Lord permits is all right by me. Good luck to you, my friend!”

“Thank you, Ralph. And I will be careful to do as you say.”

“Toodle-oo!”

“Good bye. Good luck to you, as well.”

Stepping down onto the station platform, Wilf felt a pang of regret that he had lied so shamelessly to Ralph. It was one thing to demonize and hate the enemy as he had been taught, but it was an entirely different matter to actually meet them. Ralph and Gil were kind, decent men, the type with whom you might want to share a bottle of wine, share lies, and get drunk. ‘C’est la guerre, Hermann. Remember why you are here. **Fafner. Fafner**. Now get on with it.’ Scanning the crowd for Ben without success, Wilf kept to procedure and walked over to the taxi stand.

“Where to, son?”

“The Rose Bowl Restaurant, please.”

“Sure thing. Need a hand with that suitcase?”

“No, it’s not very large. I can manage it. Thank you.”

The Rose Bowl Restaurant

Oshawa, Ontario

Tipping the driver fifty cents earned Wilf a broad smile, a, "Thank you, Sir," not "son," and an unsolicited recommendation to, "…order their fish and chips. The best in Oshawa. Just for the halibut, eh?" Perplexed, Wilf smiled nevertheless. Upon entering the Rose Bowl, he walked to the furthermost rear booth where he placed his order with the cheerful and attractive attendant, Diana, for the Daily Special: one piece of fresh halibut with chips, coffee, and homemade apple pie with a slice of Canadian cheddar. While waiting to be served, and to make himself inconspicuous, Wilf picked up a sheaf of grease-spotted two-day-old Sports pages from the *Toronto Star* newspaper, which, by their condition, a platoon of previous patrons had thoughtfully left on the table for their successors. Looking back at him was the grainy photo of a pleasant-looking young fellow named Howie William Meeker, a hockey player of great promise, it said, whom a grenade had seriously injured. The article, Wilf read, praised Mr. Meeker for volunteering to serve with Canadian armed forces overseas, and wished him a complete and quick recovery. The Toronto Maple Leafs, it concluded, considered Mr. Meeker a 'top notch prospect' when he was pronounced fit and ready, "…to return to the ice and lace up the blades, when we win this war, thanks to gutsy guys like our Howie and the hundreds of thousands of young Canadians like him."

"Here you are, dear. Ketchup, malt and white vinegar on the table. Okay?"

"Thanks," Wilf replied without looking up, now absorbed in an article about another promising player, a tough young defenseman, Bill Barilko, from Timmins, Ontario, in whom the Toronto Maple Leafs' scouts as well as some of the other NHL teams were expressing interest. A talented athlete, Wilf had played defence briefly as an army cadet until a vicious crosscheck by a Luftwaffe forward had driven him head first into the boards, putting an end of his hopes to play on the Wehrmacht team. The residual light-headedness, double vision, blinding headaches, and infrequent mild seizures about which he never said a thing to the doctors, bothered him periodically.

"Better eat up. It's not as good cold."

"Huh? Günther?"

"Who were you expecting? Father Christmas? Mind if I sit down?"

"No. Please do. Sorry, I was just reading about ice hockey…"

"Hockey. Just hockey," Günther corrected. "No one here calls it that," he confided.

"Oh, thanks. Want something…?"

Before Wilf had finished, the waitress, Diana, all leg, red lips, blonde beehive and bust in her stylish rose pink and white uniform, was at their table, pencil poised. "Hi! Want a menu?"

"No, I'll have the same, thanks," Günther replied, smiling. "And a glass of water, if you would please?"

"Pleased for sure. One fish and chips coming right up, dear. Water for you, too?"

"No, thanks. Coffee is fine," Wilf replied.

"Okey-dokey," Diana chirped as she pushed open the kitchen door with her hip.

Leaning forward, Wilf whispered, "Where in hell is Ben?"

"How would I know? Isn't he supposed to be with you?" Günther countered gruffly.

"Well, obviously he's not. He didn't get off the train," protested Wilf.

"*Scheiss*!" Günther exclaimed softly. "Only he knows the codes for contacting Johann." Pausing thoughtfully, he then continued, "Perhaps he missed the stop."

Wilf exhaled. "Perhaps he's dead. Perhaps he's an SOE double agent."

"Sssh! Not so loud!"

"Let us hope your explanation is the reason. Have you heard about the incident in New Brunswick?" Wilf whispered.

"Yes. Tom is already here and told us. Listen, Wilf, he had more news. Not so good. But we will talk about hockey for now."

"What is, 'Okey-dokey', some kind of code word?"

"No, it's common dialect for, 'Good. All right. Okay.' Talk hockey, damn it!" Günther hissed.

"Okey-dokey," Wilf nodded, attempting be upbeat. "I like the sound. So, what is this 'Stanley Cup' that I have been reading about?"

Diana flirted with Wilf while she served Günther. Günther looked around after she had returned to the kitchen. Then, leaning across to Wilf, he whispered, "Ernest is dead."

"What?" Wilf exclaimed setting down his knife and fork. "How?"

"Sssh! SOE," Günther breathed, suggesting a noose with his hand. "Kingston. In a bloody washroom of all places."

Wilf sat in stunned silence. When at length he spoke, struggling to control himself, his voice trembled. "Bastards! The bastards! What does that do to the mission? Does the Sturmbannführer, Skorzeny, know?"

"Tom maintains that it's still on. Much more difficult and risky. And no. He does not. Now hurry please and finish. Tom wants us at base as soon as possible. There are many issues that need to be reconsidered."

As if she had anticipated Günther, Diana reappeared with a Cory glass coffee pot. "Warm it up a bit, gents?"

"No. We're fine. Could we have the bills, please?" Günther asked.

"You're not going to eat your apple pie, dear?"

"I wish I could, but the fish and chips filled me up," Günther offered in apology. "We're in a hurry. But I'm sure that it is tasty."

Her voice assumed an edge. "That has to be a first for a guy: ordering and then turning down our apple pie. I'll have to charge you for it."

"But I didn't touch it" Günther protested.

"Okay, mister. Whatever. All on one or separate?" she inquired with studied indifference.

"One, thanks. Yes, it is delicious," Wilf quickly affirmed, in an effort to deflect her attention away from Günther's breach of Rose Bowl etiquette.

Slapping the slip of paper on the pink Formica tabletop, she snapped, "Pay Dimitri on your way out," and then vanished into the kitchen.

"You are an idiot," Wilf commented angrily. "Now she's sure to remember us. I'll pay. Leave her a decent gratuity, at least," he spat.

"Sorry," Günther muttered moodily. "You go ahead. Take a taxi and meet me at the house. Are you sure that you know where…"

Without replying, Wilf got up and walked to the front of the restaurant.

"Ajax, please."

"Okay. Whereabouts?"

"King's Highway Two. At the racing track. It is a house. Quite large. Field stone."

"You mean the racetrack?"

Wilf nodded knowledgeably.

"Sure. I know the place. Where the trots run on the weekends. I've been known to drop a few bucks there the odd Sunday after church."

"Help you with your suitcase?"

"No, thanks. I'll put it in the back seat."

"Suit yourself," the driver remarked with a shrug. When the cab was underway westbound on Highway 2, he turned to Wilf. "Just curious: you a trainer or something? You have that look."

Having no idea what he meant, Wilf coughed. "Sorry?"

"A trainer: the gee-gees." To illustrate his point, he uttered several rapid, low, clicking sounds, and then added for clarification, "The ponies."

Instantly, it was clear to Wilf. 'Ponies. Horses. Some type of horse man.' "Ah, no, not officially, unfortunately. Just visiting for a few days to find out if it's something I could do after the war. Then I go back to my unit."

"Good. You'll like it there, son!" Well-satisfied now that his passenger was a contributing part of the war effort, the driver was silent for the remainder of the trip, leaving Wilf to ponder the impact of Ernest's death and Ben's disappearance.

The Rose Bowl Restaurant

"Dimi, there was something fishy about those two."

"What d'ya mean, 'fishy'? Like they didn't tip ya enough?" he laughed, slapping Diana lightly on her behind.

"Cut it out, or you'll be fishing your front teeth out of the john," she warned, blowing cigarette smoke in the proprietor's face. "I mean it, Greco! You old reprobate. Shame on an old geezer like you. Do you want me to tell Voula what you tried last Sunday?"

"Okay! Okay, doll. I heard ya the first time," he muttered, wiping the grill with an oily rag.

"And don't call me doll! You're old enough to be my gramps, for heaven's sake!"

"Diana. Goddess: Protector of the weak and vulnerable. Me," he grinned mischievously.

"Baloney!"

"You could at least be nice once in a while. I could find hundreds of girls like you who'd drop their drawers to get a job here. Just kidding."

"Be my guest. Dimitri! Listen to me, you old bag of wind. I'm serious."

"I'm listening…"

"I'm positively, absolutely sure they were planning something really big."

"A bank robbery maybe? And here I thought 'Creepy' Karpis was doing life in Alcatraz."

"Oh, shut up. I think that they're, whatchamacallits, sabot…"

"Saboteurs."

"That's what I said. I heard them talking a foreign language and it sure wasn't Greek. That I would recognise."

"Oshawa's full of all sorts of foreigners. So what?"

"These guys were, well, sort of whispery. Ollie had taken his break, so I was washing up the dishes, standing at the sink just inside the kitchen door. I overheard the good-looking one say something about a mission. Then he used a word that sure as heck sounded like German: Sturm… bann…something or other. You know, what the Nazi's call Hitler."

"When he's listening? 'Der Führer.'"

"Uh huh, that's it, pops. 'Sturmbannführer.' What does it mean? Do you know?"

"I haven't a clue. Storm sewer?"

Ignoring Dimtri, Diana persisted excitedly. "I have the feeling that it's something to do with those rows of Nazi soldiers in the black uniforms and helmets you see in the newsreels: Storm Troopers?"

"Could be. So, what are you suggesting we do?"

"I don't know about you, Dimi, but I'm calling the cops. Got a nickel?"

"Help yourself to the till, kid," he shrugged, "as if you don't."

"Oh, dry up!" she tossed off, smiling nonchalantly.

Pleasant Downs

Ajax, Ontario

"Pleasant Downs. Here we are, son. Is this okay? I could drive you up closer, but I just don't want to chance it and end up getting stuck. Is that okay with you?"

"This is good, thanks. I need the exercise."

"Okay then. That'll be a buck-fifty."

Wilf tipped the cabbie generously and then began trudging up the long, winding laneway that had recently been cleared of snow. Looking far ahead, he could see a red farming tractor that appeared to be spewing a stream of snow sideways, creating a high bank on its right. As Wilf watched in fascination, the tractor came to a full stop. Then, nimbly swinging one hundred eighty degrees, it started toward him, bearing down at what Wilf estimated to be three-quarter throttle speed. As it loomed closer, noisily churning snow in its path, Wilf made a swift, life or death decision. Throwing his suitcase ahead, he leapt up onto the snow bank, and promptly fell face down. Rolling onto his back, he could almost make out the driver's grinning face inside the enclosed cab. "Idiot!" Wilf yelled. The vehicle stopped. "Tom?"

"*Bitte sehr*! You're welcome! Get in, Wilf!"

The Rose Bowl Restaurant

"Look, Sergeant, I know this may sound, what do you say, paranoid, but I swear these two guys were plotting something. Something bad. Pardon? No, not exactly. Hey, maybe they're planning to blow up the Motors, for all I know. In German. Yes, positive. Yes, two. Like I said, in civvies. One was maybe twenty-four or so. The other character was in his forties. Can I give descriptions? You bet! You will? That's great. Yes, the Rose Bowl Restaurant. It's on King... oh, you know it. Okay, I'm Diana Holt. H-o-l-t. I work here. Fifteen minutes, or less? Terrific. I'll be here. Thanks. 'Bye, Sergeant," she signed off breathily.

"Done," she announced to Dimitri. "They're sending over a radio car right away. 'Scusa me while I go to the powder room."

"Look good to me. Don't she to you, Reg?" Dimitri commented, playing to the regular at the counter. "I thought you knew all the cops in town!" he called after her.

"Don't start, you two."

Pleasant Downs
Ajax, Ontario

"Follow me downstairs to the basement," Tom ordered. Wilf blinked as he tried to accustom his eyes to the interior lighting. Walking closely behind Tom, Wilf was unprepared for the sight that greeted him when Tom opened a lower hallway door. Inside was a large room, panelled, well-provided with leather chairs and thick area rugs. Framed paintings, photographs and sketches of horses filled two walls. An array of silver trophies lined the long mantle above a large granite stone wood-burning fireplace. On his left, a well-stocked mahogany bar was adorned with Tyrolean figurines and a prominent blue and gold draft beer handle, bearing a familiar golden lion rampant. Behind the counter stood Günther, smiling, holding out to Wilf a half-litre covered ceramic mug, while wishing him, "Wilkommen!" In the far corner of the room, a figure was bent over what appeared to Wilf to be an unusually colourful type of table from which was emanating the sound of bells and thuds, accompanied by flashing lights.

"Gentlemen. Look who I found in a snow bank! Our Kamerad!" Tom announced.

The man at the pinball machine stopped pounding the side of the machine. "Wilf! What took you so long?"

Astonished, Wilf stated, "Ben! I thought that you were…," gripping Ben's extended hand. "Tell me what happened."

"I slipped up, Wilf. By mistake I got off the train in Bowmanville. Then I had to double back. I walked a long way down to Highway 2 and begged a ride to Oshawa. I took a taxi here. You'll never guess what I saw at the Bowmanville train station, Wilf."

"I can't. What?"

"One hundred or more German officers lined up in columns beside the tracks! Some Afrika Korps, many regular Wehrmacht, even more Luftwaffe, but the majority were Kriegsmarine. No SS as far as I could tell."

"Really?" Wilf asked. "Doing what?"

"The man who picked me up when I was thumbing said that there's a major PoW camp in north Bowmanville. He told me when I asked that it holds over five hundred of our men. It was a sad, sad sight to see, I tell you."

"Did you recognise anyone?" Wilf queried.

"I couldn't. They were facing away from the station as though about to march away. Besides that, I wasn't keen on hanging around."

"Maybe we should raid the place and release them when we're finished at the… target," Wilf joked.

"Not so loud!" cautioned Tom, pointing upward with his forefinger. "There's only the old housekeeper upstairs, and she's half-deaf, but keep it down anyway. Just to refresh your minds, we are supposedly here to learn about horse training. We're Zombies - Home Service. Remember? The owner, Baron von Schröder, Bernard, or Bernie, as he prefers, is of the old Prussian nobility, with ties to Kaiser William II's Royal House of Hohenzollern. Bernie emigrated from Germany after the Great War. Nearly penniless. Together, he and his two sons built this house. Now they're well-established, very successful house builders. Whether or not Bernie is an actual 'Baron', nobody seems to know. And no one asks or cares. Anyway, the important thing is, he is a sympathiser, which is the main reason that we are here. He is away on business, buying and selling horses, among other things. We are safe here for the time being, but let's not get carried away.

"Now, please refill your steins and then come and sit down at the round table. We have some serious issues to discuss before we can make our final plans. We can relax and speak German in here. Nowhere else, though."

"First. Wilf, you know about Ernest. Correct?" Tom asked.

"Not in any detail, Tom," Wilf replied, "beyond the fact that you discovered him dead in a washroom. In Kingston, Günther said."

Günther nodded.

"And you suspect that it was the work of SOE, Tom?"

"Yes. Without doubt. It was the manner by which he was garrotted. Clearly, their signature was all over it."

"So, what does it mean, Tom? For **Fafner**, for us, that is. Is it your belief that Ernest's death was connected to the incident at Binder's?" Ben asked.

"I should tell you this frankly, men. I do believe that Canadian security and the SOE are, or will soon be closing in. I don't think one needs to be a brain surgeon to draw that conclusion. As I see it…" Stopping mid-sentence, Tom looked over to see the contents of Wilf's stein forming a dark pool on the carpet. "Wilf, can't you be more careful? Watch your beer!"

Irritated by the distraction, Tom was about to resume his monologue when Ben interrupted. "Tom! Look! Wilf's passed out!"

Tom sprang out of his chair. "That's enough fooling around, Wilf! You're cut off, soldier!" Wilf slumped awkwardly in his chair, the contents of the stein in his limp right hand dripping slowly onto the carpet. Wilf! Are you alright?" Concerned now, Ben and Günther watched as Tom bent over him closely. "Wilf! What is wrong, man? Is it a heart attack?"

Unable to answer, Wilf's eyelids fluttered briefly. After several seconds, he slowly raised his head, his index fingers massaging his temples. "S, sorry, boys. A touch of my Petit mal. I should remember by now that I cannot drink when I'm overtired," he lied. "I'll be back to normal in a few minutes. Truly! Just let me sit here, please. May I have some water?" Wilf had regarded the U-boat training exercises as a trial that would test his capacity to survive the voyage to New Brunswick. Resolved to cope without arousing either Major Skorzeny's or his comrades' suspicion, his worst fears were put to rest when he found it was possible to adapt to the vessel's motions.

"Günther! Get him water!" Tom ordered. "Everyone relax." Inwardly, Tom's heart sank. His foolish actions with the tractor, intended to be a harmless prank, had shown that Wilf, his 2IC, had been hiding a serious condition that could be set off at any time, as a delayed reaction to stress, endangering the others and the mission. 'Lord! Why wasn't I told? Did

Skorzeny know? Did anyone know?' As **Fafner's** Technical Specialist, Wilf was the mission's explosives expert, although all four team members had received basic instruction. If Wilf were out of commission, Tom reflected, as mission commander, he must be prepared to accept the possibility of failure. Neither he nor Ben, nor Günther, for that matter, possessed the precise knowledge or the skills necessary to safely handle, set or detonate the charges needed to cause maximum damage to the plant's machinery. Resolved not to reveal his misgivings at this time, Tom sat back, calmly sipping his beer.

The Rose Bowl Restaurant

Diana was ready. Prepared to do her duty, she sat primly, perched at the front window booth, painted, polished, and primed. Seeing the police car draw up, she made a quick check of her lipstick in the shiny metal side of the napkin dispenser. Crushing out her Black Cat cork-tipped cigarette in the metal ashtray, she waited. Seconds later, an attractive, plain-clothes detective, grey fedora and matching overcoat, accompanied by a younger, uniformed constable, entered. Dimitri showed them to her table.

"Miss Holt?"

"Yes." Looking up, she smiled. "Diana Holt." Pegging the detective for the early forties and old school: 'A gentleman, for sure a car door holder and old enough to be my father, but not past it. Definitely a very good catch, if he's not already,' she conjectured. 'And those dreamy blue eyes! Just like Frankie Sinatra's.'

"How do you do, Miss Holt. I'm Detective Inspector Paul Cummins. This is Constable Alex Muir. May we sit down?" As he addressed her, Detective Cummins removed his hat revealing a steel grey 'classic cop cut', by her system of haircut classification. Constable Muir, wide-eyed and red-faced, although several years Cummins' junior, quickly followed suit to show a monk-like brownish fringe, either an early victim of male pattern baldness, or a result of wearing his peaked cap too long, she surmised.

"Yes, please do. Coffee, gentlemen?" On cue, Dimitri arrived at the table bearing a tray holding three cups of coffee, and a plate of freshly baked

Danishes. Thanking him, Cummins politely requested that they be left alone. Getting the message, Dimitri retreated to the splendid isolation of the front counter where he made the pretence of being wrapped up in reading his Bible, the *Daily Racing Form.*

"Miss Holt. Or would you prefer Diana?" he inquired quietly. Nervously, she nodded assent. Constable Muir, who had taken a small note pad and pencil from his breast pocket, made a notation, and then waited expectantly while Cummins continued. "Would you please be good enough to tell Constable Muir and me exactly what took place this afternoon that led to your telephone call to the station? Constable Muir will be making notes. I hope that doesn't bother you. No? Very good. It's a necessary part of, ah, conversations like this. Please. Be as thorough as you possibly can, Diana. No detail is too small or irrelevant. Take as much time as you need. Let's begin with a description of each of the men, shall we? Start with the younger, good-looking one. As I believe you told the sergeant," he commented, with a smile. Muir coughed.

Smiling shyly, Diana began with a description of Wilf. Inspired by Detective Inspector Cummins' kindly, down-to-earth manner, and under the spell of his hypnotic delft-blue eyes, she continued, recounting the episode in such detail that Cummins' few interruptions were for Muir's benefit.

Cummins thanked Diana warmly, congratulating her for coming forward, assuring her that her disclosure would be treated with the greatest discretion and seriousness. Giving her his business card, he asked that she contact him immediately should the two suspects reappear and that she treat the entire affair in the strictest confidence, discussing it with no one, including Dimitri. Otherwise, he cautioned, the investigation and possibly the safety of others could be put at risk. She agreed without reservation. Pausing briefly to have words with Dimitri, Cummins and Muir then left the Rose Bowl. After Muir had pulled out, melding with the traffic, Cummins uttered three words. "Floor it, Alex!"

"Yes, Sir," Constable Muir replied with a grin. "I always wanted to see what this baby could do."

"No siren, just the roof light. And stop for traffic signals. Otherwise, go ahead." Cummins thought about Diana's statement, while keeping a vigilant eye on the road. At length he asked, "So, what's your opinion, Alex?"

"About the lady, Miss Holt. Her story, that is?"

"The very same. Did you find her account: credible, somewhat credible, far-fetched, bizarre…?"

"Credible. And you, Sir?"

"Entirely. And that concerns me a great deal. Let me out here, at the front, please, Alex. Have your notes typed up and on my desk by the end of your shift. Can you do that?"

"Absolutely, Sir."

"Good man. See you inside. I have a telephone call to make." Swinging open his door, Cummins paused. "Thanks for your help, Alex. She was pretty too, didn't you think?"

"I thought the Inspector might have noticed that," Muir replied.

"You can leave that particular insight out of your report, Constable First Class Muir," Cummins remarked, before closing the passenger door.

Muir beamed. "Of course, Sir. Thank you very much, Sir!"

"Thank Chief Bell. Not me, Alex," Cummins commented. "He signed the paperwork yesterday in the OG."

Puzzled, Muir asked, "The O G, Sir? Oh, the Oshawa General Hospital."

"Congratulations. Oh, one other thing. The same goes for you as for Miss Holt. Not a word to anyone about this matter. Alright?"

"Detective Inspector Paul Cummins. City of Oshawa Police Department. Cummins. No, Oshawa, not Ottawa. Yes, I'll wait. Thank you… Hello,

Commissioner Reynolds! Paul Cummins… Yes, the murder at The Genosha Hotel, Sir. Marco Palermo, the Italian secret agent from Camp X. Yes, that's correct. Room 301. I must say that you have an excellent memory, Commissioner. Yes, it was quite a messy business, but you kept it... Ted. Thank you. That's right. I was Detective Sergeant then.

"Commissioner Reynolds, er, Ted, the reason that I'm calling is to let you know that I interviewed a young lady today. Her account of a meeting between two men in the restaurant where she works as a waitress might be an indication that something serious may be about to take place. Espionage? Yes, highly probable, I'd venture. Perhaps sabotage. She swore that they spoke German occasionally. She heard the term, 'Sturmbannführer'. Major, I think… I agree, Sir. It is unusual. Hardly conversational German, at all. The woman, a Miss Diana Holt, gave my Constable and me a very thorough and persuasive statement. There's quite a lot more to go on than that, of course. I'll have a complete transcript by, ah, 6:00 pm… Three copies? Of course. Camp X. Tomorrow morning, 9:00 am... Yes, I remember Colonel Findlay. That is excellent… Miss Holt? Yes, I'm sure that she'd be pleased to meet you. Yes, the owner is a Mr. Dimitri Greco. Yes, I cautioned both of them… The Official Secrets Act? And Muir? It's Constable First Class Alexander Muir. And me, as well? I see. I can call the restaurant from Camp X, and make the arrangements. If that suits you…

"…Chief Bell? My goodness, you remember Bill? That's right, Commissioner. He was Captain Bell at the time. Well, Chief Bell is currently recovering from a mild heart attack. I'm filling in, Acting. Chief Bell says for only as long as it takes to browbeat the doctors into pronouncing him fit to rejoin the fray… Quite well, actually. Thank you… Until today, that is, " Cummins chuckled. "I look forward to seeing you and Colonel Findlay tomorrow morning… You too, Commissioner. Goodbye."

Stabbing an intercom key, Cummins ordered Constable Muir into his office.

Pleasant Downs

Following the evening meal, after Wilf had reassured Tom that he was well again, Günther ushered the group along the hallway to a rear entrance. "Boot and coats. On the rack. Put them on. Hurry." Opening the door, he shone the narrow beam of his flashlight onto a faintly visible trail on the snow-covered field. Then, pointing it in the distance, Günther whispered, "The stable. Follow me. Single file. Quickly." As they were approaching the large white and black wooden outbuilding, Günther slowed and stopped. Turning to Tom, he pointed to the roof. "The ridge is perfectly aligned with the munitions works. With reason. As a marker for our bombers." Knowing this to be factual, Tom nodded in acknowledgment. "Not that much farther," Günther urged, as he continued making a path through the newly fallen snow. Twenty metres from the front of the building, he stopped abruptly, almost creating a pile-up with Tom and the others.

"Watch it! What's wrong?" Tom hissed.

"Sssh."

"I can't hear a damn thing except the bloody wind. Can you, fellows? Let's get going, Günther. We're freezing!"

"I'm simply being cautious, Tom. For all our sakes. Fact is, some of the stable hands play cards and carouse until dawn," Günther asserted, resentfully.

"Good for them. Carousing would work for me. Who in hell would want to live in a barn full of horses?" Tom remarked wryly.

With a long-suffering sigh, Günther shrugged as he resumed plodding, leading them around the barn to a large driving shed. After kicking away the accumulated snow, he pried open a door, motioning them to follow. Recoiling at the dank odour, Wilf was reminded of the U-boat's unpleasant stench. Seeing the assortment of farm vehicles and implements fleetingly revealed by Günther's flashlight, Wilf smiled, as he thought of Ralph, his companion from the train. 'He'd think he was in tractor salesman's heaven, here.'

Günther, who had vanished into a remote corner now called them over to where he was standing by an open trap door, which, he informed them, led to a sub-basement. As he was speaking, the flashlight slipped out of his hand, tumbling and then shattering the lens and bulb on impact. Dismayed at this unexpected turn of events, Wilf and Ben peered downward cautiously. There was nothing but a gaping, pitch-black hole.

"Come. Follow me: Wilf; then Ben; Tom, you last. Reach up and close the door." Tom looked at Günther hesitantly. "Don't worry. It will open. I promise. I've been up and down here more times that I can count," Günther confirmed.

Cautiously, they crept blindly down the steep, narrow wooden stairway. Reaching the bottom, Günther muttered, "Hold on," and fumbled for several seconds until he found the switch on a dangling 60W light bulb. "There. Was it not worth it?" he asked smugly. "Our Ali Baba's cave of treasures."

They were dumfounded. Blinking, Wilf clenched his hands, his fingernails digging into his palms. He refused to accept the onset of a wave of vertigo as the swaying light fixture cast illusory light and shadows on a sizeable arsenal.

Overwhelmed at first, Tom stared incredulously. "Is this all meant… for us?" As he spoke, his gaze took in rows of carefully stacked, labelled crates and open containers of mortars, grenades and grenade launchers, rifles, handguns of every description, machine pistols, bayonets and knives, plastic explosive, an assortment of wire, fuses, switches, dry cells, and detonators, with huge quantities and types of ammunition.

"No. Of course not," Günther asserted. "Are you not impressed, Tom?"

Tom nodded in approval "Yes. Very."

"Where did it all come from, Günther?" Ben queried.

"Some of it was stolen. For the most part, it was purchased on the black market."

"In Canada? A black market? In arms? Really?" Wilf interjected. "But wasn't it difficult? Not to mention highly risky?"

"Normally, yes. But not if you have the right connections. Bernie's associates are businessmen, pillars of their communities: Montreal, Toronto, Windsor, reaching well down into the United States of America. All of them are first-class bandits and scoundrels: secretive, discrete and highly dependable, for the right price. Bernie, his colleagues and I have been slowly building up these stocks since 1937. War is hell and at the same time, very, very good for big business. It's a fact of life that works in our favour," Günther responded. "In Germany, we call it the corporate state, Fascism. Here in North America, it's known as free-wheeling, unfettered capitalism. I would defy any economist here or there to explain the difference," Günther sniffed.

"Look about to your hearts' content while I show Ben the radio equipment. Then we will go back to the house, have a hot rum or two while we get down to finalizing the plan. That is, if it's all right with you, Tom."

"Pardon?" Carefully removing the wrapping from a mint Colt revolver, Tom answered distractedly, "Oh, yes. That would be fine. A question, Günther. All of this is very impressive. However it's not going to do us a damn bit of good unless we can get into DIL. Do you have an operative inside? Because if not, we're helpless, blind, impotent. **Fafner** will be finished, my friend, and so will we. Kaput. We are committed to achieving its objectives, however, we are not suicidal. That was the agreement between yourself and Berlin. No?"

Stunned by the forcefulness of Tom's tone, Ben and Wilf watched, waiting for Günther's response. It was sharp and direct. "Damn it, Tom! Do you think me an utter fool? Of course I do! Highly-placed, at that!"

"Fine then. Just asking," replied Tom calmly. "I want to meet your man. Make the arrangements. Another thing: with one exception, most of the items you have here are useless."

"Useless! What do you mean, useless?" Günther exploded.

"For Mission **Fafner**. With the exception of the *plastikstoff*. Unfortunately, there is not enough of that to do the job, properly. I can see only one partial case. Major Skorzeny promised that all of the necessary materiel would be ready for us."

“That is unfair, Tom! I did the best I could, under the circumstances.”

“I’m sorry, Günther, but your best in this case is not good enough. We need more *plastik* if we are going to destroy the plant! Get in, plant the charges, get the hell out and don’t wait to watch the place go sky high!”

“Since when…?” Günther paused, perplexed. “I was instructed that we are to take out the machinery. Not the whole damn place, surely!

“Never mind that for now, Günther. We need more *plastik*. At least twice the amount you have here.”

“Sweet Jesu, Tom. Where do you suggest I get it?”

“I have no idea, Günther. You’re the expert,” Tom retorted.

“Well, there is one place I can think of,” Günther suggested tentatively. “It is nearby and…”

“What?” Where?” demanded Tom.

“Camp-X.”

“Camp-X. What the hell is Camp-X, Günther?”

“An SOE training school.”

“Listen to me, Günther. Do you have someone in this Camp-X?”

“Yes,” Günther lied, “I do.”

“Problem solved! If it is an SOE school, there must be a tonne of the stuff in the magazine. I need all that your ‘someone’ can steal. Major Skorzeny’s orders are very clear: ensure that **Mission Fafner** is successful. Period. And I intend to do just that. Get it. Earn your pay, man! How you do it, does not concern me. I have seen enough for now. Let’s go back up.”

Camp-X

Entering his residence, without stopping to remove his greatcoat and boots, Colonel Hamish Findlay strode into the parlour, announcing breezily, “Good morning. Terribly sorry I’m late, gentlemen: ten minutes past due. Just returned this instant from bashing about in the wilds of Peterborough County. A bit of scheme to see how well this crop of Yugoslavian chaps are able to manage to navigate without maps, compasses, or supplies. Seat of the pants stuff. You know, that sort of

Boys' Own Annual roughing it thing. Grand! I see Miss Robertson has taken the bit and served biscuits and tea. Just let me throw this coat and boots in the front closet. There we are.

"Commissioner Reynolds, jolly good to see you again. Yes, of course, Ted. Hamish.

"And Detective, I should say, Chief Cummins. Hamish. May I offer my congratulations? It was at the outset of the investigation into Major Samson's rough justice at the Genosha Hotel, was it not? Best forgotten, that. Commissioner Reynolds, Ted, if you would begin, please?"

At length, Hamish commented, "Well. This certainly could come a cropper, imminently," Findlay mused aloud. "I spoke with Robert Brooks in Toronto after you telephoned, Ted. He told me that he and Eric Williamson had briefed Major Grey in Manhattan several weeks earlier. Now, Eric wants him to be inserted into the plant. Yesterday. "By whatever means," Brooks said, adding, "In whatever role or position affords him the broadest perspective, without arousing suspicion, naturally." The specific means they leave to our discretion and ingenuity, of course."

"Of course," Ted echoed. "Tell me this, Hamish. My sources inform me that the Major had a rather nasty football accident in the Fall. Double compound fracture of the right leg, was it? The story is that your lads almost beat the tar out of the visiting American boys for it, so I was told. Is he capable of carrying out this or any assignment, Colonel?"

"In a word, Commissioner: yes. Most emphatically!" Findlay paused. "Let me dispel any rumours concerning the Major's fitness for duty. Yes. He was injured. To clarify: it was a single, not a double compound fracture. Second. We did manage to prevent a restaging of the Battle of Queenston Heights, although I must admit that it hung in the balance, 'touch and go,' if you will, for a minute or so. As for the Major's present condition, I repeat, 'yes'. Actually, although he still gets about with the aid of a cane, it would be advantageous. We could employ that as his entrée to DIL!" concluded Hamish enthusiastically.

"How so, if I may?" asked Paul.

"I think I see your ruse, Hamish. Cunning devil," Reynolds chuckled.

Paul looked from Hamish to Ted and then back.

Sensing Acting Chief Cummins' discomfort, Hamish interjected," Paul, with your permission, I have been instructed to forward a copy of your *excellent* report to Robert Brooks at Toronto HQ. May I?"

Brightening, Cummins responded, "Certainly. I brought an additional copy for that purpose, Colonel. I called Chief Bell at the General and he gave his authorization. Can't be too careful, I suppose, one could say…"

"Absolutely, old man. When in doubt, always obtain the higher-level go-ahead. That way, some other poor sod will be wearing the stripes as well, as if that's any consolation. Thanks. I'll ask Betty to transmit this by secure wire directly to Toronto and Manhattan, as well. I think it would be timely to invite the Major to join the party. Right? One minute, please, while I speak with Betty," Findlay commented with a meaningful glance at Reynolds.

As soon as Findlay had left the sitting room, Cummins looked at Reynolds, and asked, "Sir, should I excuse myself?"

"Excuse yourself? Why, Paul?" Reynolds countered.

"Honestly? Because I'm feeling somewhat awkward. Colonel Findlay's remark, although he probably meant it as a joke… But more than that, I'm afraid I might be, well, unwelcome. The way in which this is shaping up, it's well beyond my mandate."

"You would be more comfortable sitting it out then, Paul? You were sworn this morning, so the Colonel and I are not concerned about you talking out of turn. And, it was your prompt action that brought us here. However, I do see your point. Perhaps you might use the time to telephone Mr. Greco and Miss Holt at the restaurant. Tell them we will be around within... two hours at the most. I suggest that you step outside now and have a breath of fresh air before Colonel Findlay returns. When you come back in you can become acquainted with the delightful *Miss* Betty Robertson."

"Thanks, I will, Commissioner. I feel tremendously relieved."

As Cummins was about to leave, Reynolds, grateful that the police officer had taken the imitative, stated reassuringly, "Good, I'm glad, Paul. I'll explain your decision to Colonel Findlay, then. All right? Should he want you back in here, be assured that he won't hesitate to ask."

"Commissioner Reynolds, may I present Major Blake Grey," declared Findlay, ushering Blake into the salon room.

Arising and offering his hand, Reynolds was impressed by the fine-looking Major's youth, vitality, bearing and the firmness of his handshake. "A pleasure, Major Grey." 'I was expecting someone much older.' Reynolds reflected that the cane seemed less of an appliance than a stylish accessory. "Colonel Findlay tells me great things about you, Major."

"Commissioner Reynolds, a pleasure. 'Blake', please, Sir. The Colonel is very kind, but he does sometimes have an over-active and vivid imagination," Blake replied, smiling. Looking at the chair that Cummins had vacated only minutes earlier, he asked, "May I?"

"Yes, of course, Blake," replied Findlay. "Commissioner Reynolds…"

"Ted, please," Reynolds interjected.

"Ted, rather, and I were just discussing the briefing which you had in Manhattan with Erik and Robert. Do you recall the details, Blake?"

"Yes. Clearly, Colonel."

"Hamish."

"Hamish," Blake replied, acknowledging Findlay's courtesy.

"So, if an attack by indigenous fifth columnists and Nazi saboteurs is imminent, as our most up-to-the-minute intelligence strongly supports, would you be prepared to go in?" Hamish proposed solemnly.

"Go in? Gung ho. Guns blazing? Under the present circumstances, I think it best to respectfully decline, Sir."

"Hardly that, Blake. Over-active and vivid imagination aside, I'm proposing that we, I, send you in undercover."

"In what capacity, if I may ask, Hamish? I'd be willing to bet that they don't particularly want a semi-invalid lurching around a munitions works with gay abandon…"

"But that's exactly the point, Blake. It would be perfect. Not lurching. Lurking. Consider this: here you are, a veteran, partially disabled by an injury sustained at, let us say, El Alamein. You are a bit down on your luck – disability pension cock-ups - or what have you, and looking for immediate employment. We would concoct a false identity and get you set up with the gods of Personnel in Montreal, using Ted's influence. All you'd have to do basically is show up, do as you're told and be on the qui vivre for anybody or anything that doesn't seem kosher. And I'm willing to wager a quart of Grand Old MacNeish that our friend Canaris has an agent or two well-buried inside. You'll find him, her or them and use your talents to gain their confidence and find out just what's what. Naturally, we'll set up a dead letter drop to keep us both on top of things. What do you think?"

"I'll do it. Set it up and I'll start soonest."

"Good show. I knew you would."

"On one condition…"

"Which is?" Findlay asked cautiously, winking knowingly at Reynolds.

"That you and Ted promise here and now that you will pull every string and kiss every backside necessary from here to Baker Street, to bring Adara here."

Although Ted's eyebrows were now raised in either disbelief or astonishment, or both, Hamish replied on his behalf, "We will."

"Thank you. Now, if you'll excuse me, gentlemen, I'm off for my daily limp."

My Darling Adara,

It seems like a lifetime that I have been away from you, although in reality, it has only been a few short months. I have been meaning to write to you for some time but something urgent always comes up just when I plan to sit down and start. I'm grateful to the Colonel for contacting you to pass along the news of my ridiculous accident. The healing has taken much longer than expected, but never fear, I am nearly fully mobile again. (Well, almost!)

So many questions: how is Canary? I hope that he is completely mended by now. Any word yet on the villain(s)? Are you and Granny well? Please bring me up-to-date on what you have been doing. I've been working on a number of minor projects of late - mostly contributing to the paper chase - but I do expect and am looking forward to becoming actively involved again in a things, which will likely keep me gainfully employed and fully occupied.

Now for the big news! If the gods are smiling, it is possible that my colleagues will be able to arrange for your transfer here! Nothing set in stone, yet. All fingers crossed, Cara Mia. Hope you look forward to that day as much as I do, my love!

Please give my best to Canary and that crowd. Hoping to hear from you very soon.

À la prochaine,

Love, always

Blake

By the River Thames, Adara Zekara wept, remembering Casablanca.

Ajax-DIL

“First rate, as always, Lil. You know, our workgroup’s production and quality are tied now with the highest in the plant.”

“Thanks, Bonnie. That really is good news. Say, I meant to ask you this before now. Have you and June made plans for Christmas?”

“Nothing much, Lil. Church on Christmas Eve...”

“Why don’t you and June come over to the new home for Christmas dinner? It was actually Jim’s idea to have you both there to celebrate our first Christmas in the company house. There’s plenty of room and it would be so nice for you to get away from the residence, don’t you think? What do you say? Jim, bless him, volunteered to cook the turkey and all the fixings if I make his favourite Christmas pudding. Now, now, you simply must come. You know you have the knack for making hard sauce. Mine never turns out the way it ought to. I suppose that’s why it’s called ‘hard,’” she smiled.

“Well, Lil, that is very kind of you and Jim. I don’t think June has anything special planned. At least, not that she’s mentioned to me. So, I’m going to accept your offer on her behalf as well and say, ‘Yes, thanks’,” Bonnie smiled cheerfully.

“That’s the girl! Tell you what, why don’t I have Jim pick you up Christmas Eve, at six, say, then we can have dinner, chat or listen to the radio and go to church together.”

“That sounds wonderful, Lil. The plant shuts down at four, so it would work out perfectly.”

“I’ve been thinking, Bonnie. You know that new night cleaner, Blake, I think his name is?”

“The nice looking, tall, dark fellow, with the problem walking?”

“So you have noticed him. Some of the girls were saying that he’s a Zombie. So, I told them. Shame on them! Did they realise that he’s a veteran of El Alamein, in North Africa. Did you know that, Bonnie?”

“Really? No, I didn’t,” Bonnie replied. “Why do you ask, Lil?”

"I was just thinking how nice it would be to do something special for him. He seems to be so nice: polite, and well spoken. Jim told me that he's a bachelor. All his family's in Saskatchewan, apparently. It will be lonely for him here, alone, at Christmas. He has to work Christmas Eve, too. Vets, especially the wounded ones, deserve better than that, don't you think?

"I agree. I've noticed recently that he's becoming quite pally with Arnie, the Finlander," Bonnie observed.

"Oh, him. The little twerp. He gives me the creeps. Nothing I can put my finger on. He just has that way about him. A bit too, too…friendly. Nevertheless, according to Jim, he's a real hard worker. Perhaps I'll speak to Jim and ask him if I can invite Mr. Blake for Christmas day. The more the merrier, don't you agree, Bonnie?"

"I'm sure you'll get no objections from June. She's already convinced herself that he's a cross between Errol Flynn and Clark Gable, minus their moustaches," Bonnie commented, with a laugh.

"Oh, he's much better looking than those two and younger. More like Tyrone Power. It's his eyes. Coal black diamonds, they are. Like they can drill right through you. Ooops! Now look at me! I almost dropped that casing thinking about those peepers. Concentrate, old girl!"

Arsenal of Democracy

Chapter 10

Call me BG. Everyone else does

Ajax
Pleasant Downs
Friday December 17 to Monday December 20 1943

So ein Feigling! (Spineless coward!) I don’t want to hear your pathetic excuses, Arnold!” shouted Tom. “Find a way to be there. It is firm: Christmas Eve. Invent a reason. Any reason. For your sake. You are a resourceful man, I assume. The men and I are depending upon you to bring us into the plant. And, to have the key to the gunpowder room. No negotiations; no more excuses. We are already missing one member of the team. Do not make this worse, I warn you,” stated Tom, eyeing Arnie coldly.

His voice now a barely audible whisper, Tom continued. “Let me ask you this: Do you have any idea of what Sturmbannfüher Skorzeny’s reaction will be if I am forced to report that Mission **Fafner** was a failure because of one gutless coward? Then, let us not forget Admiral Canaris, upon whose generosity you and Günther have been living quite comfortably in Canada. For how many years?”

“Ah, four, almost. Look, Tom, it is not that I don’t want to co-operate, it’s just that my girlfriend… I hadn’t realised …,” Arnold replied bleakly.

Exploding with rage, Tom interrupted, “Your girlfriend? What does your girlfriend have to do with anything? In case you have not noticed, there is a war going on, Casanova. This is outright treason. Betrayal of the Fatherland! Do you think for one minute that I am about to wish you, ‘Fröliche Weihnachten’ and let it go at that? Not a chance in hell,” he fumed. “You are an Abwehr Leutnant, not a freelance civilian, and therefore I expect that you will obey my orders, now! Or forfeit your life! I mean what I say. And as for you, Günther, I will hold you personally accountable as a co-conspirator.”

Günther flinched, his face ashen.

"But, but, let me explain, please?" Arnie pleaded.

"Explain what?" Tom remarked coolly. "Make it good and make it quick, or you go into the storage basement. Permanently."

"It's the girl…" Arnie began, almost in tears. "She's important to…"

Tom cut him off. "Cherchez la femme. Please! Spare me the sordid details, man!"

"No, no. With respect, Tom, that is not what I was going to say. It, it's more than that. Just listen, please?"

"I'm listening," Tom commented. Looking at his Bulova timepiece, he wound it slowly, glancing meaningfully at Ben and Wilf. "Thirty seconds…"

"She, she has access to the master keys. She is the head secretary in the Plant Manager's office. I swear."

"So. Is the mystery lady... one of us, perhaps?" queried Tom, leaning forward in his chair.

"No, she is not one of us and that's only one part of the problem, Tom. To tell you the truth, she, she is not really my girlfriend. She is very happily married, unfortunately, but, very simpatico... friendly. Her name is Dorothy Bowen. I am working very hard at gaining her confidence, but it's taking more time than I thought. If I can just have few more days, I'm sure that I can find a way to get hold of her key to the master key cabinet, make the impression and hand it over to Günther for duplication, then…"

"Stop there," Tom asserted. "I have heard enough. Listen carefully: today is Friday, December 17 Exactly one week from today, December 24, precisely 2030h: you will be waiting for us inside the fence at the location about which only Günther and I know, at this point. You will have the key to the gunpowder storage room. Punishment for failure to perform will be swift, and terminal. Trust me in this: I *will* find you. Any questions, Leutnant?"

"No, no, none, Sir." He paused. Then gathering his courage, Arnold plunged onward. "But, I do have information. Important information."

“Such as?” demanded Tom impatiently. “Well, don’t stand there dumbly. Tell us your precious information! And I don’t have time to hear about your fantasy escapades with the secretary.”

“It’s very serious, Sir! SOE or another Allied intelligence group have an operative, male, inside the plant.”

Looking at him with a mixture of contempt and disbelief, Tom uttered, “Continue.”

“He, he is posing as veteran. Injured in North Africa, appropriately enough,” asserted Arnold.

“What? How do you know that?” Infuriated that this information had been withheld until the last, Tom rose from his chair and took two steps toward the Leutnant.

“I, I know be, because I was paid to assassinate him by a woman who said that she represented a German-American league of friendship,” blurted Arnold. “I was told very little else except the Abwehr wanted his head on a platter in revenge for events that took place in Algeria. In, in North Africa.”

“I know where Algeria is located, Leutnant,” Tom commented dryly. “Go on.”

I was told, that is all I needed to know. And I almost did. Shoot and kill him, that is. On a train. Between Montreal and New York.”

“Almost!” spewed Tom disgustedly. “Your record of performance speaks volumes about the Abwehr, Leutnant. Who is this person?”

“Major Blake Grey. Canadian Army. He goes by his nom de guerre, Mr. Blake.”

Günther shuffled his feet uncomfortably. Confronting him, Tom demanded, “Do you know anything about Major Grey?”

“Yes, Tristan...”

Throwing up his arms in frustration, Tom interrupted, “Günther, Günther. Are you usually this thickheaded? How many times must I tell you! Code-names only! That goes for everyone in this room. Very well. Continue.”

"I apologize, Tom. Major Grey is a graduate of the SOE secret training school in Whitby."

"Your source of the *plastik*," Tom commented. "Correct?"

"Yes, quite right. At present, he is Second Officer. Grey is a fully-fledged assassin, bright as hell, with a thug mentality. Dangerous, a menace. Grey is bad news, Tom. Very bad, I am afraid. A man of his calibre is generally problem enough, but Grey's in a class by himself."

"Explain, please."
"He was trained at the SOE School, STS 103, sometimes called Camp-X, by Robert Samson and William Underwood, who are reputed to be the world's master practitioners of the most lethal forms of unarmed combat. Underwood allegedly tells anyone who will listen that he considers Major Grey his most talented student. But that is only scraping the surface of this fellow's formidable array of skills."

"Well, not only that, but it seems that he can dodge bullets as well, eh, Leutnant?" Tom remarked, smiling thinly. "Keep him under surveillance, Leutnant, and exercise extreme caution. For God's sake, *do not do anything to arouse his suspicion*! Furthermore, *do not* attempt to engage him in combat. The last time, you missed. If Günther's information is accurate, which I believe it is, you will not come out of another confrontation intact. One question: If this Grey is so damned clever, how is it that he hasn't throttled you yet? Tell me that."

"Simply because he never caught sight of me, directly. Oh, there was one point when I thought he had, but I slipped out of the railway car just in time. I shot twice into his sleeping compartment, in the dark. Damned if he didn't very nearly succeed in grabbing my wrist, but he lost his balance and took a fall. I just managed to escape."

"You were acting alone?"

"No. I had an accomplice. Female. Together, we had engineered a diversionary tactic. There's more. However, that is the essence…"

Raising his voice, Tom asserted, "If Grey has to be neutralized before the 24th, I will take care of it. So, no heroics, Arnie. Understood? Now, I suggest that you get out of here and start working your charm on Frau Bowen. Remember: 24 December 2030h. Dismissed, Leutnant."

Chastened, but with fresh resolve and thankful to have avoided harsher sanctions, Leutnant Arnold Huber, saluted, turned, and exited hastily.

Calmly, Tom continued. “Let’s get back to the details, shall we? Günther, spread out the photos. My apologies, by the way, for that bit of theatre. You are not to be blamed. Yes, on the floor. Quickly, please. I want to get back down into the storeroom and see to the explosives. Wilf, are you feeling all right? Good. It is after sunset, so why don’t you go ahead and continue organising the components? As you complete assembling the packets, place them in the four canvas carrying bags that are stowed beneath the stairs.

“Do not forget the flashlight. On the mantel. Off you go. We will be with you in a while. Now, Ben and Günther, let us have a closer look at Lines 1 and 2. It appears that here has been a modification of some kind. Here. Günther, as an engineer, please explain what it means to us in terms of any possible effect that it may have on the placement of the charges. We cannot be indecisive once we’re inside. In and out in forty minutes, maximum.”

DIL A Men’s Residence

Alone in the DIL residence, Blake sat on his bedside rereading Adara’s gracefully florid handwriting for the second time:

`My Darling Blake`

`How wonderful to know that you are recovering! Somehow, I can imagine the sight of you with a cane: Très élégant, non, chéri? Oui! Mais certainement!`

`Our dear Canary, you will be delighted to know, is in top form again, and keeping me occupied with errands and ongoing research projects [neither of which have come to fruition as yet, although` we have not given up hope that there will be a resolution, soon!]

Canary has sworn that he will do everything within his power to make the arrangements. I can hardly wait to be back in your arms! The very thought makes me feel as though I'm a weak-kneed schoolgirl [once again]. Altogether, too deliciously romantic to contemplate! [I know that I can count on you to have the bath water drawn and a fine vintage uncorked, with those biscuits morsure-classés [bite-sized biscuits], ready upon my arrival].

Please be careful, and keep well out of harm's way, mon chéri. Waiting impatiently for the magic day,

Je t'adore

Adara

Setting aside the personal aspect, Blake inferred that Adara's message was intended to convey two stark realities: little or no progress had been made in tracking down Clifford's assailants, *nor* had British Intelligence successfully curtailed the flow of South African Blue Fibre asbestos shipments to Professor von Bressler's North Sea 'vengeance weapon' A4 rocketry project, **Wotan**. 'On the other hand,' he reflected, 'perhaps the status of Doctor Annemarie Mahler's atomic fission weapon program is defunct. And yet,' he reflected uneasily, 'there is the unresolved matter of the two SOE agents. Likely in Gestapo custody, if they've survived this long. What were, I mean *are* their names - Daedalus and Icarus? No, wait a minute: Roman poets - **Terence** and **Seneca**. Yes, Mission **Amethyst.** According to Erik Williamson**,** they had been solely responsible for transmitting the only first-grade **Wotan** technical intelligence, until they were compromised and either turned or…Damn it all! Good people like those, left to rot. I…'

The entrance door slammed. "Mr. Blake! What's new?" Arnie bellowed.

"Not much, Arnie. What about you?" Blake replied without looking up, hastily stuffing Adara's letter under his pillow. "Arnie, since we're getting to know each other, you can call me BG. Everyone else does."

"Okay, BG. What does it stand for?" Arnie asked innocently.

"Nothing, really," Blake replied, shrugging. "Just a nickname. I've had it since I was a kid."

"BG. Fair enough. I think I'll take a stroll. Maybe drop in to see Mrs. Bowen in Caldwell's office, pick up my mail. Want to come along?"

"Thanks, but I doubt that I could get anywhere near the office. I'm only a night shift cleaner, remember? After all, you're the Night Section Lead Hand."

"Oh, don't be so down on yourself, BG. Come, the fresh air will do us both good. I will get you in. And I promise not to walk so fast."

"Well, okay. But let me finish making my bed first. There. Done. I have to go to the john. I'll just be a jif."

"Sure thing. Take your time, BG," Arnie commented, carefully combing his brilliantined hairdo in the hall mirror. Smirking, he muttered, "BG… Blake Grey."

"What? I can't hear you!" Blake called over the sound of the toilet flushing away his beloved's letter. "Sorry. What did you say?" he asked, emerging.

"Do you pay attention to the major league baseball?"

"Some, I guess. Football's more my style," Blake replied. "Why?"

"Have you ever heard of Stan Musial?"

"Stanley Frank 'The Man' Musial? Sure, who hasn't? St. Louis Cardinals. Rookie year, 1941. Batting average: .426. Astounding. 1942. Sophomore year: 315. Want more?" Blake smiled.

"Pretty damn good. I am… impressed. Ready? Let's go," Arnie commented breezily, as Blake put on his threadbare overcoat and galoshes. "Here's your cane. Watch, it. The stairs are very damn icy."

"You go ahead, Arnie. So when I fall, I'll take you down with me," Blake chuckled, concentrating on navigating the slippery steps, one at a time. Once on the boardwalk, negotiating the ice-slicked planking, he reflected, 'Arnie's syntax is somewhat screwy. 'I promise not to walk *so* fast. *Very* damn icy. Do you *pay attention to the* baseball? Well,' Blake shrugged mentally, calling upon his extensive linguistic studies at Cambridge, 'He's from Finland. Linguistically, his speech patterns aren't typical of the Uralic languages. More Indo-European. Germanic, perhaps.'

In spite of his stated intention, Arnie had forged well ahead. While attempting to pick up his pace, a random thought occurred to Blake. 'What is it about the back of his head? Wait a minute! What though? The man in the club car! Augie. The Bund. His back was toward me, but that head of greased-back hair. Unmistakable.

'And the cheap cologne. Maybe, yes, it's his hair…some sort of gooey pomade. That's the scent! The reek in my sleeping compartment after the shots were fired: Eau de cordite and axle grease. This character, Arnie, is Augie's Strawman! How did he escape from the train? Then who was the poor devil that got puréed under the wheels? That was never resolved, in spite of the hours of investigation by the State Troopers. On the other hand, was it?

'Well, Herr Strawman. You certainly know who I am. And why I'm here. So, are you leading me into a trap? A dilemma: classic case study. I wonder what Erik Williamson would say?'

Recruit: *Should I kill him, Sir? Now? At the first opportunity? Before he kills me?*

Erik: *No. No. No. Not yet. You have been selected to study the art and science of espionage. You are training to become a spy, not an assassin. Use your sense and senses. Your task is twofold: deception and intelligence. Blend in. Gather information. In this particular example, find out everything he knows about the attack. Play dumb, thick, if necessary. Draw him in to draw him out. Remember, the truly effective spy is the one who has the ability to get close to the enemy, without detection.*

In The Art of War, *Sun Tzu says it this way: What enables the enlightened rulers and good generals to conquer the enemy at every move and achieve extraordinary success is foreknowledge.*

Foreknowledge cannot be elicited from ghosts and spirits; it cannot be inferred from comparison of previous events, or from the calculations of the heavens, but must be obtained from people who have knowledge of the enemy's situation. It is subtle, very subtle! To be successful war must be based on deception.

Recruit: *Get closer? Isn't that contradictory, Sir?*

Erik: *Not at all. You must cultivate him, playing for time, for the time being. Do* not *let him know that you know.*

Recruit: *Then kill him*?

Erik: *Only if and when necessary. In closing: The enemy's spies who have come to spy on us must be sought out, tempted with bribes, led away and comfortably housed. Thus they will become converted spies and available for our service. It is owing to his information, again, that we can cause the spy to carry false reports to the enemy.*

"BG!" Arnie shouted. "Are you all right? I'll slow down."

"No, no, I'm doing okay, thanks. I'll catch up in a minute!" Blake called. "Or you can wait for me at the entrance." 'All right, Erik, Sun Tzu. I'll do it your way. For now.'

Without looking back, Arnie waved and continued on.

Sitting outside the office, Blake watched through the glass partition while Arnie carried on an animated conversation with Mrs. Bowen. Then Arnie vanished. 'Where did he go?' Minutes later, he reappeared, carrying a stepladder. 'He's bringing the ladder from the storeroom. What else is in there? Now he's climbing it. She's handing him the end of a Christmas streamer… a garland? Now she's looking at me. She's smiling. Sexy smile. Flirtatious. Good figure. Now she's beckoning me. Nice fingernails. Red for Christmas. Arnie, you dog. I know you're up to no good.'

"Hullo, Miss Bowen. BG Blake. How can I help?"

"Well, hello, Mr. Blake. We finally get to meet. I saw your name on a list of new hires. Maintenance. Right? Could you possibly just put your foot on the ladder, Mr. Blake? Can't have Arnie breaking his… I'll run across the hall and powder my nose."

"Sure thing, Mrs. Bowen. But please, call me BG. All my friends do."

"BG. It has a nice ring. Kind of, sporty. I'm Dorothy," she smiled.

Complying with her request, Blake looked up at Arnie. "You're doing a swell job, Arnie."

Arnie muttered something unintelligible, which Blake assumed was the military equivalent of, "Go! Now!"

"Yes, isn't he? Thanks, BG. Back in a jiff." Taking her purse from a desk drawer, Dorothy exited.

"Very nice, Arnie. Making any progress?" asked Blake innocuously.

"Get lost!"

"Huh?"

"You heard me, BG. Bugger off!" Arnie insisted more strongly. "Are you too stupid to see what's going on? Meet me in Coles Cafeteria for coffee. Well, go on, man! I'll be there in a few minutes."

"Okey-dokey. I'm going. Have a nice fall," Blake commented flippantly under his breath on his way out. Pausing at the top of the stairs to hook his cane on his left elbow, as he was about to take hold of the railing, Blake turned to look back into the office. Neither the ladder nor Arnie were to be seen.

The quick clack of high heels on the wooden floor, accompanied by a heady aura of perfume announced Dorothy's return. "Going already, BG?"

"Yes. Arnie said he doesn't need me, Mrs. Bowen."

"I guess he's finished. I don't see him or the ladder."

"Merry Christmas, Mrs Bowen."

"Dorothy. Merry Christmas to you, BG. Come and visit again, after Christmas, why don't you?"

"Thanks, Dorothy, I will. If I'm on nights, I usually sleep until two pm, so it would be sometime in the late afternoon. I'm starting to pick up afternoons, a bit."

"Oh, you poor nightshift folks. I don't think I could stand it. What a life! See you again then?"

"Wouldn't Mr. Caldwell mind?"

"He's usually on the run. Busy, busy. Here and there. Hither and thither," she giggled, with a slight hint of an appealing lisp. "Bye!"

"Bye." Blake waved and then proceeded down the stairs, thinking, 'Well, Arnie, Strawman, whatever you were doing in the back room, I'm sure it was either illegal, immoral or both and you can bet that I'm going to find out."

DIL Coles Cafeteria

"Sorry, I'm late," Arnie remarked nonchalantly, pulling out a chair.

Blake pushed a cup of coffee toward him. "It's probably cold. Finish what you were doing?"

"Yes, all finished," Arnie answered noncommittally, brushing imaginary crumbs off the faux Formica tabletop. "Look, BG, I am sorry to have been rude. I meant no offence. Nothing personal. Okay?"

"There are times when a man has to do what a man has to do," Blake remarked, adding with a knowing smile, "Cherchez la femme, eh?"

"Yeah."

"Ei arvoitus. Te areena polveutua Suomi, aari te, Arnie," Blake stated in Finnish. (No problem. You aren't Finnish are you, Arnie.)

With a blank stare, Arnie was seized with a paroxysm of coughing. After several seconds, during which, Blake was just able to maintain a poker face, Arnie gasped, "S, sorry, I didn't hear you."

"No problem. I was just muttering," Blake shrugged.

As Arnie's red-rimmed eyes darted around the cafeteria, the fingers of his right hand drummed a nervous tattoo on the table edge. Distractedly he looked at his wristwatch and announced, "Nearly five o'clock. Listen, BG, I have to take the car to fill up the gas tank and run some errands. I would invite you to come along for the drive, but you are on C shift, nights this week, am I right? So, why don't you have an early supper now that you're here? Are you all right to get back to the residence on your own?"

Assuring him he was more than capable, Blake watched Arnie hastily exit the cafeteria. Taking a final sip of coffee, Blake retrieved his cane, rose from the table and began threading his way around the incoming dinner crowd towards the cafeteria's rear, seemingly unaware of the admiring glances and whispers of Val and many others. He carefully negotiated his way down three linoleum-covered steps, and continued along the drab hallway, past the kitchen doors and the washrooms, to a bank of three payphones on the end wall. Selecting the one farthest from the three doorways, he deposited a nickel, waited for the coin to drop, then dialled '0'. "Yes, Operator, Please connect me with Special Operator 2-5-1-1. Yes, Special Operator 2-5-1-1. Thank you."

Following a two-second pause, his nickel tumbled out of the coin return slot, falling onto the red and grey-flecked linoleum tiled floor to roll under a crate, dubiously labelled, **Apex Forever Fresh Lettuce**. "Damn!"

An uninflected female voice interrupted, "Operator 2-5-1-1. Please hang up and remain at your location." Then the line went dead. Faintly amused as he replaced the receiver, he wondered if his oath had contravened a section of the Criminal Code. While he waited, he checked up and down the hallway. It was empty. On the first ring, he picked up. The disembodied voice instructed, "Please hold." The line became filled with static, followed by an electronic 'ping', indicating that a secure link-up with Hydra, the Camp-X communications centre, had been established.

"103. Name," Hamish stated flatly.

"CENTURION," he responded tersely. While he waited for confirmation, Blake pictured Yorkie and the Hydra boys switching on the voice recognition and wire-recording apparatus.

Presently, a metallic-voiced Hamish came back on the line. "Say again, please."

"Centurion."

Seconds later, Hamish stated, "Go ahead, Centurion."

"Status: Alpha One Plus. Request shadow. Do not engage. Subject: German national. Abwehr. Five feet, ten inches, 170 pounds, hair: black, eyes: brown. Wearing a dark blue, grey fur trimmed parka. Driving a black, late model Plymouth coupe. Licence plate: Ontario. Whisky 8-6-9-6. Assumed name: Able Roger Nan Item Easy. Last name: unknown. Subject departed DIL at 1705h. I repeat: departed DIL, 1705h. Destination and purpose, unknown. Out."

Blake depressed the hook with his index finger to break the connection, pleased to have been in contact, even briefly, with his friend and mentor, Colonel Hamish Findlay. Replacing the receiver, he recalled two occasions when Hamish had advocated for him with BSO Manhattan and Toronto Headquarters. 'Well, Arnie,' he reflected with satisfaction, 'or whomever you are, non-Finnish, Abwehr stooge, I think we shall soon see what you were doing in Dorothy's drawers.'

Taking his cane that he had propped against the wall, Blake began making his way along the corridor when the telephone he had been using rang shrilly. Pausing, he looked back. 'That's curious.' He was about to resume walking when it rang twice in quick succession. 'No, that's Findlay.' Quickly, he picked up the receiver. "Hamish?"

"Don't go anywhere," ordered the familiar voice. "I have someone here who wants to speak with you. Hold, please."

"Okay." Through the static, Blake thought he could hear Betty Robinson's voice indistinctly in the background. Then, silence. "Hello! Hello! Is someone there?" As there was no response, he suspected that Findlay had set him up again with another of his infamous practical jokes. Annoyed but mystified, he blurted, "Hamish! This is no time for fun and games!"

"Those will come later, darling."

Astonished, Blake mumbled, "Adara?"

"Yes."

"Where are you?"

"Here. 103."

"Really?"

"Really. I assure you," she confirmed softly.

"That's amazing. You know, I just received your letter today!"

"Oh, I wrote that more than three weeks ago. The Lord, my sweet, works in mysterious ways."

"And so does Canary, obviously. Can I see you?"

"You'd better," Adara asserted. "Hold for a minute would you, darling? I'd best let the Colonel explain the details. À bientôt, chéri."

"À bientôt."

"Hello, old man. Thought I was pulling your leg, did you?" Hamish commented jovially. "Be outside the main gate when you've finished your shift. Doug will be waiting. Shortly after 0800h tomorrow morning. He will have commandeered a taxicab, to dispel tittle-tattle and such. Adara and I will be waiting with bated breath at the Blue Swallow Inn."

"Fine. But what should I tell the security guard?"

"Good Lord, man! Do you think that you're in prison?"

"No, of course not. I'm only concerned about keeping up appearances. Friendless, etcetera, etcetera."

"Say that you have an eye examination scheduled for 0900h with Dr. Ted Johnson in Oshawa. After that, you're going to knock about town, and will be back with time to spare for your shift."

"Will do. Hamish, I have to go. I can hear people coming down the hallway. I'll thank you for this when I see you. Take good care of Adara for me. Bye."

"Like gold, old man. Like gold. Cheerio."

Findlay's oblique reference to Great Britain's gold reserves, which were in storage in the Great Room beneath Camp-X, was not lost on Blake. "I certainly hope so." Chuckling, he hung up.

"Excuse me. Mr. Blake?"

Instinctively gripping his cane tightly, Blake turned around to be confronted by Val, June and their coterie.

"Hi, Mr. Blake! I'm June. I sure hope you won't think we're being forward, b, but the girls and I were wondering if you've had supper. Y, yet. That is, if you're not busy," volunteered June sweetly. "We know you're new around here, a war hero and all…"

Taken aback, Blake smiled self-consciously, stammering, "A, actually, I, I, haven't had supper. And I'm not. Busy. For a while, that is. And a war hero, June, I most definitely am not."

"Well, would you like to join our table?" inquired Val. "I'm Val by the way. The chatty one, June, you already know. This is Carole and she's May." Val punctuated the introductions with a casual flip of her red mane.

"I'm BG. Thank you very much. That's very thoughtful of you, but I…"

'Thoughtful has nothing whatsoever to do with it,' mused June. "We solemnly promise to behave. Cross my heart," she beamed, deciding, 'Tyrone Power. Yes. Positively!'

'What's the worst that can come of this? Perhaps I'll hear some useful gossip,' Blake speculated. "Very well, ladies. I'll follow you upstairs. Slowly. If you don't mind."

"That always works for me," Val observed offhandedly, cracking her chewing gum.

"Stop it, Val," protested the girl named May in a stage whisper. "Why do you always have to embarrass us?"

Stepping in to soothe their collective discomfort, June ventured, "So, BG, how do you like it here at DIL, so far?"

"Couldn't be happier, thanks."

"And how do you get along with your Shift Leader, Arnie? We promise we won't tell," Val confided, winking.

"Arnie? He's okay. Good guy to work for, as supervisors go, I suppose."

"Want to know what we think?" asked June conspiratorially. "We think he's weird and a creep. So do most of the women here. He's always acting like he's God's gift. And that, he's not. That's def, eh, girls?"

"Sometimes, he just appears, out of nowhere, standing watching you. He gives me the willies. Downright peculiar," Carole chimed in. "He's a squinter, too. Makes you feel like he's examining your tonsils, or something," she giggled. The others nodded in agreement. "You won't say anything, will you? It could get us written up."

"Don't you worry. Not a chance. Trust me. One hundred percent, "Blake solemnly affirmed. 'If only they knew.'

Val piped up, "Good man. This could be the beginning of a beautiful friendship, eh, girls? To celebrate, dinner's on us, BG! Come on and order up!"

"How could I refuse?" Walking to the cafeteria counter with Val, Blake ventured casually, "Notice anything else 'peculiar' about him?"

"Well, if he's a Finlander, I'm from Mars."

"Oh? Why do you say that?"

Val lowered her voice to a whisper. "Listen, Stan, this is really hush-hush. Okay?"

"Okay..."

"I heard him on the telephone downstairs a day or so ago. He was speaking perfect German. I know a little bit, thanks to my step-mom, enough to get around anyway, if I ever visit there someday and what I heard had to do with stealing a key or keys. I told my husband, Gus, when I got home. He's with the OPP but, you know, I think he forgot about it. Never said anything, at least to me," she shrugged.

"No kidding. Maybe Arnie's a car thief on the side," Blake quipped, thinking, 'Now I know what he was doing in the office!' "So, what do you recommend, Val?"

"Just about everything, Stan, except the 'mystery' meat loaf and the sausages. We call them 'Hitler's secret weapon'."

"Thanks. I'll keep that in mind."

Blake returned to the residence at 1910h. Finding no sign of Arnie, he set his alarm clock for 2315h, kicked off his shoes, lay down on the bedspread and began to read *The Oshawa Times-Gazette* that he had bought at the cafeteria. Though the reports from the European Theatre were censored, of necessity, he realised, Blake gleaned the impression that the Canadian forces were distinguishing themselves. In particular, the Ontario Regiment (Oshawa) which had been heavily involved in the July invasion of Sicily and now as part of the 1st Canadian Armoured Brigade was making headway in the fiercely contested Italian campaign, battling for the approaches to Ortona. Casualties were dishearteningly high, the article explained, not only because of the difficult terrain, but also because of the high-walled villages that were being vigorously defended by battle-hardened SS Divisions. By 2000h, Blake had drifted off to sleep, only to be awakened shortly after 2100h by the faint sound of breathing close by. Suspecting that it was Arnie hovering over him, Blake opened one eye, softly calling out, "Arnie. Is that you?"

As though startled, the dark shadow drew away suddenly. "Uh, huh."

"Get everything done that you planned?"

"Ya, more or less. Damned gas rationing. I could get only five gallons. New, tighter government regulations, the fellow at the White Rose station told me."

"Oh, I hadn't heard that," Blake commented, thinking, 'That's interesting, seeing that the only White Rose service station that I know of hereabouts is Barnie's. And it's only a stone's throw from Camp-X.'

"To top it off, I got pulled over by an OPP police car!" Arnie complained.

"How come?" Blake asked, feigning mild interest. 'Why did they stop him, when I distinctly told Hamish, shadow only?'

Thoroughly disgruntled, Arnie explained, "Broken taillight. It sure as hell was not broken when I was clearing off the snow in the parking lot, after I left you at the cafeteria. I bet one of them kicked it in."

'No doubt.' "Did you get a ticket?" Blake asked innocently.

"No, a warning. I must have it fixed and present myself at the Whitby station, within twenty-four hours. The officers were nice about it, but they kept me for fifteen minutes while they checked everything: my license, insurance, headlights, even the horn. Can you believe that crap? I almost missed my appointment!"

"Hm. I didn't know you had one. Oh well, none of my business," Blake sighed, leaning back on his pillow.

"What about you, BG? Did you stay for supper?"

"Yes, and I was adopted by four lovely young women, who treated me. They all said they know and think very highly of you: Val, June, Carole and May." Blake smiled in the darkness.

"Son of a bitch! I've been trying to get a date with that June for weeks now and you get invited. Like that!" Snapping his fingers, a bewildered and angry Arnie shook his head. "No offence, Stan, but I outrank you here. It should have been me!"

"Shoulda, coulda, but it wasn't," Blake replied matter-of-factly. Pleased to have upset Arnie, he continued, "Oh, by the way, I thought I'd better mention that I'm off tomorrow morning after work to have my eyes examined in Oshawa."

"You sure as hell don't need an eye examination. Maybe those women do," countered Arnie sarcastically.

"You know, Arnie, you're right. You outrank me in every way. That is for sure. Now if you'll excuse me, I'm going to get a few minutes shuteye." Turning onto his side, Blake reached down in the darkness to pat the sheathed Samson dagger strapped to the calf of his left leg. 'As my Brit friend, Michael Heaviside would say: If you try anything dodgy tonight, old son, there'll be another kind of knife in your gut before you can say Jack Robinson.' "Have a good sleep, Arnie. See you tomorrow afternoon." There was no reply.

The Blue Swallow Inn

Whitby, Ontario

Approaching the junction of Highway 2 and Thornton Road, Private Doug, the 'taxi driver', took an envelope from the glove compartment which he handed to Blake, commenting, "Oh, Major, Colonel Findlay told me to give this to you. He said you should read it before we get to your destination, Sir."

"Thanks, Doug." Opening the envelope, Blake smiled. The almost illegible handwriting was unquestionably Hamish's personal brand of scrawls, splotches and squiggles. After reading and refolding it, he placed it in his breast pocket.

Upon arriving at the registration desk, Mr. Wesley Curtin, one-half of The Blue Swallow Inn's owner-management team, greeted him effusively. "Well, good morning, Mr. Blake. A warm welcome back to the Blue Swallow Inn, Sir. Your suite, ahem, the usual one," he confided, "is ready. Everything is arranged, Sir," stated Wesley, beaming in anticipation of approval.

The Blue Swallow Inn

Taken aback for a moment by the thought that the worthy proprietor had divined the true purpose of the rendezvous, Blake thanked him cordially.

Taking the key, he proceeded up the mahogany staircase to the Camp-X reserved suite.

Once inside, it was obvious to Blake that Wes or more likely, his wife, Wilma, had faithfully followed instructions from Colonel Findlay. An exquisite cut-glass vase of fragrant coral and yellow oleander, Adara's favourite flowers, adorned the dark mahogany dresser. Laid out neatly on the bed along with a fresh change of underclothes, socks and a white Oxford cloth cotton dress shirt, were a complete shaving kit, slippers, four enormous bath towels and washcloths, along with a large bar of English bath soap, which Blake knew to be Hamish's favourite. An inspection of the closet revealed Blake's regimental tie, grey trousers complete with a navy blue blazer and hand made Italian black loafers. Knowing that a check of the labels was unnecessary, he did so nonetheless only to confirm that all items were first class and exactly his size. "Ah, Hamish, my friend, you treat me too well. Frankly, I am just as happy, not to know which budget paid for your extravagance. Of course, I'll have to return everything," he acknowledged with a smile.

Undressing, he removed his wristwatch, placing it on the dresser beside the flowers, and then picked up a towel, washcloth, soap, and the shaving kit and walked slowly, without his cane, to the bathroom door.

Opening it, he let the leather shaving kit fall onto the tiled floor. There, like a Botticelli Venus, Adara lay partially submerged amidst a riot of bubbles. "Could you add a little more hot water, my darling?" she asked, kicking the water delicately with the tips of her toes.

"Adara!" Overcome with emotion, taking her outstretched hand, Blake knelt beside the bathtub, lightly kissing her fingertips, the palm of her hand, her shoulder, her neck, and breasts, until at last his mouth smothered her eager lips.

After an eternity, they drew apart. Adara asked softly, "Well, my handsome hero, are you coming in or not?"

"In."

"Overdue. Longtemps, mon chéri. Then come," she whispered in her enchanting lilting manner, shifting in the bathtub to make space. "Mmm, Blake, the champagne, glasses and we mustn't forget the little biscuits things, on the counter, bring…"

"Dessert."

The Blue Swallow Inn

Private Dining Room 1500h

Findlay fiddled with his napkin ring while Wilma Curtin lit the fireplace and took their orders. When she had returned to the kitchen, he cleared his throat, then, after a long, and uncomfortable silence, spoke. "Well, you two are looking fighting fit, I must say."

Sensing his awkwardness, Adara touched his hand, saying, 'Thank you sincerely, Hamish. For everything."

"Yes, thanks indeed," echoed Blake.

"You are both very welcome," replied Hamish smiling faintly. "You have had some difficult times, of late. It was Erik Williamson's suggestion to…" Hesitating, he looked up as Wilma returned with a tray bearing a silver soup tureen.

"I, I have to confess that I have an, uh, ulterior motive for this, this get-together," he resumed, after she had finished serving her highly prized specialty: garden fresh leek soup. "We know with some certainty when the attack will be launched."

"Yes?" Blake inquired.

"Between Christmas Day and New Years. However, we do know the exact time. 2100h. Hydra has picked up some radio traffic which nails that down."

"Well, today is December 20th," Blake remarked. "I just hope that we're ready for it. And you're certain of this?"

"Yes. Absolutely."

"Then, why don't we interdict it before then? Now?" Blake queried.

"Because, Blake, I'm sure you'd agree that we want to round up the entire band of outlaws. We do know that your co-worker, Arnie is Abwehr, low level, and definitely not the ringleader. We also know that one of their bunch was allegedly murdered in Kingston. Commissioner Reynolds reported that details are very sketchy to this point: mysterious circumstances, etcetera. Not our doing, however. Nor does Ted have a clear picture of the 'why'. They have left quite a trail of mayhem. SOE London is concerned about the recent disappearance of a female agent, stationed on the East Coast. Vanished. Naturally, foul play is not only suspected, but is written all over the case.

"Just what they're all about, running loose here is another kettle of fish that Erik is frying," Hamish remarked, unconsciously mixing metaphors. "Furthermore, we know that they're lying low somewhere in close proximity to DIL. Exactly where, we're still not sure. Reynolds and others are working on that lead. We suspect that a group of Canadian and American businessmen have been acting as their pipeline for illicit weapons. For several years now. Therefore, we can reasonably expect that they will have accumulated a significant stockpile. And that, it goes without saying, must be seized, immediately."

"So, what is to be my role?" Blake inquired. "I'm only a lowly night cleaner, as you know."

"All the better. You both will be involved," Hamish stated. "Here's how I see you operating. Oh, by the way, I wouldn't suggest making any plans for Christmas, or New Years, for that matter. First, you, Adara. Your part…"

"Excuse me," Wilma interrupted politely. "Your salads."

Ajax DIL
Ajax DIL
Ajax DIL

Chapter 11
All the Creatures Were Stirring

STS 103 Camp-X

22, 23 December 1943 0650h

Oh, dear God. Donny?" Setting down his rifle, Sergeant Mac McDonald knelt on the grass beside the inert form of Private Donald Ellsbridge. "Donny. It's me, Mac. Donny! Can you hear me?" Reaching out to check for a carotid artery pulse, Mac quickly withdrew his hand, horror-stricken, in the realization that his fingers were blood-covered. "Merciful heavens! His throat's been slit!" Ellsbridge's lifeless eyes stared at him blankly. "Oh, you poor, poor soul." Making the sign of the cross on his comrade's forehead, Mac gently closed Donny's eyes. Glancing at the shattered wooden door of the old Sinclair farm root cellar, now the munitions magazine, Mac whispered a prayer as he scrambled to his feet.

Muttering repeatedly, "Get the Colonel; get Findlay!" he ran pell-mell down the laneway. Approaching the second 'H' hut, Mac caught sight of Sergeants Maloney and Greene outside the Mess. Waving his arms frantically he hailed them, "Maloney! Greene! Stop! Maloney! Greene! Emergency!" Summoning his last ounce of reserve, McDonald broke into a mad dash.

The Mess, Camp-X

Turning to see the source of the commotion, Greene remarked, “It’s Mac. Wonder what has him all fired up?” Seconds later, red-faced and gasping, Mac, drew up in front of them.

Accustomed to McDonald’s stock-in-trade pranks and practical jokes, Maloney, winking slyly at Greene responded, “Gees, Mac! Why the big rush? Let me guess: Churchill, Roosevelt, and Stalin are at the gate.”

Greene chimed in, “With Harry James, Betty Grable and… Mac, what’s wrong?”

“Donny Ellsbridge is dead!” sputtered Mac, now exhausted. “The m, magazine’s been broken into. Get the Colonel. Right away!”

“Wait! Slow down, Mac,” Maloney implored. “Did I hear you right? Donny’s *dead*?”

“Yes. His throat’s been cut. And the magazine’s been breached. It, it’s a disaster! Get the old man. Now, please?”

“Okay, Mac, I’m on it!’ Maloney declared. “Greene, go to the magazine. Wait there for Colonel Findlay and me.”

“I’m going back too!” asserted Mac.

Placing his hand on McDonald’s shoulder, Maloney quietly asked, “Are you sure you want to go back there with Greene, Mac? I know how much you liked Donny. You don’t have to.”

Mac nodded in affirmation.

“Mac’s coming with you! No one else except the Colonel and me is to come within one hundred feet! Shoot anyone who tries,” Maloney called out to Greene.

“Got it!” Greene shouted back.

Mac set off after Greene as Maloney sprinted towards the Colonel’s residence.

Yes, Miss Robertson,” Hamish intoned with barely-concealed irritation.

"I'm so sorry, Colonel. Sergeant Maloney is here, Sir."

"I see..." Findlay pronounced into the intercom. "You do realize that I'm on the line with Mr. Brooks at HQ Toronto. Tell Sergeant Maloney that it will have to wait until I'm finished, please."

Without hesitation, Miss Robertson declared, "Normally I would, Colonel. However, Sergeant Maloney says that we have a crisis. Urgent."

Covering the mouthpiece, Findlay muttered, bristling, "Urgent! What isn't?" Regaining his composure Findlay asked evenly, "A crisis, Miss Robertson? What kind of crisis?"

"He says it has to do with the magazine, Colonel."

"Ruddy hell! No, no. Sorry, Robert. Listen, Sergeant Maloney is outside my door in a lather. Something or other to do with the magazine. I had best check it out, all right? I will ring you back, soonest. My apologies. Thanks.

"Send him in." With a baleful look at the anxious intruder, Findlay enquired, "Sergeant Maloney, what in the devil is so ruddy earth shaking? Do you know that you've interrupted my daily SITREP with HQ Toronto?"

Gulping, Maloney launched into the account. "With respect, Colonel, you're needed at the magazine. Urgently. It's Private Ellsbridge. He, he's dead, Sir."

"Dead? Dear God. How?"

"Violently, Colonel. From McDonald's report, Sir, it looks as though he was killed defending the magazine."

Ashen faced, Findlay punched the intercom button. "Miss Robertson, hold the fort. Sergeant Maloney and I are heading to the magazine."

Arising, Findlay sombrely declared, "Here, take my coat, Sergeant. Cover him. Where's McDonald?"

Complying, Greene replied, "Thank you, Colonel. He's inside, Sir," inclining his head toward the entrance. "I thought it best if he was kept busy. I have him checking the inventory. Begging the Colonel's pardon, but Mac's in a state of shock, Sir. He and Private Ellsbridge were good chums. Very close. Private Ellsbridge hated midnight shift, Colonel. He said it made his blood run cold. He often told us how he could hear things rustling in the bushes behind the magazine. He could not wait for Mac or another one of us to appear at the end of his shift. To think it came to this."

"Indeed," Findlay commented gravely. "Keep a sharp look out, Sergeant Greene. This is a crime scene. No intruders and mind that you don't bollocks up the evidence: footprints, blood spatters, cartridge casings and whatever else might be scattered about."

"Very good, Sir. Count on it," replied Greene grim-faced.

"Sergeant Maloney, go fetch the Majors immediately and have them meet us here. As soon as you've done that, tell Miss Robertson to summon Doc Miller to come at once." Without waiting for a reply, Findlay stepped carefully around the body, ducked his head and entered the magazine. Surveying the disarray, he muttered, "Well, this is a right mess, isn't it?"

Under the faint glow of a single overhead light bulb, Mac looked up, his pale features reflecting his state of agitation. "Thank God you're here, Colonel."

"Hello, Mac. I'm terribly sorry about Private Ellsbridge."

"Thank you, Colonel Findlay. Donny, Private Ellsbridge is... was a good chum. We all liked him a lot."

"Yes, I know, Mac. Can you tell me what you saw? Start at the beginning, man. Take your time." Findlay spoke calmly, while eyeing the overturned cases of ammunition and explosives.

"Thank you, Sir. I had just arrived for my shift when I saw Private Ellsbridge lying in front of the doorway. My first thought was that he had fallen asleep, but I told myself, that wouldn't be Donny. Anyway, when I got closer, well…I..."

"That's fine. Thank you, Mac. We will talk about it another time. I want you to book off for the remainder of the day. And tomorrow, if you feel the need. Major Heaviside will rejig the Guards' schedule. I'll see to arrangements for Private Ellsbridge's funeral as soon as Doctor Miller releases his body. So, off you go, Mac. Just before you do, did you find any discrepancies in the stock? Judging from the way things are tossed about, somebody has had a field day."

"Thank you, Sir. Well, I had just started straightening up and counting the inventory. Right away, I noticed a clear difference between the last count on Thursday and now. It's the RDX. I can't be certain, Sir, but it appears that some, quite a lot actually, is missing."

"I see. How much is unaccounted for, Mac? One ounce? Two?" Findlay queried, suppressing his rising anxiety.

"Mmm... more than five pounds, roughly..."

"That is not happy news, Sergeant. Keep it to yourself. If word were to leak out, we would have the entire Town of Whitby up in arms. And justly so. Right, I'll take over from here. The logbook, please. Thank you, Mac. Good job. Have Sergeant Greene step inside.

"Sergeant Greene! Any sign yet of Majors Heaviside, Jones and Mason?" Hamish inquired.

"Not yet, Colonel. Oh, wait, they're..."

Major Heaviside appeared in the doorway. "Colonel, may Major Jones, Mason and I enter?"

"Yes, yes, of course. Step carefully. Mike, send Sergeant Maloney to take over the gate. Instruct him that no one but Doctor Miller is to leave or enter. The Camp is to be locked down, until further orders. No one enters or leaves. And I want a Camp-wide roll call carried out immediately. Get Captain Connors onto it: Clients, a head count; NCO's, Section Heads of Hydra, Business and Operations the same. Connors will report to you, Major Heaviside. Oh, and I want you and Captain Connors to set up a temporary Guard's schedule, taking into account that Sergeant McDonald may not be available for a day or two. Private Ellsbridge will require a permanent replacement. I'll be speaking to Mr.. Brooks in Toronto this morning to contact General Constantine at Military District 2 HQ to request an immediate transfer. I'm thinking out loud, here, but perhaps it would be best to have Mr. Brooks and the General decide how best to inform Private Ellsbridge's family.

"Majors Mason and Jones, you will remain here. I want the entire magazine inventory checked thoroughly. Every item. Beginning with the plastic explosive. I am going up to my office to attend to matters.

"In summary then, gentlemen, the word will go out straight away that until further notice, that, pending a full investigation, the magazine is off limits to all personnel with the exception of assigned guards, you and me. Nothing is to be touched until it is cleared with Doc Miller. At any sign of suspicious activity, any at all, inform all guards that they are under my direct orders to challenge any intruder or intruders, then, by whatever means necessary, swiftly incapacitate, disarm and arrest him, or them. Take note. I want this suspect or group, taken alive. For interrogation. Got that?"

"Yes, Colonel," responded the Majors solemnly.

"In one hour, all officers will report their findings to me in my study. Put the word about. Oh, and one more thing, I must repeat that I want the Camp in total lock down, immediately and until further notice. Entry and exit prohibited, excepting Doctor Miller. No one leaves for any reason. Questions?

"Ah, Doc! Good of you to come on such short notice."

"I'm glad to be of whatever assistance I can, Hamish. I was about to leave the hospital when I received Miss Robertson's call and sped over here directly."

"Thanks for your promptness. As you can see, Doc, we have a situation," Findlay remarked. "I'll be with you momentarily.

"Very well, Major Mason, Major Jones, report to my office in one hour. Carry on."

The Commandant's Residence

"Captain Connors, Major Heaviside, your report please, gentlemen," began Findlay.

With a nod from Major Hcavisidc, Captain Connors arosc from his chair. "Thank you, Colonel. All Department and Section Heads report nil absences. Similarly, NCO's and Client-trainees. All personnel are present and accounted for, Sir."

"Thank you. Well done, Captain Connors.

"Major Mason, Major Jones, your inventory report, please."

Hugh Mason, recently appointed to Major (Acting), in Blake Grey's absence and Adjutant-Quartermaster Major Brian Jones arose. "Thank you, Colonel Findlay. Major Mason and I only wish that our report were more encouraging," Jones declared. "Taking into account my logged withdrawal of two ounces of RDX for a training exercise at 1348h yesterday, Major Mason and I have concluded that we have a deficit of… ten pounds."

The silence was electrifying. Looking askance at Majors Jones and Mason, seeking confirmation, Colonel Findlay enquired, "You are saying, gentlemen, that you are absolutely certain of your reckoning then, are you?

"Yes, Colonel. Major Jones and I are certain," Hugh responded.

"This is an unprecedented emergency, gentlemen. It certainly goes with saying that the capture of the perpetrator or perpetrators and the stolen explosives is not only our priority, it is our only priority.

Commandant's Office

Camp-X

"Doc, have you been able to make some headway?" Findlay inquired.

"Yes, Hamish, I have, bearing in mind, if you will gentlemen, that forensic pathology is both an art and a science. In accordance with Sergeant Greene's account, that he and Sergeant Maloney encountered a distraught Sergeant McDonald at 0705h, and his statement that McDonald habitually reported for duty at the magazine at or about 0645h, I can provide an ETD, that is, an estimated time of death. Based upon current rule-of-thumb calculations for rectal heat loss following death of one and one-half to two degrees Celsius in the first hour and one degree thereafter, along with other variables, including ambient temperature and clothing, which I shan't burden you with, I estimate Private Ellsbridge's time of death between 0500 and 0530h, today. Plus or minus thirty minutes. Evidence of the onset of rigor mortis tends to confirm this. Thank you."

"Thank you, Doc. If I may, I'll just make brief mention that our examination of the body and the scene would lead us to believe that Private Ellsbridge was attacked from behind, without warning. We are quite certain that the perpetrator is left handed, wearing size 12 European Alpine-style snow boots at the time. Off the record, gentlemen, the weapon used was serrated, one of ours, a Samson dagger, or something quite similar.

"How soon can the body be released to John Kellam at McIntosh-Anderson for the funeral, Doc?" asked Findlay.

"Quite soon, Hamish, providing that you can transport Private Ellsbridge to the Oshawa General Hospital for the autopsy this morning," Miller replied, knowing from previous experience that Camp regulations prohibited all civilian vehicles, including a hearse or an ambulance, on the property. "I will be conducting the post mortem examination personally."

"Excellent. Say the word, Doc, and it will be done," confirmed Findlay. "And given the unusual circumstances, the men whom I dispatch to deliver the body to the OGH will be ordered to guard the Autopsy Room and then accompany it to John at McIntosh-Anderson in Oshawa. Standard procedure. Do you have any objections, Doc?"

"No, none at all, Hamish. That's quite satisfactory."

"Very good. Thank you. Now, if you'll excuse me, gentlemen, I have a long-overdue return telephone call to make and other matters to attend to.

"Major Jones, I am placing you in charge of Camp security. Please conduct an inventory of all officers' daggers and those in the Armoury, as well. Straight away.

"Major Heaviside, take over as chief ops (operations) officer until I return."

Pleasant Downs,

Ajax, Ontario

1945h Christmas Eve 1943

"So, is everything ready?" asked Tom.

"Yes, we're ready, Tom," replied Günther.

"Good man. This time you remembered. Code-names only. You have the knapsacks?"

"Yes, everything, Tom. Haven't we gone over this a hundred times?"

"Look, Günther, I don't care. Until I am certain that we are all on the same page, I will go over it six hundred times. If I have to," snapped Tom. "We're starting out at disadvantage having a critical shortage of *plastik*, Günther. No thanks to you and our illustrious Abwehr Leutnant, Arnie."

Leaning over to Wilf, Günther asked in an undertone, "Can you talk to him, please? He'll listen to you."

"What are you two whispering about?" Tom demanded. "Well? Speak up one of you. I'm waiting."

"Tom, Günther was just saying how sorry he is that things didn't work out as he hoped and he wasn't able to get the additional *plastik* explosives," explained Wilf. "I can tell you this, as **Mission Fafner's** explosives specialist: I have no doubt that we can get the job done with what we have if we are mindful about *where* we place it and *how much* is needed. That is my job. Trust me in this, Tom. Look, at us. We are ready. Physically and mentally. We are as ready as we ever can be. With the greatest respect, Tom, but we have trained hard for too many months to make a botch of things now with recriminations and doubts. We *do* have absolute confidence in you, Tom. We believe we *will* be successful. And I believe that one month from tonight, Der Führer will be wining and dining Major Skorzeny and us in the Reich Chancellery. What say you, Sir?"

Turning slowly, Tom's stern facade had given way to a broad smile. "Wilf, as usual you are right, my friend. I say, let's do it. Heil Hitler!"

2000h

Stepping outside, they were not fully prepared for the bitter blast of bone-chilling December night air and the penetrating dampness typical of Lake Ontario winter weather. Tom stopped and looked up at the sky. 'Quarter moon. Excellent,' he thought. 'Christmas Eve: I hope everyone at home is sitting in front of a roaring fire, mulling wine and enjoying being with their kids. I wish I were,' he reflected longingly. 'Who am I fooling? They're all probably in an underground bomb shelter.'

Upon reaching Bernie's four-door Chrysler luxury sedan, Tom opened the trunk and waited as each man placed his knapsack inside. Closing the compartment, he threw the key ring to Günther, stating, "You drive. I will sit on the passenger side. Ben and Wilf, in the back. Keep down. Let's go.

"You know your way around here, Günther, so I'll navigate. You're going to turn right onto Highway #2, and drive to Church Street in Pickering." Tom instructed. Then, blowing on his hands, he asked, "Does this car have a heater?"

"Tom, I know exactly where I'm going. I have spent a lot of time scouting the area while I was awaiting your arrival to Canada. I have also lived in this area for several years. We're going to drive to Church Street in Pickering, and then we'll drive south towards the lake," explained Günther. "And yes, for your information, this car is equipped with a heater. However, at this moment and for the time being, it is on defrost. Be patient, please. One, two, minutes more."

"Very good," Tom remarked, rubbing at the frosted lace pattern on his window with the cuff of his jacket. "One less problem." Ten seconds passed. "Günther, you know it is important that you keep the speed down."

Complying without comment, Günther's facial muscles twitched slightly, betraying his aggravation at another example of this SS-Hauptsturmführer's overbearing, arrogant manner. Despite his best intentions to ignore Tom's sarcastic, thinly veiled hostility, Günther realized that he had reacted twice within the hour, or less. They drove the rest of the way to Pickering in silence. As agreed, upon turning left onto Church Street South, Günther extinguished the headlights. Tom nodded in tacit approval.

Slumped in the back seat, Wilf and Ben were silent, absorbed in their thoughts, sensing that any comment, however trivial, would be taken as a sure sign of 'nerves', uncertainty, or a lack of courage. Travelling south in the darkness along Church Street, Ben thought of how eerie it was to be driving an unfamiliar road in the near pitch-blackness once again. 'At least this time we don't have Mata Hari in the trunk.'

Abruptly, Tom spoke up. "Drive slowly, Günther. We should see the signal at any moment now."

"I can hardly see a thing with my lights out, you know, Tom. I hope for all our sakes that I don't drive into the ditch," he muttered.

Tom looked over, noting that Günther's chin was almost grazing the top of the steering wheel. "Relax, Günther. You're doing well. Slowly does it. Keep going. ...

"Anyone see it?" As he searched for a light in the east, the fingers of Tom's left hand incessantly drummed the top of Günther's seat back. Following several seconds without a response, he slammed his fist on Gunther's seat back and declared, "If we go much farther south, we'll be in the lake, dammit! Arnie, where are you? You did give him the instructions about where..."

"Do you think that I'm totally incompetent? Of course I told him," Günther retorted.

"Okay, okay, Günther. Sorry. Just checking," Tom replied quietly. "It's possible he ran into a patrol, God forbid."

"I see it, Tom! There it is!"

"Where, Wilf?"

"There…at forty-five degrees. Directly abreast of us," Wilf explained, pointing with his right hand.

"Yes, I see it. Stop the car, Günther. Ben, get out. Here, take the flashlight and confirm the code," Tom directed, noting the time, '2014h 32s, precisely', on the Bulova's face.

While the others waited nervously inside the car, Ben walked to the opposite side of the road and flashed a Morse signal in the direction noted by Wilf. Swinging open the passenger door, Tom stood on the running board, calling softly across to Ben, "Well? Damn it, Ben! Is it him? Or is it a trap?"

"Wait. He is still sending… It's okay," Ben announced. Turning, he smiled, "It's him."

"You're certain of that, Ben?" Tom whispered.

"Affirmative, Tom."

"Okay, good." Dismounting from the running board, Tom ducked his head and re-entered the car. "Günther, pull off the road. Not too far though," Tom ordered, mindful of the near-disaster in New Brunswick. "After we complete the job, we have to get out of here, *schnell*! They will not be searching over this far. At least, not right away. Next stage: we have to get across Duffin's Creek. Günther, report?"

"I checked it yesterday, Tom. It is pretty well frozen although I did see some open spots where trees have fallen in. We should be all right, though. We'll just have to be watchful."

"Good. Gentlemen, the sooner we get this over with, the sooner we can get our German butts the hell out of Kanada. I'm looking forward to getting back into the car and heading east as soon as possible," Tom stated, adding, "I am sure you feel the same way. Günther, open the trunk, please. Stealth mode, gentlemen. Skorzeny style. To review quickly: Ben, behind me. Then, Günther, followed by Wilf, who has the most to carry. Okay, boys, let's go."

Exiting and closing his door silently, each man claimed his rucksack, then quickly fell into single file behind Tom. As he was about to give the hand sign, Tom glanced skyward. Noting with satisfaction that the quarter moon was now partly cloud covered and checking his watch, '2023h 44s', he dropped his right arm. On his signal, the men began the trek across the crusted snow towards Duffin's Creek. Staying one metre apart, moving without any sound but their own breathing, as Skorzeny had taught them, they made rapid progress.

Although Günther had offered to assist him, Wilf had willingly shouldered two canvas shoulder bags laden with explosives and equipment in an effort to demonstrate to Tom and Ben that, far from being a liability, he was a capable and dependable teammate. Privately, when his condition resurfaced, Wilf had struggled to come to terms with Major Skorzeny's prediction, finally accepting that he was the least likely to walk out of DIL unscathed, much less return to the Fatherland. He had given his speech on dining with the Führer in an effort to buoy up the team, not that he believed it.

Wilf trudged on, preoccupied, hoping that his condition would not reappear under fire to prevent him from doing his duty for Germany, his beloved Wehrmacht and most importantly, his **Fafner** teammates. "*Gott*! What was…? Jolted back to reality by a sudden, silence-shattering shriek overhead, Wilf quickly caught sight of a Snowy Owl clutching a baby snowshoe hare in its talons. Ashamed, he could only whisper, "Sorry."

Approaching the stream bank, Tom halted the column. "Ben, alert Arnie."

Flashing the light on and off rapidly in Morse code, Ben signalled, '**Fafner** coming in.'

"Give Günther the flashlight, Ben. Take us across, Günther. Keep the beam down. As low as possible. Don't let it shine up, I said!" railed Tom.

"Calm down! I heard you the first time, Tom," Günther snapped back.

Ignoring him, Tom continued, "Ben, first. Wilf, then me. Stay in single file behind Günther." The men began to make their way warily across the frozen surface of Duffin's Creek.

"Careful… Hole on the right. Stay behind me. We're almost there," Günther noted calmly.

Within a metre of the far bank, they heard a loud whisper. "Günther! Lads!

It's me, Arnie. The side is slippery. Here, take the end of this rope. It's tied to a tree so you can pull yourselves up the slope. Quickly! This damn place is crawling with patrols."

Greeting each mission team member with a backslapping hug as he reached the top of the bank, Arnie remarked to Tom, "Glad you made it! I was beginning to wonder."

"Likewise," Tom countered. "What took you so long to signal?"

"Like I just said, Tom. Guards…."

"More than usual?"

"I'd say so, but no cause for alarm," Arnie replied. "I heard my secretary friend Dorothy Bowen on the phone with some big shot in Montréal saying that they always step it up when the plant is shut down for a holiday. Normal operating procedure, it seems. But I had enough spare time to figure out their schedule."

"Do you have the key to the gun powder storage room, Arnie?" inquired Tom.

"No, don't you have it, Günther? I left the wax impression exactly where you told me; in an envelope taped underneath Bernie's mailbox at the Downs."

"Not a problem, Arnie. I picked it up *and* I have the key. I took it into Highland Creek to get a copy made at the machine shop where I used to work. Germany still has a few good friends left there," Günther remarked. "They did it in honour of two of their fallen comrades, Christoph and Rolf, without any questions."

"Well done both of you," Tom commented. "Now, how do we get in there from here? With all this chit chatting we're getting off-schedule… running three minutes behind."

"The fence is about eight hundred metres from here. I am glad to see that you dressed warmly, because once we get to the fence; we are going to have to hide in the bushes until the guards make their pass around the perimeter. By my calculation, they should be coming by in approximately twenty minutes," replied Arnie.

"Good. Then we'll get started," Tom instructed. "It's cold enough just standing out here."

Ajax – DIL

2038h Christmas Eve

"Damn, this bush has thorns," complained Ben.

"They're not thorns, Ben. They're burrs," explained Günther patiently.

"Well whatever they're called, they're in my hair and down my collar. They're probably poisonous too!"

"It's a weed. Burdock and it's harmless. Now will you two shut up?" Tom scolded when twin beams of light skimmed the top of the clump of bushes. "Keep down. There they are, Arnie. Two men to a truck."

"They likely won't look over here, Tom," Arnie whispered. "This complex is huge. I don't know how many kilometres it is around the perimeter, but it normally takes an hour to make one circuit. That gives you a pretty good idea."

"I had no idea it was *that* large. Let's hope there are no more surprises," Tom commented. "Can we go now?"

"Yeah, the coast should be clear. I chose that building directly ahead of us as our marker when I cut through the fence."

"So, the hole is straight ahead, right? Good thinking, Arnie.

"Okay, listen everyone. You have rehearsed and memorized your tasks so that you can likely walk through the operation in your sleep. You know your building and your attack points inside out. As soon as you have completed placing your charges, you will report directly to Wilf who will set your time delays. He knows your target locations. Then, do not wait around. Wilf will look after it all. Is that clear? Make your way directly back here, take cover and wait. We will muster here in precisely one hour, 2150h. Check?"

"Check," each man replied.

"In the event that we are not all here in exactly one hour, those that are here are to leave," ordered Tom. "If Günther or I do not return, there is an extra set of car keys in a small magnetic box under the left front fender. Got that?"

"But what about those who don't return on time?" asked Günther. "What are they expected to do? Or are they..."

Interjecting before Günther could finish, Tom stated, "Make it back to Maisonette Point the best way you can. Locate Johann Binder and he will hook you up with us, somehow. I am sure that Skorzeny can convince Kapitänleutnant Kettling to delay the U-boat's departure a bit. Right, gentlemen. Godspeed. See you all back here in an hour. Or sooner. Heil Hitler!"

With quiet determination, the five men made their way across the field, crawled through the fence opening and headed off in their separate directions.

Cautiously, Tom entered his building, Line 1. Pausing, he took stock. It was exactly as Skorzeny's plans had shown. "No surprises," he sighed gratefully and gave silent thanks to the Sturmbannführer for his attention to detail. Tom knelt. Carefully setting down his rucksack, he unfastened the top flap. As they had rehearsed, he lay on the floor and began to crawl to his first designated location. Creeping crab-like, dragging the rucksack, Tom worked his way rapidly from station to station. Placing thumb-sized pieces of plastic explosive in a strategic position on each piece of equipment, he then pressed firmly on the RDX to ensure that it stayed in place before inserting the wires and moved on, stringing the wire coil to the next location, while taking extra precaution to ensure that the wires were concealed.

Undeterred by the acrid fumes and odours, which reminded him of his SS barracks in Nuremberg, nor the machine oil and industrial lubricants that coated the equipment and concrete floor, Tom found himself enjoying the challenges that each installation presented.

He was confident that if each man was properly doing his part and Wilf performed his technical wizardry, then, the strategically placed chain of explosions together would ensure the destruction of the munitions factory. He recalled a private discussion with Major Skorzeny on board *U-4720* about **Case Fafner** setting back the Allies' timetable for an attempted invasion of Europe a year or more while creating critical shortages on the front lines in the short term.

Checking his watch, Tom noted with satisfaction that he had completed seventy-five percent of his assignment in less than fifteen minutes, more quickly than he had anticipated. His pulse raced with the very real possibility that within hours, perhaps early Christmas morning, the Führer would receive a communiqué from Otto Skorzeny in the Atlantic hailing the success of their accomplishment, the successful completion of **Mission Fafner.**

Sweat trickled into his eyes, or was it tears? Tom wondered momentarily, envisaging Wilf, Ben, Günther, Arnie and himself as heroes, feted nationally, being awarded the precious Knight's Cross of the Iron Cross with Oak Leaf Clusters, by the Führer Adolf Hitler, Admiral Canaris, and Sturmbannführer Otto Skorzeny, himself a recipient of the Iron Cross for Bravery and in September 1943, the Knight's Cross of the Iron Cross. Perhaps, he reflected, their exploits would be recorded in history books for generations of young Germans to read about their gallant, key role in the Third Reich's ultimate victory. As Sturmbannführer Skorzeny had said so well in his final address, they were the new order's noble Siegfried's, the dragon slayers, akin to the heroic Teutonic Knights of old, brothers in arms to Generals Ludendorff and Hindenburg, who had inflicted a crushing defeat on the Russian Army at the Battle of Tannenberg in 1914.

'Enough dreams of glory, Tristan. Ten minutes more and you are finished here. Then check that Günther has set the charges in the gunpowder storage room, give Wilf the go ahead to place and arm the detonators and get out,' Tom reminded himself, as he methodically worked his way toward the back of the building.

Crouching to lay a series of charges on the steel rollers beneath the main shell conveyer belt, Tom abruptly stopped. 'What is this? Am I going insane?' Unable to comprehend what he was seeing, wiping his brow, he bent over to look more closely. Then, it was obvious: the line was charged and wired, professionally. Leaning back on his heels, struggling to understand, Tom could only assume that one of the others had become confused and entered the wrong building. 'Ben? No. Rock steady. Günther? Possible. Arnie? No. He knows his way around here, better than anyone does. Wilf? He has been acting okay recently though. Maybe the pressure was too much for him', Tom speculated, thinking of his sudden outburst on the way. "God, I hope not. We're sunk if he is not capable of setting the… Hello, what's this?' Unnoticed before, a flashlight was lying on the floor. 'It must be Ben after all, or Günther. Who had it last?' Tom reached forward to retrieve it. He immediately recognized the brand: Wehrmacht issue. He inspected it, noting that a discoloured piece of surgical tape, bearing the initials, 'JJ', had been attached below the thumb switch. 'JJ? JJ? Who the hell is JJ? Wait! No, it cannot be. Jon Jensen? Binder!' "I'll be damned! Binder, you old fool!" he muttered. "Where are you?"

Without warning, Tom felt the butt on a pistol in the small of his back. "Good deduction, Hauptsturmführer Zeiss. Tom, that is. Binder's not here, though. Hands up. High!"

Struck cold, Tom complied. "This is impossible!"

"*Nothing* is impossible. Major Skorzeny taught us that, Tom. Keep your hands up. Turn around, very slowly. I will kill you if you play games," Ernest ordered, waving the Luger to add emphasis to his directions. "Ah, yes, games," he laughed. "If I remember correctly, that was your very term in the restaurant lavatory, Hauptsturmführer Zeiss. Well, you have just been red carded. You are out of the match and… Wha…?"

"Ernest. You were never as fast as me," remarked Tom matter-of-factly, executing a lightning fast manoeuvre, resulting in the Luger skittering across the floor and leaving Ernest, screaming in pain, kneeling with his forehead almost touching the concrete floor.

"Stop the caterwauling, Ernest and I'll release my thumb lock," Tom ordered. "I said, shut up! That's better. Look. Here, behind you. See this? It's a dagger and I will do you up for good, if you don't obey me. Got that? Or maybe you'd prefer that I finish you off with *my* garrotte."

"No. I'll obey," he muttered weakly. "My thumb, Tom. You promised! God, it feels like you've twisted it out of the socket!"

"Soon. Now, start talking, Ernest. How did you fake that heartbreaking scene in the washroom? It was well done, mind you. I forgot to check your pulse, though, dammit. Why, and what are you doing here? I swear I'll finish you off, if you try to con me," remarked Tom calmly, prodding the nape of Ernest's neck with the tip of the knife.

Struggling to turn his head, Ernest whispered, "Tom, I really didn't expect you. I did not think you could pull it off. Sorry…."

"Keep talking, Ernest. You're still alive, for now."

"Okay. I convinced Sturmbannführer Skorzeny that he needed a backup plan, in case you were not able to pull it off. He agreed, a little reluctantly at first, if that helps. So, I had to make my separation from the group final and as realistic as possible. That is why I concocted the idea of staging my own death. Skorzeny was not only aware of it," explained Ernest, "he helped with some of the props, you know, the theatrical aspects. He loved it. We chose the garrotte for a couple of reasons. One, to make you think I was a victim of the SOE, and two... "

"Interesting. Was the woman's death part of the scheme?"

'You mean the SOE agent in New Brunswick?"

"Yes."

"No, unrelated. Damn it, Tom, this is uncomfortable."

"Where have you been staying?" Tom continued.

"Release your grip on my thumb and I'll tell you."

"Answer that first and I'll consider it."

"I was staying in Highland Creek at a safe house. I was in constant communications with Skorzeny on *U-4720*."

Tom, convinced that Ernest was telling the truth released his thumb lock, keeping the dagger tip on his neck, as insurance.

"And the *plastik*. Where did you get it?" Tom demanded coolly. "God knows, we tried."

"Thank you, thank you. Well, Major Skorzeny told me that you were going in on Christmas Eve. I could not risk going in either earlier or later, as you may have been successful and I might have fouled up your efforts, one way or another. So, I had to go in at about the same time.

"As for the explosives and detonators, I was able to get wire, wire cutters etcetera from the machine shop close to where I was staying. I broke into the SOE training school in Whitby, Camp-X and stole a supply of *plastik,* RDX, from the magazine. Unfortunately, I had to kill a young man while doing it. He fought bravely, but I had the drop on him. I managed to bring back a souvenir, a Commando dagger!"

"Where is it?"

"In my bedroom at the machine… Oh! Damn! Okay, it's in my boot."

"Left or right?"

"Left."

"Do not breathe. I'll get it. Yes, so you did! Was it the young man's?"

"No, he wasn't carrying. Just his .303. It was lying under a case of ammo in the magazine. As if someone, maybe a guard, had stolen and stashed it. Do you want to hear the rest?"

"Yes," replied Tom tersely.

"Tonight, I came in from the opposite side of the complex again to make sure that I didn't mess up your plans. Just in case…"

"I see. Skorzeny didn't trust us."

"Yes and no. He's not a Waffen SS-Sturmbannführer for no reason, unlike Binder, is he, Tom?"

"Sturmbannführer Johann Binder is Allgemeine SS. There is big a difference."

"Okay, okay. My mistake. It's the old saying about one's eggs in one basket. He could not risk it all on you, without a **Plan B** on tap. He trusted me and that is why he chose me for the back-up mission. Hey, what the hell, we're both here aren't we and we're carrying out the mission? So, don't be upset, Tom. It was a solid military strategy."

"Listen, Ernest, we are running out of time. Second, you are starting to believe your own fairy tales. Frankly, I don't believe anything you've said about Skorzeny. You're a renegade. Pure and simple. So, save your breath and can the B. S. Me? I have been in here forty nine minutes and I'm not finished…"

"Yes, you are, Tom, Hauptsturmführer Zeiss!" announced a voice in German as all banks of overhead fluorescent lighting came on full power. "Drop your weapons and hit the floor, boys! *Mach fix*! Make it snappy! We have rounded up all of your comrades: Gunther, Ben, Wilf and Arnie. So, no last ditch heroics, please," continued the amplified voice, evenly. Tell them, Arnie!"

"Er, Tom, Ernest," Arnie's voice crackled through the P.A. System. "The Colonel is telling the truth. We are finished. Come out peacefully... I urge you... Do not say any more… The room is miked…." His voice cut out abruptly.

In disgust, Tom muttered, "You always were a weakling, Arnie."

"Ten seconds to eternity," Hamish continued. "Walk out or die. Your choice. Counting now…"

"We surrender," shouted Tom and Ernest, complying with Hamish's orders.

"Very good. Hands clasped on top of your heads. Single file, walking to the entrance. You will be shot at the least provocation. Is that clear?"

Ernest shrugged in resignation, as Tom shouted, "Clear, Sir. We're coming out!" Tom turned, looking dejectedly at Ernest. "Coming?"

"I might as well shoot myself than go out there, Tom. I just confessed publicly to murdering a Canadian soldier. Wait until they find out about the woman. What's the use? At least you stand a chance. I've heard that the Canadians are lenient on Germans. And just for the record Tom, about the secret deal I made with Skorzeny? It's true. I swear it, with the same conviction as the oath of loyalty I took to the Führer! Go, Tom!"

"Okay. I believe you. I am Waffen SS, Ernest, and you heard what Binder said about that. We are the worst of the worst. I will be shown no mercy."

"Gentlemen," Hamish stated, "you have three seconds more and them we will come in and take you out. Think carefully."

"Get the hell out, Tom. You'll be okay. You have committed no capital crime. Go! Now!"

"Alright, Franz, my comrade-in-arms. If I can't die like a good Roman soldier and fall on my sword, I'll do the next best thing." Removing the Samson dagger from its sheath, he handed it hilt-first to Ernest. "Here," Tom pointed to his chest, just to the left of his sternum. Make it clean and make it quick."

Confused and shocked, Ernest shook his head, muttering, "I, I can't, Haupsturmführer Zeiss!"

"Yes, you can, Leutnant Haldemann. You have killed twice in three weeks. As your Kommandant, I am issuing you a direct order. Do it!" Tom roared, standing erectly.

"Yes, Sir. May God forgive me," Ernest whispered, plunging the dagger into Tom's chest.

"Ah…" Tom looked down at the handle protruding from his rib cage as he reached out with his right arm as though to cling to Ernest's shoulder. Looking Ernest in the face, he gasped once. Then uttering, "Death before dishonour," he collapsed, falling sideways onto the now bloodied floor.

"Time, gentlemen," Hamish announced. "Squad, prepare to enter. Major Grey. Permission to use all necessary force. Forward!"

Flinging open the doors, Blake, cane-less, revolver drawn, held up his left hand. "Squad halt. Search the premises! Andy, Maloney take the left side. Mac, Greene the right. Major Heaviside, come with me. Down the middle. Hold!" Blake shouted, seeing Tom's bloody body crumpled on the floor. Bending over Tom's prostrate form, he checked for a carotid pulse, pronouncing, "That's Tom or Tommy Fralick. SS-Haupsturmführer Tristan Zeiss. Dead. There's one more inside here," Blake stated calmly.

"Ernest. This is Major Grey. Give it up, man! There is no way out." Blake warned, swiftly scanning the building's interior. Holding his left forefinger to his lips, he pointed with his right hand in the direction of the main shell conveyer area. Signalling Mike Heaviside to follow silently, Blake proceeded cautiously to the far end of Line 1.

Blake halted. Ernest, seated on the floor, the barrel of the Luger pistol in his mouth, looked up wide-eyed at Blake. Uttering something too garbled to be understood, which Blake later guessed was an apology, Ernest then pulled the trigger. The shot rang out deafeningly, reverberating from ceiling to floor, wall to wall. Kneeling, Blake carefully removed the pistol from Ernest's clutched left hand. As a formality, he reached over to check the pulse, noting that the 9-mm bullet's projectile impact had blown away two-thirds of the back of his head, depositing blood, bone and brain tissue on the wall three metres behind. "I guess he saw a way," Blake remarked. "Ernest Dixon. A.k.a. Leutnant Franz Haldemann, Mission 2IC. This is the one who killed Private Ellsbridge," Blake commented in an undertone to Heaviside. "Take his Luger, please, Mike. And do not say anything about his ID to Mac, Greene or Maloney, just now. Oh, remove the Samson dagger from our friend Tom's chest. Somewhat embarrassing. If it wasn't reported lost or missing, it's a bit of a mystery, as to whose it is and where this lad found it."

"Well, Major Grey, Major Heaviside. Good job. That puts paid to **Mission Fafner**, eh?" stated Hamish Findlay. "I rather expect some heads to roll in Berlin. Hitler's wonder boy, Otto Skorzeny's for one. Canaris' as well, conceivably. Things could get a mite ugly in the Reich Chancellery."

"I would imagine you're right, Colonel," Heaviside replied.

"Blake, would you mind seeing that Captains Mason and Connors have everything under control outside? Prisoners searched, seated on the ground and manacled. General Constantine and Robert Brooks suggest that we lock then up temporally in the underground firing range, until they can make arrangements to have them incarcerated in suitable high security accommodations. I agreed. See to it, Blake, please. Triple the usual guard," Findlay ordered.

"I will. What's your best guess regarding their final destination, Hamish?" asked Blake.

"I don't wish to second guess Robert Brooks and the General, Blake, but I would think that the majority will end up at PoW Camp 30 Bowmanville. If the vetting committee recommends it, however, they might be sent up to Camp 20 Gravenhurst. If harsher justice prevails, and I wouldn't want to second guess that one, they could stand trial for espionage."

"Conviction would carry a mandatory sentence of from twenty-years to life imprisonment, or execution, then," Blake commented, seeking clarification.

"Correct. May I ask why? You appear to be terribly interested in their fate, Blake," Hamish inquired.

"That fellow, Wilf, Hermann Klein, the army explosives specialist, I'd very much like to have a crack at him. I have a feeling that he could prove helpful, if you and I approach him the right way...using the tried and true Findlay carrot and stick technique," Blake smiled.

"If you think so. Very well, I'll see what I can do. No promises, mind. You know the military justice mentality. Now, let's wrap this night up and get over to my residence.

"Major Heaviside, Michael, please see that the buildings are secure, then you may stand down the squad. Have Andy open the bar. On my chit," Hamish declared.

"Sergeants Maloney and McDonald, bring out the bodies. Sergeant Greene will see to fetching two stretchers. We will keep them in cold storage for the time being. In the magazine. Under lock and key." Walking outside, Colonel Findlay was buttoning his somewhat stained greatcoat, when he encountered Dave and Jim. "Ah, Mr. Caldwell, Mr. Montgomery. Thank you for dropping by. A bit of excitement. However, it's all under control."

Shaking Findlay's hand, Dave Caldwell and Jim Montgomery stood shivering in the biting cold. "Colonel Findlay, if I may be so bold to ask, wasn't that cutting it a bit close?" proposed Dave.

"Not at all, old man," replied Hamish. "You see, we had to make sure they were all here and accounted for. We simply could not afford for one of them to get away and make contact with their handlers. Now, we must act swiftly if we're going to round up the others. Minor players, nuisances mostly, rest assured, but dangerous to have these villains running about, free range, on the loose, nevertheless. Tonight's Operation Clean Sweep, is a significant achievement in shutting down Admiral Canaris' vaunted Abwehr in Canada," replied Hamish.

"But how did you know that it would be tonight, for sure, Colonel?" asked Jim.

"Our chaps intercepted a message to their handlers advising that it would take place on Christmas Eve. That is all I can tell you. Security reasons. Now, what time is it, gentlemen? Good, Lord. 2253h."

"Ten fifty-three p.m., Jim," Dave clarified.

"Adara, my dear! Come over here and meet these two fine gentlemen. Now, I have a capital idea. What say we all head over to the Swallow for drinks?"

"Thank you, Colonel, but as it is Christmas Eve, we should be getting back home, right Dave?" suggested James.

"Hearth and home. Yes, you're quite right. You're excused, this time," Hamish chuckled. "Merry Christmas!" he called out to the two DIL managers as they walked quickly to their cars.

"Now, Adara, what say we hop in my jeep and head to my residence for a taddle of Christmas cheer? Now, now, don't look like that. The boy, Blake is invited, too. In fact, all the officers will be there. Even Robert Brooks, a fellow bachelor, from HQ Toronto, will be partaking. He's rushing back madly from Manhattan, at this very moment, mad as he, well, quite upset to have missed the show here. It's a jolly fine two-year old Christmas Eve tradition at the Camp, it is."

"It's not that, Colonel," she smiled. "Blake said…it's…"

"Yes…?

"It's your driving. He says it's…"

"Wild, unrestrained, reckless?" Hamish suggested, straight-faced. "Foolhardy…?

"Life threatening, actually."

Pausing, downcast, Hamish then roared with laughter. "The nerve of that cheeky blighter! He hasn't flown with me, yet. Come, get in. I solemnly promise to adhere to all rules and regulations of the road, my dear Adara," Hamish vowed, holding out his hand to assist her.

"There is one other thing, Colonel."

"Hamish, my dear. And what is that?" Hamish inquired, starting the engine.

"Oh, nothing."

"Go ahead."

"You won't be angry with me?"

"I promise. Try me."

Leaning over, Adara kissed him tenderly on the cheek. "You have given me the greatest gift I could ever have imagined or wished for. Thank you for Blake. Merry Christmas, Colonel Findlay," she whispered.

Surprised, moved and slightly befuddled, Hamish was silent for a moment, then, in control again, replied gently, "You are most welcome. Merry Christmas, Adara. Now, can I tell what HQ has in mind for you two?"

Well now, how would you feel about returning to Casablanca, or perhaps Caracas, Venezuela. Peenemünde, perhaps…?

"Timbuktu... The Road to Mandalay…Bora Bora. No, Tahiti. No Abwehr villains in Tahiti, are there?" she asked, giggling seductively.

"Not that I know of. However, to be serious for a moment, if I may, Adara. I was informed that SIS London has passed along some rather chilling news to BSO HQ, New York. It concerns your chum, Clifford Jackson, the South African/ Venezuelan Blue Fibre asbestos cartel, Wilhelm von Bressler, the rocket chap and another top German scientist, Maria Mahler. In short, Jackson has disappeared. Vanished, as they say, without a trace."

Adara winced as Hamish drifted a corner, causing the jeep's rear end to fishtail, narrowly avoiding a snow bank. "Oh, no!"

"Sorry. Was that my driving or the news?"

"Both. Could you pull over for a minute, Hamish? Please?" Adara pleaded. "Thank you."

Driving onto the shoulder, Hamish stopped. "I a, apologize, Adara," he stumbled.

"Oh, it wasn't the driving," she smiled faintly, "I just need a moment to think. I am very concerned. What can we do to help find Clifford, Hamish? When he drove me to Croyden Airfield, he seemed the chipper old Cliff, although when I think of it now, it all seemed a little, how do you say, *forced*? He kissed me like an uncle, as usual, and then wished me a good flight. I asked if he was going to be all right. He hesitated, and then replied, 'No worries, darling'. I confess that I didn't think much of it at the time."

Hamish (l.) and Private Andy with Hamish' prized Jeep.

Placing his hand on her arm, Hamish stated, "Adara, Clifford Jackson is a staunch friend and ally. Moreover, I do share your concern. Yet, however much I might wish to help, I have neither permission, nor the level of security clearance necessary to delve into this. The message that I received from Manhattan was clearly intended for information only, not action. Perhaps, just perhaps, it is all a ruse, a cover. You can understand that my knuckles would be soundly rapped for meddling in British security affairs. This is a matter for Erik Williamson and Sir Will Cunnington."

"I understand your position, Hamish, really I do. Nevertheless, I am convinced that his disappearance is directly related to the Abwehr's habit of settling old scores. I feel personally responsible and I can guarantee that Blake will as well. We know…"

"Adara, I confess that I had an ulterior purpose in mind for inviting Robert Brooks here tonight," Hamish interjected.

"Colonel, no disrespect, but Mr. Brooks does not know Clifford Jackson as well as Blake or I do. If you or Mr. Brooks suspect that he defected, went over to the other side: German, Japanese or Soviet, it *is not* possible. Clifford may be many things, but he is not a traitor. It's ludicrous for anyone to even suggest that."

Taken aback, Hamish protested, "I haven't suggested that, Adara. It may be a dark shadow in the background, but that's not my…"

"Good. Then, you will not object when I request that Mr. Brooks sit down with Blake and me, privately, tonight, will you? I promise not to involve you."

"Au contraire, mademoiselle," Hamish smiled, "I can assure you that I'd like nothing better than to 'have a go' with you two. Whatever comes of your pow-wow with Brooks, count me in. Promise, Adara?"

"I solemnly promise."

"Good show. Oh, my! The time! It's nearly Christmas Day! We must get back or they'll be thinking that you and I have run off together!" Hamish remarked as the Jeep sped away into the darkness.

End

To be continued 2006: *Mills of the Gods*

Ajax DIL
Ajax DIL
Ajax DIL

THE Junior Commando
VICTORY IS OUR BU...ESS!
OF DEFENCE INDUSTRIES LIMITED • AJAX • ONTARIO

No. 6 AJAX, Ontario AUGUST 15th, 1944

The Shells You Make

A Condensation of the broadcast from Normandy made by Matthew Halton, C. B. C. war correspondent.

This is Matthew Halton of the C.B.C., speaking from France.

This is a talk about guns, guns, guns, guns — all day and all night the incessant thudding and pounding of the guns. All day and all night the roaring and thunder of the guns and the screaming tempests of steel, thousands of guns blasting the way for the fighting men; thousands of guns and millions of shells helping to win this close, bloody and ferocious battle in Normandy; making the face of France a pitted and hideous thing, yet helping to shorten the war, saving lives and fair cities, even as they destroy lives and cities.

Listen! Always the guns... (and the sound of Canadian guns, firing Canadian shells against the Nazis was heard across the Atlantic).

Always the guns, and yet never enough guns; never enough guns and shells. Watch the Infantry cross the field just once and you'll know there are never too many guns.

Let's go back to the morning of July 4 when four Canadian infantry regiments, with tanks, attacked the German strongpoint in the village and airdrome called Carpiquet, which is now a Canadian name, full of Canadian sweat and blood. To support that attack we used 600 guns. In the first four hours of that attack, 600 guns fired 1,800 shells a minute. That is 432,000 shells — 432,000 fierce spouts of flame and roar as the guns fired; 432,000 demons whistling through the air; 432,000 evil, thought-splitting c-c-r-rumps, as the shells exploded.

Had all those guns been 25-pounders, our light field gun, the weight of shells dropped in that first four hours would have been nearly 11,000,000 pounds. But they weren't all 25-pounders, by any means. There were many regiments of mediums, the 4.5's and 5.5's, which throw shells weighing 100 pounds; and regiments of heavies, the huge guns that fire much heavier shells. The weight of shells that morning was probably 25,000,000 pounds. Twenty five million pounds of splitting steel. Listen... (and again Matthew Halton paused so that his listeners could hear the sound of artillery fire, using the shells that had been made and filled in Canadian factories).

Lay down the shells. Tens of thousands of them will do no damage... just simply make small holes in open fields or

(continued on page 4)

Canadian-Filled Ack-Ack Shells Down Buzzbombs

First it was the Luftwaffe that ran smack into the terriffic ack-ack fire over London and learned to keep its distance.

Canadian filled shells played a major part in that aerial show and many of them made fatal contact with German bombers over Britain.

Now it's the buzzbombs, those pilotless bombs that fall indiscriminately on the British Islands, that are being knocked out of the sky by Canadian-filled 20mm. shells.

Once again the R.A.F., together with the R.C.A.F. and the U.S. Army Air Corps, are fighting a new type invader in the sky. And once more anti-aircraft guns by the thousands are hoisting their explosive-filled metal high into the air to form a protective fence around Britain's cities. The attack on the buzzbomb is double barreled. British and Allied airfract, equipped with sensitive detectors that tell when and where the buzzbombs took off, chase the destroyers over the channel and shoot many of them down before they reach land. For those that finally get over Britain the ack-ack are waiting.

Canadian-filled 20mms. helped bust the Luftwaffe. They're doing a job again on Hitler's Vengeance Weapon No. 1.

DIL Commando August 15 1944

Ajax DIL
Ajax DIL
Ajax DIL

Junior Commando
VICTORY IS OUR NESS!
OF DEFENCE INDUSTRIES LIMITED • AJAX • ONTARIO

No. 20 AJAX, Ontario NOVEMBER 30th, 1944

Ammunition Shortage Held Back Allies At Aachen, Gen. Eisenhower Declares

5,000 Pounds Of Shells Per Minute Poured Into Enemy Lines

Allied Supreme Headquarters, Paris. (A.P.) — The reduction of the German fortress city of Aachen was delayed by a shortage of ammunition, Gen. D. Eisenhower said today.

Gen. Eisenhower declared also that "Allied fighting men have achieved in Europe since June 6 one of the remarkable military victories of all time. They have eliminated more than a million German soldiers."

APPEAL BROADCAST

The Allied Supreme Commander appealed to munitions workers in the United States to turn out ammunition, especially artillery shells, at top speed. In an address on the army hour program, broadcast in the United States over NBC, Gen. Eisenhower emphasized the enormous drain on ammunition resulting from the stepped-up tempo of the war.

"Today we are firing ammunition that we would not have used until next February or March if we had been content with slower advance, with less crushing victories, or if we had been ready to sacrifice soldiers to save materials," he said.

In the capture of Aachen, he reported, the 1st Army used 300,000 rounds of 105-millimetre ammunition in a two-weeks' period "and even the reduction of that place was delayed because of shortage of ammunition."

USED IN ALL WEATHER

"Now we are hammering at the massive crust of armor surrounding the German fortress," Gen. Eisenhower added. "Appaling conditions of rain, fog, snow and mud make difficult the employment of our air forces and the manoeuvre of our tanks, even of our foot soldiers. But wretched weather cannot stop artillery shells. More than ever before we need ammunition."

Expenditure of ammunition has "raced ahead of our receipts from home, but I know that you do not want to give the enemy one second's rest", he said.

The supreme commander said 5,000 pounds of ammunition are being poured into German defences every minute. Six million rounds of artillery fire and 2,000,000 rounds of mortar fire are being hurled at the Germans each month.

SOLDIERS WANT MORE

The following day Gen. Eisenhower revealed plans to steadily increase pressure on the Hun. To do this, the supreme commander said, "I want more supplies than we are getting and I think the soldier wants more than he is getting, both now and in the future.

"Unless everyone all the way through the nations—those at the front and those at home—keep on the job everlastingly and with mounting intensity, we are only postponing the day of victory", Eisenhower declared. He explained that his remarks were not designed as a criticism of what has been done on the home front but rather as an inspiration to produce the extra shells essential to victory.

HIGHLIGHTS

Shells now being used on western front would not have been until February in a normal advance . . .

6,000,000 artillery shells and 2,000,000 rounds of mortar ammunition are being hurled at enemy each month...

Shell consumption on western front is at a rate of 5,000 pounds per minute . . .

In battle for Aachen 300,000 rounds of 105 mm. ammunition were used in two weeks.

Commando November 30 1944

Atlas Tag (2005)

Harwood Point Historical Gardens, site of ***HMS Ajax*** *, RCAF and DIL Memorials.*

HMS Ajax *Memorial Plaque*

DIL Memorial Plaque

DIL Memorial Plaque

RCAF Memorial Plaque

Ajax DIL
Ajax DIL
Ajax DIL

Historical Ajax

Graf Spee *Memorial*

Ajax DIL
Ajax DIL
Ajax DIL

The Writing/Production Team

Lynn Philip Hodgson

As co-author of the ***Inside Camp-X*** Series with Alan Longfield, Lynn has spoken to over sixty thousand public and high school students in the past three years, enlightening them of their rich historical heritage in Durham Region. He is a Director of the Scugog Historical Society, a volunteer at the Camp-X museum in Oshawa and a Director of the Scugog Shores Historical Museum, Director of the Kawartha Conservation Authority, Director of the Military Heritage of Durham Region and Director of the Scugog Township Heritage Committee. He is also an elected Councillor for Ward 3 in Scugog Township.

He has spoken to every Lions, Kiwanis, Probus and Rotary Clubs in Durham Region. He has also addressed the National Press Club in Washington D.C.:http://www.SpiesCafe.com/menu.htm and The Bletchley Park Trust in Milton Keynes, England. He was the only Canadian invited to the 60th anniversary of the OSS (CIA) in June of 2002, which was held inside the famous CIA HQ at Langley, Virginia.

http://webhome.idirect.com/~lhodgson/OSS.html

Lynn has spoken to over 60,000 Public, Separate and High School students in Southern Ontario and has been recommended by numerous teachers as a valuable teaching resource. http://webhome.idirect.com/~lhodgson/teachers.html Lynn has appeared in many documentaries including the hour long documentary called 'Family Secrets' which appeared on Global Television across Canada and 'The True Intrepid' which has been shown many times on History Television.

On March 7 2005, Lynn Philip Hodgson won the "Lifetime Achievement Award" for 2004. The award is issued by the Ontario Heritage Foundation.

Lynn has succeeded in giving Canadians a sense of their wonderful heritage and history.

Visit Lynn at http://www.camp-x.com

Alan Paul Longfield

Alan Paul Longfield, B. A. (Queen's), M. Ed. (Toronto), has been researching and writing about Camp X in partnership with Lynn Philip Hodgson since 1977, as described in Lynn's best selling, ***Inside Camp-X*** (1999, 2002).

Born in Toronto, Alan has lived in Whitby, Ontario for thirty years. His wife, The Honourable Judi Longfield, P.C., is Member of Parliament for Whitby/Oshawa. Michael, their son, is with **Alliance Atlantis Cinemas** in Toronto.

After a thirty-eight year career in education as an Elementary, Junior High, and Secondary School Science Teacher-Consultant and Principal of three elementary schools with the Toronto District School Board, Alan retired in 1998, to devote himself to writing and consulting. During his ten year term as a Science Consultant with North York, Alan served as Adjunct Professor with both the York and University of Toronto Faculties of Education and was the Educational Editor of two Intermediate Science textbooks with Oxford University Press: ***Science: The Nature of Things*** and ***The Measure of Things***.

Ajax Arsenal of Democracy is his sixth production with **Blake Books** in the ***Inside Camp X Series***. Previous works include: ***Camp-X The Final Battle** (2001)*, ***Camp-X Silver Dagger*** *(2002)*, ***Camp 30 Word of Honour*** (2003), and ***Camp-X Vengeance Weapon** (2004)*. Alan served as principal writer of the biographical, ***Almost** (2000)*, the memoirs of Joseph J. Gelleny, a Camp X-trained Canadian secret agent, with Joe and Lynn.

Through his company, ***APL Consulting***, Alan has now ventured into the field of graphic design. ***Arsenal of Democracy***, is his first commercial production, using ***Adobe Creative Suite®***.

Alan would be delighted to hear from our readers and may be contacted at

alongfi@sympatico.com.

Introducing the *Special Agent Blake Grey* Series

Unlike many examples of the espionage genre, each book in the ***Special Agent Blake Grey*** series will place Major Blake Grey at the centre of actual events in authentic locales during World War II and into the dawn of the Cold War era in the early 1950's.

Drawing upon the current surge of public interest in espionage and special operations, as evidenced by the success of the Washington D.C.-based International Spy Museum, while retaining the distinctly Canadian flavour of the ***Inside Camp X*** titles, the ***Special Agent Blake Grey*** Series will focus upon little-known, covert operations in which Canada's role is largely unacknowledged in the official record. These include: Dieppe, D-Day, Nazi Germany's intercontinental V2 rocket Project **Wotan,** atomic weapons Project ***Thor***, The Manhattan Project, the war in the Pacific theatre and the origins of psychological and biochemical warfare in top-secret Western and Soviet research establishments. Each episode will depict Grey's evolution from brilliantly gifted understudy into the inheritor of Erik Williamson, *Stalwart's* mantle, to become Canada's pre-eminent, enigmatic master spy in the fascinating and often deadly shadow-world of espionage and clandestine operations.

***Camp X Vengeance Weapon,* (2004),** is the first in this new series featuring the Canadian Special Agent, Blake Grey. Toronto-born Major Grey, Second Officer at Camp X, is a graduate of Beaulieu, Great Britain's WWII elite 'finishing school' for special agents. Grey has risen from the alleyways of Toronto's Cabbagetown, becoming a Cambridge scholar, linguist, and a leading disciple of Bill Underwood, world-renowned master of the deadly arts of unarmed combat and assassination. (http://www.defendo.ca/).

There can be no doubt that German rocket technology and engineering, as embodied in Adolf Hitler's pet V2 'vengeance weapon' missile program, was superior to any the world had witnessed. Similarly, few historians doubt that Hitler would have used the atomic bomb, had its development not been thwarted.

In 1943, Grey is selected by *Stalwart*, Erik Williamson, Chief of British Security Operation, with the personal approval of British Prime Minister Winston Churchill and American President Franklin Roosevelt, to not only infiltrate and destroy **Wotan** *and* **Thor**, Adolf Hitler's ultimate terror weapons, which if launched, will devastate not only Great Britain, but Washington, New York and Ottawa, but abduct the Projects' top scientists.

To do so, he must first demonstrate his ability as an *agent provocateur* by infiltrating the top secret Manhattan atomic bomb Project at Los Alamos, New Mexico. then, fly to Casablanca, Morocco, posing as Caracas tea merchant, Mr. Blake, to intercept a shipment of a critical component, the rare South African Blue, needed to put the last touches to Adolf Hitler's intercontinental rocket program. Betrayed, he believes, by the mysterious Moroccan beauty, Adara, mistress to Graziano, his wealthy and unscrupulous underworld contact, Grey must use his wits, linguistic skills, and deadly proficiency as an expert practitioner of combat by special means to escape imprisonment and torture to fulfill his mission, before **Wotan** and **Thor** can be combined in one fearsome super weapon.

Followers of the ***Inside Camp X*** series will be delighted to be reacquainted with many of their favourite characters. Hamish Findlay, CO of Camp X; 'Mac' and Maloney, Camp guards and keepers of the King's Gold; 'Yorkie' Hardcastle, of Hydra, along with a new cast of 'gentlemen adventurers,' such as Clifford, 'Call me Canary, old man,' Jackson of Special Operations Executive; German rocketry titans, Dr. Willi von Bressler and General 'Sig' Hoffman, whose questionable allegiance to the Nazi regime might play into Grey's hands; Dr. Annemarie Mahler, dedicated Nazi chief of Germany's atomic bomb development program **Thor**, along with a supporting cast of rogue double and triple agents, hired thugs from the Casablanca *demi monde*, who may not be as they appear.

. Grey's involvement with the enigmatic Algerian enchantress, Adara, possibly an agent of German Intelligence, or SIS, or both, threatens to compromise his mission and consign Western civilization to ashes.

By combining elements of authentic and reconstructed history, ***Vengeance Weapon*** is a thought-provoking, smashing good read, in the tradition of ***Final Battle*** and ***Silver Dagger.***

Review *Vengeance Weapon* (2004)

Mr. Hodgson and Mr. Longfield deliver a whirlwind world tour involving espionage, deceit, and intrigue. They not only stir the imagination with the actual locations in which dramatic events were shaped or played out, but have again created a memorable cast of characters who range across the human spectrum from valiant, principled and courageous to unscrupulous, corrupt, and treasonous, whether friend of foe.

It is not only enjoyable to read, but exciting to experience the role Canada's masters of secret warfare played in the prelude to events which, if unchecked, would have turned the tide against the Allies and plunged the world into a chillingly - possible second Dark Age, ruled by tyranny and evil, during the madness of World War II.

Chris Janusitis, Producer Rogers Television Durham Oshawa, ON

Ajax Arsenal of Democracy* (2005),** a tribute to Ajax on its 50th anniversary and the men and women of Defence Industries Limited, [DIL], proposes: If Adolf Hitler's intelligence chief, Admiral Wilhelm Canaris, had developed a plan to sabotage and destroy DIL, by what means and by whom would it have been executed? And, how and by whom might it have been averted? The familiar ***Inside Camp-X series cast is enriched with a host of new characters in authentic settings as varied as the Reichs Chancellery in Berlin, aboard *U-boat 4720* and a night train to Manhattan as well as the shop floor of Line 3, DIL, while the multi-plotted story's twists and turns reach a thrilling climax on Christmas Eve, 1943, in Ajax.

Mills of the Gods* (2006).** Is Clifford Jackson a Soviet 'mole' and Adara a double agent? In the third instalment of the ***Blake Grey series, with the sudden disappearance of 'Canary', Clifford Jackson, while Nazi Germany's ominous Projects **Thor** and **Wotan** are nearing completion, Major Grey, a.k.a Mr. Blake, Adara and Hamish Findlay must go undercover in the best spy-thriller tradition to hunt down and destroy the links, if they exist, between Jackson, Moscow, and Hitler's top scientists to prevent Armageddon. **Slated for release in Spring 2006!**

Arsenal of Democracy

Ajax DIL
Ajax DIL
Ajax DIL
Ajax DIL

BLAKE BOOKS DISTRIBUTION PRESENTS
THE *INSIDE CAMP-X* SERIES

Thank you for this opportunity to introduce our ***Inside Camp-X*** series, of which ***Ajax Arsenal of Democracy***, released **May 2005** (please see previous Section-***Blake Grey***), is the sixth instalment since the introduction of ***Inside Camp X*** in **1999**.

Inside Camp-X The Series

***Inside Camp X* (1999)** Non-fiction. Over 28,000 copies sold

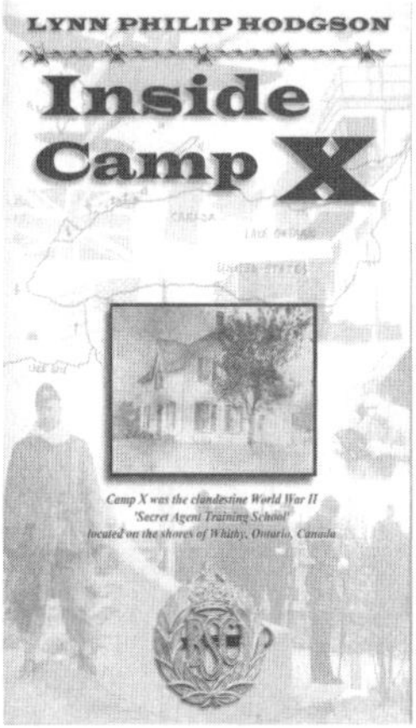

Scrupulously documented, this Canadian best-seller brings to light in authentic detail the day-to-day operations at Camp X, (STS 103) Special Training School 103, situated on the shore of Lake Ontario in Whitby, Ontario. Thoroughly researched, and enriched with first-hand accounts and 108 never-before-published photographs provided by Camp X alumnae, ***Inside Camp X*** unlocks the secrecy of this unique Canadian establishment, which served as the inspiration for the WWII American Office of Strategic Services that became the CIA.

ISBN 0-9687062-0-7. Mass Market $11.95

ISBN 0-9687062-5-8. Paperback $24.95

ISBN 0-9687062-6-6. Hard Cover $39.95

Camp X The Final Battle **(2001)** Fiction. 4,800 copies sold.

ISBN 0-9687062-3-1. Paperback $24.95

Triumphant in the epic 1941 Battle of Britain, Adolf Hitler arrives to proclaim possession of his most prestigious conquest, The British Reich Protectorate. Somewhere, a lone female assassin, sent from Camp X, lies in ambush as the Fuhrer's aircraft skims the River Thames in preparation for setting down upon Westminster Bridge, while in Canada, Great Britain's gold reserves are being transported for safekeeping in the century-old network of catacombs and tunnels that lie beneath Camp X. A thrilling blend of historical facts and speculative fiction, **The Final Battle** is based upon documented events with portrayals of actual personages of the era, opening a deeper understanding of how Camp X might have contributed to the battle for Great Britain's liberation.

Camp X Silver Dagger **(2002)** Fiction. 2,800 copies sold.

ISBN 0-9687062-7-4. Paperback $24.95

Continuing the story and characters of ***The Final Battle***, ***Silver Dagger*** leads the reader from a dramatic hostage rescue in a Whitby church by Camp X and RCMP officers, to a bold daylight murder in downtown Toronto, to Hitler's Bavarian mountain retreat, The Eagle's Lair, to a climactic confrontation in the *Fuhrerbunker* buried beneath besieged Berlin. The astonishing revelation in the **Epilogue**, founded upon recent disclosures from Moscow, has until recently been the subject of heated speculation fuelled by six decades of official Soviet silence.

Camp 30 Word Of Honour **(2003)** Non-fiction.

ISBN 0-9687062-8-2. Paperback $24.95 ISBN 0-9687062-9-0. Hardcover: $39.95

Eastward down the Lake Ontario shoreline from Camp X, a boy's correctional institution is commandeered by the Canadian military to be transformed into an internment camp for more than 800 German officers. ***Camp 30 Word of Honour*** is the never-before-told story of Prisoner of War Camp 30 at Bowmanville, Ontario. In richly detailed, realistic narrative, ***Camp 30 Word of Honour*** is told through the eyes of two prisoners whose experiences change their beliefs, their futures and life through the humane treatment by their Canadian captors. With unprecedented access to the records and personal recollections of living Camp 30 survivors, the authors have painstakingly recreated the Camp's setting and atmosphere in authentic, first person detail to include the prisoners' inventive pastimes behind barbed wire, both legal and illicit, their brilliantly-engineered secret tunnel schemes, highlighted by the gripping account of one U-boat officer's breathtakingly daring daylight escape and flight across eastern Canada to rendezvous with a waiting U-boat and a three day uprising remembered as the 'Battle of Bowmanville'. ***Word of Honour*** illuminates the astonishing bond between the Canadians and their prisoners, embodied in the German officers' code of honour, *Ehrenwort*, Word of Honour.

Marlene Hodgson President

Blake Books Distribution

P.O. Box 153 Port Perry, Ontario, Canada L9L 1A3

Phone (905) 985-6434 **Fax** (905) 985-6435 **Email** lynniso@idirect.com

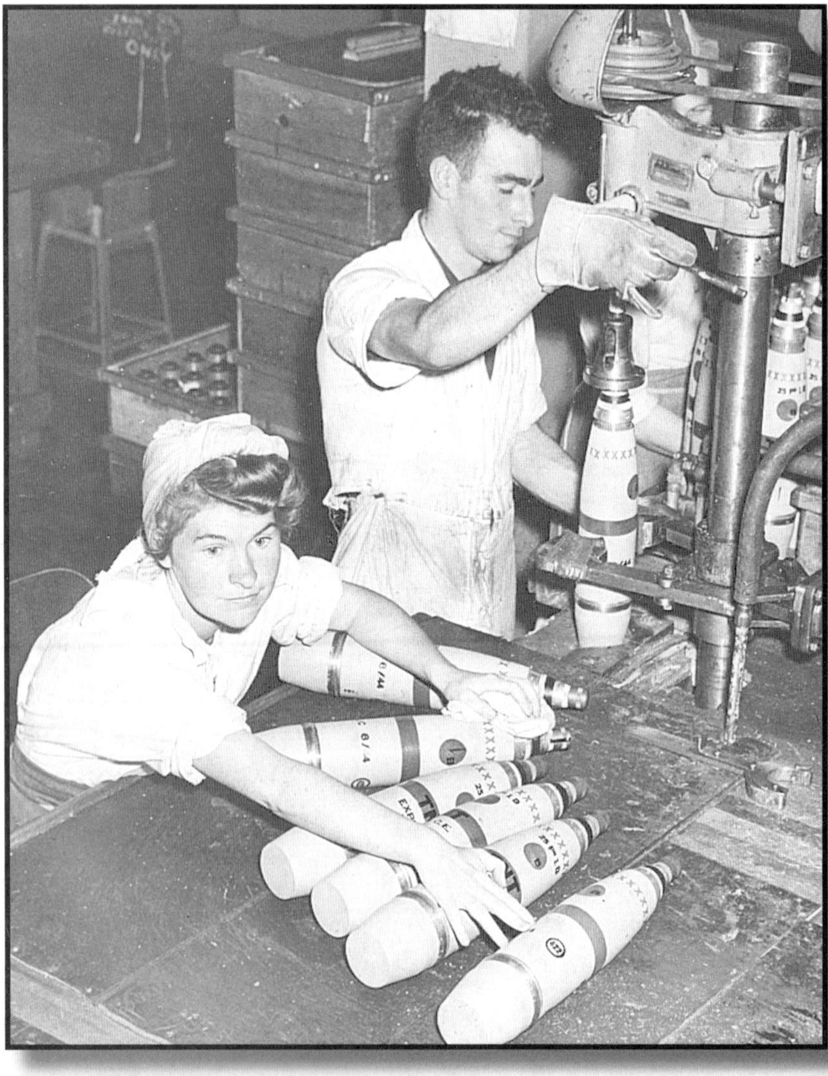

We sincerely hope that you enjoyed this book, the second in the Blake Grey series and that you will look for **Mills of the Gods**, to be released in Spring 2006. Thank you.

Alan, Lynn, Marlene